Ethics
for CPAs

MEETING
EXPECTATIONS
IN
CHALLENGING
TIMES

Ethics for CPAs

for

MEETING EXPECTATIONS IN CHALLENGING TIMES

Dan M. Guy, CPA, PhD   D. R. Carmichael, CPA, CFE, PhD   Linda A. Lach, CPA

WILEY

JOHN WILEY & SONS, INC.

For general information on our other products and services, please contact our Customer Care Department within the US at (800)762-2974, outside the US at (317)572- 3993 or fax (317)572-4002.

Wiley also publishes its books in a variety of electronic formats. Some content that appears in print may not be available in electronic books.

To order books, or for customer service, call (800)-CALLWILEY (225-5945).

ISBN 0-471-27176-4

Printed in the United States of America

10 9 8 7 6 5 4 3 2 1

CONTENTS

PREFACE

Ethics for CPAs: Meeting Expectations in Challenging Times will help CPAs, both in public practice and not in public practice, to understand and apply the guidance on ethics. It is designed to be a comprehensive and integrated analysis of ethics requirements that is easy to read and easy to use.

The book integrates the various requirements of the AICPA's Code of Professional Conduct, the SEC, the Independence Standards Board, the Department of Labor, the GAO's Yellow Book, and state societies and state boards. The book also contains information on ethical standards for consulting and tax services, and provides a clear and concise analysis of international ethics requirements.

The book provides invaluable guidance on how a CPA should respond to an ethics investigation. An overview of the Joint Ethics Enforcement Process is presented, along with steps to take if selected for a disciplinary action. The book also features a chapter on Enron and the ethics issues involved.

The book is presented using the Information Mapping format. This format separates information into small units based on purpose or function for the reader, rather than by topic. It allows a reader to either go through the book in detail or scan quickly for relevant points to resolve an ethics question or issue. The format has been successfully used in hundreds of training, procedural, and reference manuals, in both paper and on-line modes.

The book includes numerous examples and graphics designed to illustrate complex ethics issues that CPAs and their firms face. Each chapter contains a section that provides guidance on the authoritative sources for the topics discussed in the chapter. The book also provides information on where CPAs can go to get more information on ethics issues. Finally, a glossary provides a quick reference for key definitions.

Low-cost self-study continuing education for eight hours of CPE is included within the book.

The authors bring to this book over seventy years of experience of accounting and auditing, and the ethical issues involved in these disciplines. Mr. Guy and Mr. Carmichael, both former vice presidents at the AICPA, have served as consultants to the SEC on ethical issues, represented CPAs in state board of accountancy ethics investigations, and testified as experts on ethical matters. Ms. Lach adds her expertise as the former director of professional development at the AICPA, responsible for all of the AICPA's continuing education programs.

This edition of the book is current through all pronouncements issued as of December 1, 2002. Updates will be provided on the John Wiley & Sons, Inc. website at www.wiley.com/ethics within thirty days of the issuance of a new pronouncement.

We welcome comments, suggestions, and questions about this book. Please direct all correspondence to

Dan M. Guy, PhD, CPA
314 Paseo de Peralta
Santa Fe, NM 87501
Dmguy@worldnet.att.net

Douglas R. Carmichael, PhD, CPA, CFE
Baruch College, CUNY
Department of Accountancy
17 Lexington Avenue
New York, NY 10010
Douglas.carmichael@worldnet.att.net

Linda A. Lach, MS, CPA
21 Papurah Road
Fairfield, CT 06432
LindaLach@aol.com

Dan M. Guy
Douglas R. Carmichael
Linda A. Lach

December 2002

ABOUT THE AUTHORS

Dan M. Guy, PhD, CPA, lives in Santa Fe, New Mexico, where he has a litigation consulting practice. He is also a consultant to KPMG Audit Committee Institute. He completed an 18-year career with the AICPA in New York City in January 1998, where he had overall responsibility for, among other things, the Auditing Standards Board and the Accounting and Review Services Committee. Dr. Guy was Vice President, Auditing, at the AICPA from 1983 until 1996, when he became Vice President, Professional Standards and Services. Dr. Guy has written numerous books on auditing, sampling, and compilation and review. He has represented the profession on numerous occasions before Congress, various regulatory agencies, and at the international level. Prior to joining the AICPA, Dr. Guy was a professor of accounting at Texas Tech University and a visiting professor at the University of Texas at Austin. He was in public practice with KPMG. In 1998, he received the John J. McCloy Award for outstanding contributions to audit quality in the US. The award was presented by the Public Oversight Board of the SEC Practice Section of the AICPA's Division for CPA Firms. In January 2001, he received the Distinguished Service Award from the Auditing Section of the American Accounting Association.

D. R. Carmichael, PhD, CPA, CFE, is the Director of the Center for Integrity and is the Wollman Distinguished Professor of Accountancy in the Stan Ross Department of Accountancy of the Zicklin School of Business at Bernard M. Baruch College, City University of New York. Until 1983, he was the Vice President, Auditing, at the AICPA, where he directly participated in the development of accounting and auditing standards. Dr. Carmichael has written numerous books and articles on accounting and auditing. He acts as a consultant on accounting, auditing, and control matters to CPA firms, public corporations, attorneys, government agencies, and financial institutions. Dr. Carmichael has served as a consultant to the AICPA, the Securities and Exchange Commission (SEC), the General Accounting Office (GAO), the Federal Deposit Insurance Corporation (FDIC), the Federal Trade Commission (FTC), and other federal and state government agencies. He has also investigated numerous cases involving allegations of fraudulent financial reporting and provided expert witness testimony on those matters.

Linda A. Lach, CPA, is the Associate Director of the Center for Financial Integrity at Baruch College and is a coauthor with Dan M. Guy and D. R. Carmichael of the *Practitioner's Guide to GAAS*. She is the former Director of Professional Development for the American Institute of Certified Public Accountants. In that position, she was responsible for conferences, seminars, and self-study courses developed for the accounting profession. She has made numerous presentations and written articles on continuing education issues. Before joining the AICPA, she held various financial management positions and worked as an auditor for Touche Ross (currently Deloitte & Touche).

ACKNOWLEDGMENTS

We are grateful to the individuals who contributed to *Ethics for CPAs: Meeting Expectations in Challenging Times*. In particular, we express our appreciation to the Independence Education Project (IEP), especially Bob Sack, Mike Sutton, Joe Godwin, Jim Detrick, and an anonymous practitioner. The IEP was sponsored by one of the large CPA firms as a public service for CPAs and others wanting to know more about independence. We are also especially thankful to our spouses, Terri Guy, Carol Schaller, CPA, and Richard Nichols, for their technical skills as well as their patience and encouragement. Finally, we wish to thank everyone at John Wiley & Sons, Inc., including John DeRemigis, Judy Howarth, and Pam Miller, for helping to make this book possible.

PART A

INTRODUCTION TO ETHICS

1 INTRODUCTION

Purpose of This Book

This book is designed to help practitioners understand and apply the ethics requirements of the AICPA's *Code of Professional Conduct*, along with ethics requirements of

- The SEC
- The Independence Standards Board[1]
- The DOL
- The GAO's Yellow Book
- State societies and state boards
- Other organizations, such as the FDIC and HUD

Applicability of Code of Professional Conduct

The AICPA's *Code of Professional Conduct* was adopted by the membership of the AICPA to provide guidance to all members in carrying out professional responsibilities.

Therefore, the Code applies to

- Members in public practice
- Members in industry
- Members in government
- Members in education

Applicability of Chapters

Each chapter indicates whether the chapter applies only to members in public practice, only to members **not** in public practice, or to all members. The following chart guides members in determining whether the guidance in a chapter applies.

Recent SEC Rules

In November 2000, the SEC issued an extensive number of new requirements and amendments to existing independence rules. Those new requirements generally were effective February 5, 2001.

---

[1] *The ISB went out of existence in July 2001. See Chapter 2 for more information.*

Format of Book

This book is presented in an information mapping format. The format separates information into small units based on the purpose or function for the reader, rather than the topic. It allows a reader to either go through the book in detail or scan quickly for relevant points.

This method has been in use in industry since 1972 and is used extensively in hundreds of training, procedural, and reference manuals, in both paper and electronic modes.

Organization of This Book

This book is divided into the following parts:

- **Part A** introduces the organizations involved in setting and enforcing ethics requirements. It also summarized the ethics enforcement process.
- **Part B** provides an overview of the key concepts of independence, integrity, and objectivity.
- **Part C** provides detailed guidance on understanding and applying the complex independence requirements of the AICPA and other organizations.
- **Part D** covers other ethics rules in the AICPA's *Code of Professional Conduct.*
- **Part E** provides additional guidance for tax and consulting services and covers international ethics requirements. It also gives the practitioner guidance on where to go for more information.

How to Use This Book

This book is designed to be easy to use. To find a topic or subject in this book, use the Table of Contents or the Topical Index on page 383. The information mapping format makes it easy to scan each chapter and find information easily and quickly.

To find the meaning of a technical term, refer to Appendix A, Glossary.

2 ORGANIZATIONS INVOLVED IN THE DEVELOPMENT, REGULATION, AND ENFORCEMENT OF ETHICS REQUIREMENTS

In This Chapter	*For information on*	*See section*
	AICPA	A
	SEC	B
	Public Company Accounting Oversight Board	C
	Independence Standards Board	D
	State societies of CPAs	E
	State boards of accountancy	F
	Other organizations	G

Overview

The AICPA establishes ethics requirements that apply to AICPA members.

State societies of CPAs and state boards of accountancy establish their own ethics codes, but the independence requirements are generally the same as those of the AICPA.

The AICPA and most state societies cooperate in the Joint Ethics Enforcement Program (JEEP) in bringing enforcement actions against their members. Each state board of accountancy independently enforces its requirements against the CPAs it licenses to practice.

The Independence Standards Board (ISB) established independence requirements for auditors of public companies.[1] The SEC enforces those requirements. The SEC also provides guidance on insider trading and advertising.

NOTE: The securities laws require that public companies file statements with the SEC that have been audited by an independent accountant. Because the SEC is charged with the responsibility to administer the securities laws, the Commission and the Staff have established and interpreted independence rules for CPAs who audit public companies.

---

[1] *The ISB went out of existence in July 2001.*

Section A: AICPA

Introduction	The American Institute of Certified Public Accountants (AICPA) is the national professional organization for all certified public accountants (CPAs).
	Its purpose is to provide the necessary support to ensure that CPAs serve the public interest in performing the highest quality of professional services.
Ethics Requirements	The *Code of Professional Conduct* ("the Code") was adopted by the membership of the AICPA to provide guidance and rules to all members.
	Membership in the AICPA is voluntary, but by accepting membership, a CPA assumes an obligation of self-discipline and agrees to adhere to the Code.
Composition of the Code	The Code contains principles, rules, interpretations, and rulings. The *principles* are positive statements of responsibility that provide the framework for the rules, which govern performance.
	Rules are broad but specific descriptions of conduct that would violate the responsibilities stated in the principles.
	Interpretations provide guidelines on the scope and application of the rules, but do not limit their scope or application.
	Ethics Rulings summarize the application of rules and interpretations to a particular set of factual circumstances.
Principles	The six *principles* in the Code are described as follows:

Article I	Responsibilities	Members should use sensitive professional and moral judgments in all their professional activities.
Article II	The Public Interest	Members should act in a way that will • Serve the public interest • Honor the public trust • Demonstrate commitment to professionalism
Article III	Integrity	Members should perform all professional responsibilities with the highest sense of integrity.
Article IV	Objectivity and Independence	A member should • Maintain objectivity • Be free of conflicts of interest in discharging professional responsibilities A member in public practice should be independent in fact and appearance when providing auditing and other attestation services.

Article V	Due Care	A member should
		• Observe the profession's technical and ethical standards
		• Strive continually to improve competence and the quality of services
		• Discharge professional responsibilities to the best of the member's ability
Article VI	Scope and Nature of Services	A member in public practice should observe these principles in determining the scope and nature of services to be provided.

Professional Ethics Executive Committee (PEEC)

The PEEC is the AICPA's senior technical committee that promulgates professional ethics requirements.

Rules and changes in rules must be approved by the AICPA membership.

Interpretations and rulings are issued on PEEC's own authority after due process procedures that include exposure to interested parties.

Coverage of Rules, Interpretations, and Rulings on Ethics

The rules on independence, integrity, and objectivity are described generally in Chapters 5, 6, and 7. Related interpretations and rulings on independence are explained throughout Chapters 8 through 27.

The remaining rules and their related interpretations and rulings are explained in Chapters 28 through 34.

Recent AICPA Rule Changes

In November 2001, the AICPA issued a number of new or amended rules and definitions relating to independence. These rules and definitions are discussed throughout this book in the appropriate chapters.

Section B: The SEC

Introduction	The Securities and Exchange Commission (SEC) is a federal government regulatory agency with responsibility for administering the federal securities laws.
	These federal securities laws are intended to protect investors and to ensure that the securities markets operate fairly and that investors have access to disclosure of all material information concerning publicly traded securities.
Relation to Independent Auditors	The federal securities laws require that independent public accountants audit financial statements filed with the SEC to protect public investors.
	SEC regulations (Rule 2-01 of Regulation S-X) provide that the SEC "will not recognize any certified public accountant or public accountant as independent who is not in fact independent."
Prohibitions against Relationships and Interests That Impair Independence	SEC regulations [Rule 2-01(b)] specifically identify the following situations that will be considered to impair independence:

- Connection to the client (or any of its parents, its subsidiaries, or other affiliates) as a promoter, underwriter, voting trustee, director, officer, or employee.

   *NOTE: The term **affiliates** is construed broadly and includes persons associated with the client in a decision-making capacity such as officers, directors, and substantial stockholders, as well as entities that, directly or indirectly, control, are controlled by, or are under common control with the client.*

   *Whenever the term **client** is used in this book in reference to an SEC requirement, the term also includes its parents, subsidiaries, and affiliates.*

- Holding or being committed to acquire any direct financial interest or material indirect financial interest in the client or any of its parents, its subsidiaries, or other affiliates.

   NOTE: These specific prohibitions are similar to those specified in AICPA Interpretation 101-1 and are described in more detail throughout this book, including particularly Chapters 10, 11, 16, and 17.

SEC Interpretations of Independence Requirements	The SEC has authority and responsibility under the federal securities laws for determining whether auditors who audit financial statements filed with it are independent.

From 1934 on, the SEC exercised its authority by having its staff issue interpretations of the independence requirements and by bringing enforcement actions for violations.

The SEC also refers auditors to independence requirements adopted by the AICPA to the extent they do not conflict with the sec's own requirements.

NOTE: SEC interpretations are codified in **Codification of Financial Reporting Policies,** *Section 600, "Matters Relating to Independent Accountants."*

These interpretations are integrated and referred to at appropriate points throughout the book.

SEC Enforcement Authority

The SEC has authority to institute enforcement actions as it deems appropriate under Rule 102(e) against auditors who appear or practice before it.

The SEC may deny, temporarily or permanently, the privilege of appearing or practicing before it to a person found to have engaged in unethical or improper professional conduct.

NOTE: "Improper professional conduct" means

1. *Intentional or knowing conduct, including reckless conduct, that results in a violation of applicable professional standards; or*
2. *Either of the following two types of negligent conduct:*
   a. *A single instance of highly unreasonable conduct that results in a violation of applicable professional standards in circumstances in which an accountant knows, or should know, that heightened scrutiny is warranted.*
   b. *Repeated instances of unreasonable conduct each resulting in a violation of applicable professional standards, which indicate a lack of competence before the Commission.*

This means the SEC may deny the ability of an individual auditor or a CPA firm to perform audits of public companies.

Recent SEC Rule Changes

In November 2000 the SEC issued new rules for auditor independence. These rules are discussed throughout this book in the appropriate chapters.

NOTE: In general, the effective date for these rules is February 5, 2001. The SEC has granted additional time to meet certain requirements.

Additional Guidance on Ethics

The SEC also provides guidance on

- Insider trading (Chapter 29)
- Advertising by investment advisors (Chapter 32)

Section C: Public Company Accounting Oversight Board[2]

Overview

The Sarbanes-Oxley Act of 2002, also known as the Public Accounting Reform and Investor Protection Act, was signed into law on July 30, 2002. Among other things, the Act created a new Public Company Accounting Oversight Board. This new five-member Board will have many responsibilities, including the establishment and enforcement of ethics standards, including independence and other standards relating to the preparation of audit reports.

---

[2] *As of December 1, 2002, the Public Company Accounting Oversight Board with the exception of a chairperson, had been appointed. The Board has until the end of April 2003 to become organized, hire staff, etc., to carry out requirements and enforce compliance. Please check for updates about this Board on the John Wiley & Sons, Inc. website at www.wiley.com/ethics.*

Section D: Independence Standards Board

Introduction

The Independence Standards Board (ISB) was the private sector standard-setting body governing the independence of auditors from their public company clients. The ISB was dissolved on July 31, 2001, because the SEC, in issuing its new independence requirements in November 2000, basically obviated the need for the ISB. Although the ISB no longer exists, some of the ISB's standards and all of its interpretations continue to apply to auditors of public companies.

NOTE: The AICPA maintains the ISB's website at www.cpaindependence.org to provide access to ISB standards and interpretations that apply to auditors of public companies and for archival purposes.

Applicability of ISB Independence Requirements

The independence requirements established by the ISB apply only to auditors of public companies.

The independence requirements of the AICPA's *Code of Professional Conduct* (the Code) apply to members providing audit, other attestation, or compilation services whether those services are provided to public or private clients.

The auditor of a public company is required to follow the *Code* to the extent its requirements do not conflict with those of the ISB or SEC.

The requirements of the SEC are generally more restrictive than those of the AICPA code.

Standards Issued by the ISB

The ISB has issued

- Standard No. 1—*Independence Discussions with Audit Committees* (discussed in the next section)
- Standard No. 3—*Employment with Audit Clients* (ISB Standard No. 3 is discussed in Chapter 17.)

*NOTE: The ISB exposed, but never finalized Standard No. 2, **Certain Independence Implications of Audits of Mutual Funds and Related Entities**. When the SEC released its comprehensive revisions to its auditor independence requirements, those revisions contained requirements covering the independence issues addressed by this standard. Therefore, the standard, by its terms, never became effective. Prior to the dissolution of the ISB, the ISB staff recommended that Standard No. 2 be withdrawn.*

The ISB has also issued the following interpretations:

- Interpretation 99-1, *Impact on Auditor Independence of Assisting Clients in the Implementation of FAS 133 (Derivatives)*
- ISB Interpretation 00-1, *The Applicability of ISB Standard No. 1 When "Secondary Auditors" Are Involved in the Audit of a Registrant*
- ISB Interpretation 00-2, *The Applicability of ISB Standard No. 1, When "Secondary Auditors" Are Involved in the Audit of a Registrant—An Amendment of Interpretation 00-1*

Required Independence Communications with Audit Committee (ISB No. 1)

ISB Standard No. 1 requires that an auditor disclose to the audit committee, in writing, (1) all relationships between the auditor and the public company that may reasonably be thought to bear on independence, and (2) confirm the existence of independence.

The auditor must also discuss independence with the audit committee.

These written and oral communications are required at least annually.

*NOTE: When secondary auditors are involved in the audit of consolidated financial statements, the secondary auditors must comply with ISB No. 1 **when a subsidiary or investee is itself a registrant**. Otherwise the responsibility to comply with ISB No. 1 rests solely with the primary auditor. In that situation, the primary auditor's report to the audit committee should include independence issues involving secondary auditors, if any.*

Section E: State Societies of CPAs

Introduction	State societies are voluntary organizations of CPAs within each individual state.
	They are self-regulatory organizations.
Code of Professional Conduct	Generally, each state society has its own code of professional conduct.
	Generally, these codes are modeled after the AICPA code but sometimes have important differences. For example, state requirements may differ from AICPA rules in the area of commissions and contingent fees.
	In the area of independence requirements, however, there are not significant differences.
Enforcement of State Society Codes	Most state societies cooperate with the AICPA in the Joint Ethics Enforcement Program (JEEP). See Chapter 3.
Contacting State Societies	Appendix B provides information on how to contact state societies.

Section F: State Boards of Accountancy

Introduction

State boards are state government regulatory organizations. Each state government issues a license to practice within the particular state under that state's accountancy statute.

State accountancy statutes are enacted into law as part of the normal legislative process in each state.

A state board in a particular state may be a component of a larger organization that regulates several professions or vocations within the state.

NOTE: The designated agency may be a part of a state department of regulation or board of regents.

Code of Conduct

The code of conduct of the state board may be a part of the state accountancy statute. Generally, independence requirements are the same as those of the AICPA.

National Association of State Boards of Accountancy (NASBA)

NASBA is a voluntary organization composed of the state boards of accountancy.

It promotes communication, coordination, and uniformity among state boards.

In conjunction with the AICPA, NASBA has developed a Uniform Accountancy Act (UAA).

The UAA is for the information of state legislators, and adoption of all or part of its provisions is up to the legislators in the individual states.

Enforcement of State Board Codes

The enforcement mechanism within each state depends on the laws and regulations of the state.

A state board has authority to suspend or remove a CPA's license to practice in that state.

Recent Legislative Initiatives

As of the date of publication of this book, many states have introduced legislative initiatives for post-Enron accounting and auditing reforms. For example, several bills have been introduced in 2002 in Pennsylvania, including one that would alter both CPAs' and non-CPAs' responsibility for wrongdoing discovered during employment. New York has introduced legislation that would prohibit auditors from providing nonaudit services to publicly traded companies and New York state retirement systems. The AICPA has compiled an update of Enron-related legislative proposals under consideration at the state level. The summary is broken down into legislation that affects the profession and other Enron-related legislative proposals. The summary can be found on the AICPA website at http://www.aicpa.org/download/info/Enron_Related_State_Activity.doc. Practitioners may find this useful in monitoring legislative initiatives within their states.

Contacting   Appendix B provides information on how to contact state boards.
State Boards

Section G: Other Organizations

Introduction	A variety of regulatory or self-regulatory organizations may be involved in the establishment of independence requirements.
Department of Labor (DOL)	The Employee Retirement Income Security Act of 1974 (ERISA) requires that the audit of an employee benefit plan's financial statements be performed by an "independent qualified public accountant." DOL regulations impose independence requirements that are stricter, in some ways, than those of the AICPA. Generally, those areas in which DOL requirements are more stringent tend to be the same as those of the SEC. (See Chapter 24.)
General Accounting Office (GAO)	The GAO establishes standards for audits of governmental organizations, programs, activities, and functions. In January 2002, the GAO established significant new requirements for auditor independence under Government Auditing Standards (i.e., the Yellow Book). The new standards apply to all Yellow Book audits for periods beginning on or after October 1, 2002, with earlier implementation encouraged. The revisions contain some differences from current AICPA independence rules. In many cases, the new GAO rules are more restrictive than the AICPA's standards. (See Chapter 23.)
SECPS	The SEC Practice Section (SECPS) is a self-regulatory group whose objective is to improve the practice of CPA firms. The AICPA bylaws state that all AICPA members who engage in the practice of public accounting with a firm auditing one or more SEC clients as defined by AICPA Council are required to join the SECPS. The SECPS currently has approximately 1,200 member firms, which either audit registrants that file financial statements with the US Securities and Exchange Commission or have joined voluntarily. In addition to quality control requirements, the SECPS has numerous requirements for members such as requiring that each proprietor, shareholder, or partner residing in the United States and eligible for AICPA membership is a member of the AICPA; required partner rotation on SEC engagements; required second-partner reviews; and CPE requirements for all professionals in the

firm. The SECPS membership requirements can be found at
http://www.aicpa.org/members/div/secps/require.htm. In addition,
Appendix L, "Independence Quality Control Policies and Procedures," of the SECPS Reference Manual contains information on
the SECPS requirements related to independence quality controls.

FDIC

The Federal Deposit Insurance Corporation (FDIC) requires that
each depository institution engage an independent public
accountant to audit and report on its financial statements. The
FDIC states that the independent public accountant should comply
with the AICPA's *Code of Professional Conduct* and meet the
independence requirements and interpretations of the SEC and its
staff. See Chapter 38 for the FDIC's website.

HUD

The Housing and Urban Development (HUD) Handbook contains
additional independence requirements. For example, the
Handbook states that an independent public accountant who
performs bookkeeping services for a HUD project is prohibited
from performing audits of the project's financial statements.

**Auditing
Standards Board
(ASB)**

The ASB issues Statements on Quality Control Standards (SQCS)
that establish requirements for quality controls, including policies
and procedures related to independence, integrity, and objectivity.
(See Chapter 27.)

The ASB issues pronouncements on auditing and other attestation
services that require independence in the performance of those
services. (See Chapters 5 and 8.)

**Accounting and
Review Services
Committee
(ARSC)**

The ARSC issues Statements on Standards for Accounting and
Review Services that require independence in the performance of
reviews. An accountant may perform a compilation when he or
she is not independent, but must disclose the lack of independence
in the compilation report (or in the engagement letter if a
compilation report will not be issued for a management-use-only
compilation).

Authoritative Sources

1. SEC *Codification of Financial Reporting Policies*, Section
    600, "Matters Relating to Independent Accountants."
2. Bylaws of the AICPA.

3. AICPA *Code of Professional Conduct.*
4. ISB Standard No. 1, *Independence Discussions with Audit Committees.*
5. ISB Interpretation 00-1, *The Applicability of ISB Standard No. 1, When "Secondary Auditors" Are Involved in the Audit of a Registrant.*
6. ISB Interpretation 00-2, *The Applicability of ISB Standard No. 1, When "Secondary Auditors" Are Involved in the Audit of a Registrant—An Amendment of Interpretation 00-1.*

3 ETHICS ENFORCEMENT—WHAT A MEMBER NEEDS TO KNOW

Overview

The AICPA and virtually all of the state societies of CPAs have joined together in the Joint Ethics Enforcement Program (JEEP). This chapter describes JEEP and the major phases and possible outcomes of ethics investigations and hearings, and provides guidance on what a member should do if notified of a potential disciplinary action under JEEP.

How to File a Complaint

The Professional Ethics Division investigates complaints against AICPA members. To find out if an individual is a member of the AICPA, call 877-777-7077. To file a complaint, write to

AICPA
Harborside Financial Center
201 Plaza Three
Jersey City, NJ 07311-3881
Attn: Professional Ethics Division

Section A: Overview of the Joint Ethics Enforcement Program (JEEP)

What Is JEEP?	The AICPA and virtually all of the state societies of CPAs have joined together in a program to permit joint enforcement of their Codes of Professional Conduct.
What Is the Purpose of JEEP?	The purpose of JEEP is to eliminate duplicate investigation of a potential matter by both the AICPA Professional Ethics Division and the ethics committee of one or more participating state societies.
Who Performs an Ethics Investigation under JEEP?	The ethics committee of a participating state society investigates a potential disciplinary matter unless it requests the AICPA to conduct the investigation or the AICPA, under established policy, has the right to conduct the investigation.
	An investigation by the executive committee of the AICPA's Professional Ethics Division may be performed by a committee member and staff member, or an ad hoc investigator appointed specifically for a particular matter.
What Are the Possible Outcomes of an Investigation?	The possible findings of an ethics committee under JEEP are as follows:
	• No violation. • Letter of required corrective action with directives. • Offer of a settlement agreement. • Trial board referral.
	If a matter is referred to the trial board, ethics committee representatives present the action as the Ethics Charging Authority (ECA).
What Is the Role of the Joint Trial Board?	A hearing panel of five members of the Joint Trial Board hears cases referred by the ethics committee and recommends appropriate disciplinary, remedial, or corrective action.
	The Joint Trial Board consists of at least thirty-six members elected for a three-year term by AICPA Council.
	NOTE: In a trial board hearing, the ECA (ethics committee representatives) act as the plaintiff's attorney, the hearing panel chairman acts as the judge, and the hearing panel is the jury.

What Is Automatic Discipline?

Members of the AICPA can be automatically suspended from membership without a hearing if they are convicted for

- A crime punishable by imprisonment for more the one year.
- Willful failure to file any income tax return that the member, as an individual taxpayer, is required to file by law.
- Filing a false or fraudulent income tax return on a client's behalf or for the member's own benefit.
- Willfully aiding in the preparation and presentation of a false and fraudulent income tax return of a client.

Automatic suspension can also result from suspension of the member's certificate as a CPA or license or permit to practice public accountancy as a disciplinary measure by any governmental agency.

What Is Failure to Cooperate?

A member who refuses to honor his or her obligation to make a substantive response to an ethics committee's written interrogatories or requests for documents is said to have failed to cooperate with the committee in its investigation.

Failure to cooperate subjects a member to an automatic charge before a hearing panel of violation of

- Rule 501, *Acts Discreditable* (see Chapter 31).
- Rule 102, *Integrity and Objectivity* (see Chapter 7).
- Bylaws of the AICPA or participating state society.

Section B: Conduct of an Investigation and Trial Board Hearing

Major Phases of Investigation and Hearing

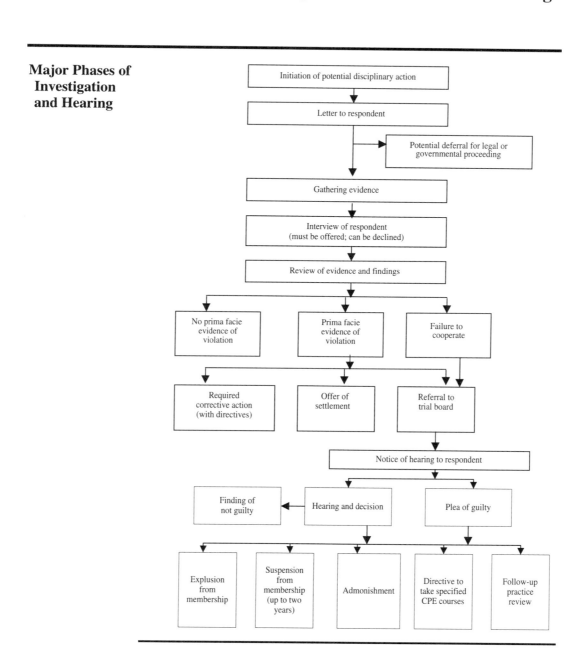

**What Can Cause
the Initiation of a
Disciplinary
Action?**

A potential disciplinary matter may come to the attention of an
ethics committee as a result of

- A complaint.
- Other information.

Other information can be any information from any source what-
soever, including

- AICPA programs and activities, such as the Division for
  Firms.
- Participating state societies.
- Federal, state, or local governmental agencies.
- Newspaper articles or other media reports.
- Announced decisions of judicial or regulatory authorities.
- Anonymous tips.

**When Can a
Disciplinary
Action Be
Deferred?**

If a member makes a written request and provides evidence of the
following, a disciplinary action will be deferred.

- A legal proceeding before a state or federal civil or criminal
  court.
- A proceeding or investigation by a state or federal regulatory agency, such as the SEC or a state board of accountancy.
- An appeal actively undertaken from a decision of a state or
  federal civil or criminal court or regulatory agency.

**How Will a
Member Know a
Disciplinary
Action Has
Started?**

The ethics committee investigating the matter will send an open-
ing letter to each member identified as a respondent.

The letter might request responses to written interrogatories and
documents such as working papers and financial reports.

**What Are the
Member's
Obligations in an
Investigation?**

A member has a duty to cooperate in an investigation by providing
a written response to interrogatories and furnishing requested
documents.

If a substantive response is not received to a letter of inquiry
within 30 days, a follow-up letter will be sent.

If a substantive response is not received within 30 days of the
follow-up request, the matter will be referred to the full committee
for action due to failure to cooperate.

What are the Member's Rights in an Investigation?

A member has several rights, including the right to

- Be represented by legal counsel, firm representatives, and an expert witness at any meetings or discussions during the investigation, and, if there is a referral, at a hearing panel.
- Have the opportunity to meet or have a telephone interview with members of the committee, and offer evidence that should be considered in making a finding.
- Have the opportunity to read and correct and comment on the written summary of the interview.
- Have the investigation conducted in a **confidential** manner and have his or her name and the findings published only in specified circumstances.

When Will the Name of a Member and the Findings of an Investigation Be Published?

The results of the investigation and the name of the member will not be published in *The CPA Letter* unless

- The matter is presented to a hearing panel and the panel finds the member guilty, or
- As part of a settlement agreement, the member agrees to publication.

When Will the Ethics Committee Refer a Matter to the Trial Board?

If the ethics committee concludes that a violation is of sufficient gravity to warrant formal disciplinary action, the matter will be referred to the trial board.

One or more of the following conditions could result in referral:

- Harm to the public or the profession.
- Disregard for standards.
- Disregard for facts.
- Subordination of professional judgment.
- Failure to act on findings of a prior quality control or peer review.
- Repeated violations.
- Reflections on the respondent's honesty.

Can a Guilty Decision of the Trial Board Be Appealed?

A respondent found guilty by a hearing panel may request a review by filing a letter within thirty days of the decision.

A review of the request is performed by an ad hoc committee of at least five members of the trial board who did not participate in the prior proceedings.

A decision by the ad hoc committee denying a request is final. If the request is granted, a new review panel conducts a hearing that may affirm, modify, or reverse an initial panel decision.

Section C: Authors' Advice to a Member
Involved in a Disciplinary Action

Introduction

A member who receives notice of a potential disciplinary action under the JEEP has to treat the matter very seriously because

- Even though the most severe penalty is loss of AICPA or state society membership, a guilty finding can significantly damage a member's public reputation and personal self-esteem.
- A companion action by a state board can cause the loss of the member's CPA license.

NOTE: Many state boards do not have the resources to perform their own investigations and rely on the JEEP investigation.

Respond on a Timely Basis to Requests of the Ethics Committee

By not responding within the established time limits, the member will be found to have failed to cooperate with an ethics investigation.

The matter will automatically be referred to the trial board as a violation of ethics rules or membership bylaws.

Engage Professionals as Representatives

A member should promptly hire competent legal counsel and an experienced expert witness before responding.

This is a right of the member that should be exercised.

The ethics committee will have the legal and technical resources of the AICPA and state society available. A member needs comparable or better support.

Go to the Interview and Be Thoroughly Prepared

The interview by the investigators is an opportunity the investigators must offer that should be accepted.

It is the best chance a member has to persuade investigators that no disciplinary action is necessary.

The member and his or her representatives should be thoroughly prepared to explain why relevant professional standards were not violated or to present meaningful mitigating circumstances.

In Written and Oral Responses, Limit the Response to the Request	Requests for information should be responded to honestly and with diligence, but the responses should not provide any information beyond what is requested. An ethics investigation is not limited in scope to the allegations or implications included in the complaint or other information that gave rise to the investigation. Any responses should avoid raising other issues by being limited to what was explicitly requested.
Carefully Consider Acceptance of a Letter of Required Corrective Action	If the ethics committee finds there is prima facie evidence of a violation after the interview, the mildest penalty is an agreement for corrective action. Even when the member disagrees with the finding, professional pride should not stand in the way of accepting the penalty because • There will be no publication of the finding and the member's name in *The CPA Letter*. • The corrective action is usually taking specified CPE courses and the member will have to take courses anyway to comply with mandatory CPE requirements.
In a Hearing, Try to Persuade a Sufficient Number of Decision Makers	An affirmative vote of two-thirds of those present and voting is required to expel a member. An affirmative vote of a majority of those present and voting is required for other sanctions. *NOTE: The goal should be to persuade three members of the five-member panel that no sanction is necessary because there was no violation of relevant professional standards or that mitigating circumstances indicate sanctions are not warranted.*
Persuasive Mitigating Circumstances or Arguments	If the facts of the case support them, the member and the member's representatives should try to make the following points: • There was no intentional disregard of the standards or the facts. • The member has acted promptly and diligently whenever a peer review or internal inspection has found the need for improvement. • The member has cooperated fully and responded honestly to all inquiries. • Any violations of standards that might have occurred were isolated events and inadvertent. • The member has consistently endeavored to remain competent and current by taking CPE courses and other means. • For all these reasons, no sanction is necessary to prevent harm to the public or the profession.

Authoritative Sources

1. *Joint Ethics Enforcement Program (JEEP) Manual of Procedures.*
2. *Rules of Procedure and Practice of the Joint Trial Board.* (Available at www.aicpa.org.)
3. *How to Respond to an Ethics Investigation.* (Available at www.aicpa.org.)

PART B

OVERVIEW OF INDEPENDENCE, INTEGRITY, AND OBJECTIVITY

4 THE FALL OF ENRON AND THE ETHICS AFTERMATH

Introduction

In a few months, Enron went from being one of the leading US corporations to the largest bankruptcy in US history. Enron Corp. announced a large quarterly loss in October 2001, in November announced a restatement of financial statements back to 1997, and in December filed for bankruptcy.

The resulting scandal and investigations which involved Enron's external auditor, Arthur Andersen, have caused some observers to call into question the integrity of independent audits and have sullied the image of CPAs as trusted professionals.

This chapter explores some of the ethics issues raised by Enron.

Close Relationships between Enron and Andersen Personnel

Andersen personnel attended office parties and Enron-sponsored events, and generally behaved in a manner so similar to employees that many Enron personnel and others believed they **were** Enron employees.

Actual employment by a client would impair independence under Interpretation 101-1, but "cozy" relationships are not explicitly prohibited. An auditor must be sensitive to impairments of independence in appearance and avoid circumstances that blur the distinction between employee and independent status. An auditor must be especially on guard for professional relationships that evolve into significant friendships and social relationships

Article IV states that independence precludes relationships that may appear to impair a member's objectivity in rendering attestation services.

Andersen Personnel Hired by Enron

Enron hired many Andersen Personnel. Enron's chief accounting officer and others in significant financial and operating positions were former Andersen employees.

The ISB, before its demise, issued ISB Standard 3, *Employment with Audit Clients*, which contained safeguards that are necessary to maintain independence when a client hires CPA firm personnel. (See Chapter 17 for more information on ISB 3.)

The Sarbanes-Oxley Act of 2002 makes it unlawful for a registered accounting firm to perform any auditing services for a public company for a one-year period starting from the date the company has hired an CEO, CFO, controller, chief accounting officer, or any equivalent position, a person formerly employed by that firm who previously participated in the audit of the company.

A CPA firm should follow the ISB 3 safeguards and institute its own guidelines to ensure audit independence and effectiveness when firm personnel are hired by audit clients.

Scope of Services

In 2000, Enron paid Andersen $27 million for nonaudit services, including tax, consulting, and extended/internal audit services, and $25 million for audit services. Some at Andersen believed the total fees would reach $100 million annually, largely from nonaudit services.

Article VI on the scope and nature of services advises that service and the public trust should not be subordinated to personal gain and advantage, but states that no hard-and-fast rules can be developed on the nature and scope of permissible nonaudit services.

A member is required to determine whether nonaudit services would create a conflict of interest in the performance of the audit function and whether an activity is consistent with the auditor's professional role. A CPA firm should be sensitive to the effect on the appearance of independence created by the nature, scope, and fees for nonaudit services. (See Chapter 14 for more information on nonaudit services.)

Internal Audit Outsourcing

In 1993, Enron engaged Andersen to perform its internal audit function. Andersen then hired forty Enron personnel, including the vice president of internal audit, to be part of Andersen's team providing internal audit services.

SEC requirements that were not in effect before Enron's bankruptcy would have limited services to 40% of total hours expended on internal audit work related to accounting systems, related controls, and financial statements.

The Sarbanes-Oxley Act of 2002 makes it unlawful for a registered accounting firm to perform several nonattest services for a public company audit client, including internal audit outsourcing services.

AICPA requirements have no quantitative limits, but have qualitative restrictions aimed at not acting or appearing to act in a capacity equivalent to a member of management or an employee. (See Chapter 22 for more information on the SEC and AICPA requirements for internal audit outsourcing.)

Accounting Advocacy— Consulting on Structuring Transactions

Enron consulted with Andersen on the structuring of Special Purpose Entities (SPE) to achieve a particular accounting result—to avoid consolidation and permit the recognition of gain or an offset to losses.

Andersen was also consulted on swap contracts involving the exchange of productive assets to achieve gains and assets given up and capitalization of assets received.

Interpretation 102-6, *Professional Services Involving Client Advocacy*, applies when a member is requested to act in support of a client's position on accounting or financial reporting issues. The interpretation does not prohibit this service, but notes the possibility that client advocacy may go beyond sound and reasonable professional practice or compromise credibility.

The Auditing Standards Board recently issued SAS 97, *Amendment to Statement on Auditing Standards No. 50, "Reports on the Application of Accounting Principles,"* which revises SAS 50 to prohibit an accountant from providing a written report on a hypothetical transaction. However, the amendment still does not apply to an entity's auditor and would not have changed the consulting that Andersen provided on the structuring of transactions to achieve a particular accounting result.

Rule 203 and Accounting for, and Disclosure of, SPEs

Enron "hedged" investments carried at fair value using agreements with SPEs that derived their value from commitments of Enron stock.

Some observers believe that Enron's related-party note disclosures of these transactions were designed to obscure rather than illuminate the transactions and the effects on the financial statements.

Even if the structuring of these transactions literally conformed with GAAP requirements, Rule 203, *Accounting Principles*, requires the auditor to evaluate whether adhering to pronouncements will result in misleading financial statements. If following an authoritative pronouncement produces a misleading presentation, the auditor should describe the situation, disclose the departure from the pronouncement needed to make the presentation not misleading, and express an unqualified opinion.

Enron's Whistleblower and Rule 102

In August 2001, an Enron vice president (Sherron Watkins) informed Enron's CEO (Kenneth Lay) and Andersen about concerns with Enron's accounting practices. Ms. Watkins noted, among other matters, that Enron had booked a $500 million gain from equity derivatives from a related party that was thinly capitalized with no party at risk except Enron.

Interpretation 102-4, *Subordination of Judgment by a Member*, deals with the steps that should be taken when a member has a dispute with a supervisor about the preparation of financial statements. It also presents a framework for the proper approach in any situation in which an employee has concerns about an employer's accounting.

Interpretation 102-3, *Obligation of a Member to His or Her Employer's External Accountant*, deals with obligations of a member to the employer's auditor.

Ms. Watkins disclosed her concerns about improper accounting or disclosure to a level of management above those that appeared to be involved and also to Andersen.

Rule 202 and the Audits of Enron's Financial Statements

A pervasive issue related to audits of Enron's financial statements is the conformity with professional standards by Andersen in performing those audits.

Rule 202, *Compliance with Standards*, provides that a member who performs auditing as well as other professional services, must comply with standards promulgated by bodies designated by Council. In the case of audits, Rule 202 requires compliance with the ten basic auditing standards and interpretations of those standards in SASs.

The existence of Rule 202 in the *Code* permits the AICPA and state societies of CPAs to take enforcement actions against members who depart from applicable professional standards.

There will also be actions by private litigants and federal state regulators.

---

5 IMPORTANCE OF INDEPENDENCE

Overview

Independence is essential when a CPA in the practice of public accounting issues a report that provides assurance on the reliability of a written assertion that is the responsibility of another party. This type of engagement is referred to broadly as an **attestation service**.

An opinion based on an audit of financial statements is a widely known form of attestation service.

This chapter explains the importance of independence when providing auditing (section A) and other attestation services (section B).

Section A: Importance of Independence in Providing Audit Services

Introduction	Independence is an essential auditing standard because the auditor's opinion is provided to enhance confidence in the reliability of financial statements that are the representations of management. If the auditor were not independent of management, the auditor's opinion would add nothing to the financial statements.
Basic Principle	A member in public practice should be independent in fact and appearance when providing auditing and other attestation services.
Rationale	No matter what technical proficiency the auditor possesses, the auditor's impartiality is the indispensable quality that inspires confidence in the dependability of the auditor's opinion, and therefore the reliability of the audited financial statements.
The Auditing Standard	The second general standard of generally accepted auditing standards (GAAS) is In all matters relating to the assignment, an independence in mental attitude is to be maintained by the auditor or auditors.
Significance of Independence to the Profession	It is of utmost importance to the profession that the general public maintain confidence in the independence of independent auditors. The prestige and trust of auditors as a professional group depend on the continued achievement of public confidence in the independence of auditors.
Consequences of Not Being Independent	If an auditor is not independent, any procedures the auditor might perform would not be in accordance with GAAS, and the auditor would be precluded from expressing an opinion on the financial statements. No matter how extensive the procedures performed by the auditor, if the auditor is not independent, the financial statements are, for all practical purposes, unaudited.

Example

In several instances in which the SEC has determined that a CPA firm was not independent, the SEC has notified the client that its annual financial statements filed with the SEC would have to be reaudited by another firm. The filed financial statements were not considered to meet the SEC's requirement for audited financial statements because of the original firm's lack of independence.

Other Possible Consequences of Not Being Independent

A lack of independence may subject an auditor or a CPA firm to disciplinary action by regulators and professional organizations as well as to litigation by clients, investors, and others who relied on the financial statements.

Penalties can include payment of monetary damages to plaintiffs and loss of the license to practice and membership in professional organizations.

Consequences to the Profession of Lack of Independence

Publicly reported instances of violations of the independence rules could damage the faith of the public in the reliability of audited financial statements.

The result could be a significant loss in the value of the audit function and a deterioration in the public trust of all members of the profession.

The Current Status of Auditor Independence

Historically, auditors as a group, and the accounting profession generally, have enjoyed a high level of public trust and confidence because of an established reputation for professional independence, objectivity, and integrity.

Maintaining public trust and confidence requires every auditor to take seriously the requirements for independence, integrity, and objectivity, and to adhere to the letter and spirit of those requirements in daily practice. (See Chapter 4, The Fall of Enron and the Ethics Aftermath.)

Section B: Importance of Independence in Providing Other Attestation Services

Introduction	In addition to an audit of financial statements, there are several other types of engagements that require independence.
	These types of engagements are described in detail in Chapter 8, Engagements That Require Independence.
	This section describes the importance of independence to the broad category of engagements generally referred to as **attestation services**.
The Attestation Standard	The fourth general standard of the attestation standards is
	In all matters relating to the engagement, an independence in mental attitude shall be maintained by the practitioner or practitioners.
Significance of the Independence Standard to Attestation Services	Independence is a cornerstone of the attest function.
	It presumes an undeviating concern for an unbiased conclusion about the reliability of an assertion no matter what the assertion may be.
Rationale for Independence	Because a practitioner providing an attestation service is giving assurance on the reliability of assertions that are the responsibility of another party, the practitioner must be free of influence by that other party.

Authoritative Sources

1. *AICPA Codification of Statements on Auditing Standards.*
   a. AU Section 220, Independence.
   b. AU Section 504, Association with Financial Statements.
2. *United States v. Arthur Young & Co.*, 465 U.S. 805, 1984.
3. *Statements on Standards for Attestation Engagements*, AT Section 100, Attestation Engagements.

6 BASIC CONCEPTS OF RULE 101—*INDEPENDENCE,* AND RULE 102—*INTEGRITY AND OBJECTIVITY*

In This Chapter	*For information on*	*See section*
	Basic concepts of independence	A
	Related requirements on integrity, objectivity, and freedom from conflicts of interest	B

Overview

CPAs need to perform all professional responsibilities with the highest sense of integrity.

CPAs also need to maintain objectivity and be free of conflicts of interest in discharging all professional responsibilities.

CPAs in public practice have additional responsibilities related to being independent when providing auditing and other attestation services. Section A explains the basic concepts related to these additional responsibilities. Section B explains the key features and relationships among ethics requirements on independence, integrity, and objectivity.

Section A: Basic Concepts of Independence

Introduction	The public relies on the independence, objectivity, and integrity of independent auditors to maintain the orderly functioning of commerce. This reliance imposes a public interest responsibility on auditors.
Basic Principle	A member in public practice should be independent in fact and appearance when providing auditing and other attestation services.
Rationale	The purpose of an audit of financial statements is to enhance confidence in their reliability. Public confidence in the auditor's report on financial statements could be impaired by • Evidence that independence was actually lacking (*independence in fact*), and • Circumstances that reasonable people might believe likely to impair independence (*independence in appearance*).
Requirements for Independence in Fact	To be *independent in fact,* the auditor must have • **Integrity**—a fundamental character of intellectual honesty and candor, and • **Objectivity**—a state of mind of judicial impartiality that recognizes an obligation for fairness to • Management and owners of a client, • Creditors, • Prospective owners or creditors, and • Others who might rely (including governments and the business and financial community).
Requirements for Independence in Appearance	To be **recognized** as independent, the auditor must be free from any obligation to or interest in the client, its management, or its owners. Such interests or obligations could cause those who rely on audited financial statements to believe the auditor is biased with respect to the client, its management, or its owners.

Example

> An independent auditor auditing the financial statements of a corporation of which the auditor is a director might be intellectually honest. However, it is unlikely that the public would accept the auditor as independent. The auditor would, in effect, be auditing decisions that he or she had a part in making.

Precepts against Presumed Loss of Independence

The accounting profession and regulators—for example, the SEC—have adopted requirements to guard against the **presumption** of loss of independence.

These requirements are stated in the from of rules and their interpretations that provide objective tests.

These requirements have the force of professional law for independent auditors.

Example

> A member with a direct financial interest in a client is **presumed** under these requirements to not be independent. The presumption relates to conformity with an objective test and not the personal qualities of the auditor. An auditor with a financial interest in a corporation might still be unbiased in expressing an opinion on its financial statements. However, the rule has been adopted to avoid situations that are likely to lead outsiders to doubt the independence of auditors.

General Standards of Independence

Independence rules and interpretations do not cover all independence issues. Therefore, the concepts of independence in fact and independence in appearance must be considered in resolving issues that are not explicitly addressed in the various rules and interpretations. In fact, these general standards should be considered in resolving all independence issues. In addition, the SEC requires auditors to consider the following general standards. Does the relationship or the service provided

1. Create a mutual or conflicting interest with the client?
2. Place the auditor in a position of auditing his or her own work?
3. Result in the auditor acting as management or an employee of the client?
4. Place the auditor in a position of being an advocate for the client?

Section B: Related Requirements on Integrity, Objectivity, and Freedom from Conflicts of Interest

Introduction

A CPA in public practice, providing auditing and other attestation services, should be independent in fact and appearance.

In providing all services, a CPA should maintain the objectivity, freedom from conflicts of interest, and integrity required to be independent in fact. However, independence in appearance is not always required or possible.

Reasons for Separate Requirements on Integrity and Objectivity

Not all professional services require independence in appearance, and CPAs not in public practice cannot maintain the appearance of independence because they are employed by others.

Examples

A CPA representing a client in tax court must be intellectually honest and objective, but is acting as the client's advocate and cannot exercise the judicial impartiality of an auditor.

A CPA preparing financial statements as a corporate controller cannot be free of any conflict of interest in making accounting judgments, but must be intellectually honest in applying accounting principles.

Responsibilities of CPAs Employed by Others

CPAs employed by others to prepare financial statements or to perform internal auditing, tax, or consulting services are charged with the same responsibility for objectivity as those in public practice.

They must be scrupulous in the application of generally accepted accounting principles and candid in all their dealings with CPAs in public practice.

Structure of the Rules on Independence, Integrity, and Objectivity

There are two related rules that are concerned with independence, integrity, and objectivity as follows:

Rule 101—Independence. A member in public practice shall be independent in the performance of professional services as required by standards promulgated by bodies designated by Council.

Rule 102—Integrity and Objectivity. In the performance of any professional service, a member shall maintain objectivity and integrity, shall be free of conflicts of interest, and shall not knowingly misrepresent facts or subordinate his or her judgment to others.

*NOTE: AICPA Rule 302, **Contingent Fees,** and Rule 503, **Commissions and Referral Fees,** also affect independence. In fact, if the auditor provides any service or product for a contingent fee or a commission, or receives a contingent fee or commission from an audit client, the auditor is not independent.*

Applicability of the Rule on Independence

Rule 101 applies to CPAs in public practice who provide professional services that must be performed in accordance with standards that specify an independence requirement.

Examples

Generally accepted auditing standards that apply to audit services include a standard that requires independence.

Attestation standards that apply to examination, review, and agreed-upon procedure services include a standard that requires independence.

Other services that require independence are explained in Chapter 8, Engagements That Require Independence.

Applicability of the Rule on Integrity and Objectivity

Rule 102 applies to all CPAs, no matter where they are employed, who are engaged in performing professional services.

Example

CPAs in public practice who render attest, tax, and consulting services, CPAs employed by others who prepare financial statements, who perform internal auditing services, or who serve in financial and management capacities in industry, education, and government are all subject to Rule 102.

Enforcement of the Rules on Independence, Integrity and Objectivity

A variety of self-regulatory and regulatory organizations enforce the requirements on independence, integrity, and objectivity.

- The AICPA and state societies of CPAs enforce the requirements against all members in a cooperative program called the Joint Ethics Enforcement Program (JEEP). See Chapter 3.
- State boards of accountancy enforce the requirements against CPAs licensed in their particular states.
- The SEC enforces the requirements against auditors who audit financial statements and against CPAs who are involved in the preparation of financial information filed with it. (All AICPA members with a firm that audits one or more SEC clients must also join and adhere to the requirements of the SECPS.)

- Other government agencies, such as the Department of Labor (DOL), enforce the requirements against CPAs subject to their jurisdiction.

NOTE: See Chapter 2, Organizations Involved in the Development, Regulation, and Enforcement of Ethics Requirements, for a more extensive discussion of these organizations.

Authoritative Sources

1. *AICPA Codification of Statements on Auditing Standards,* AU Section 220, Independence.
2. *AICPA Code of Professional Conduct*

    a. Article II—The Public Interest (ET Section 53).
    b. Article III—Integrity (ET Section 54).
    c. Article IV—Objectivity and Independence (ET Section 55).

3. FASB Statement of Financial Accounting Concepts 1, *Objectives of Financial Reporting by Business Enterprises.*
4. AICPA *Code of Professional Conduct*

    a. Rule 101, *Independence* (ET Section 101.01).
    b. Rule 102, *Integrity and Objectivity* (ET Section 102.01).

5. SEC Rule 2-01(b), General Standards, and 2-01(c)(5), Contingent Fees. *Revision of the Commission's Auditor Independence Requirements.*

7 REQUIREMENTS FOR INTEGRITY AND OBJECTIVITY (INCLUDING FREEDOM FROM CONFLICTS OF INTEREST)

In This Chapter

For information on	See section
Basic rule, definitions, and rationale	A
Guidelines for members in public practice	B
Guidelines for members not in public practice	C

Overview

Rule 102: Integrity and Objectivity states:

> In the performance of any professional service, a member shall maintain objectivity and integrity, shall be free of conflicts of interests, and shall not knowingly misrepresent facts or subordinate his or her judgment to others.

In addition to discussing integrity and objectivity, this chapter discusses the meaning of "conflicts of interest" and how such conflicts may impair independence in an engagement requiring independence.

Additional prohibitions relating to conflicts of interest are set forth in SEC rules. These are referred to as "occupational conflicting interests." These prohibitions are also discussed in this chapter.

Section A: Basic Rule, Definitions and Rationale on Integrity and Objectivity

---

Rule 102

In the performance of any professional service, a member shall

- Maintain objectivity and integrity.
- Be free of conflicts of interest.
- Not knowingly misrepresent facts or subordinate his or her judgment to others.

Definition of Integrity

Integrity is an element of character fundamental to professional recognition. It is the quality from which public trust derives and the benchmark against which a member must ultimately test all decisions.

Integrity is measured in terms of what is right and just.

Definition of Objectivity

Objectivity is a state of mind, a quality that lends value to a member's services.

The principle of objectivity imposes the obligation to be

- Impartial.
- Intellectually honest.
- Free of conflicts of interest.

Definition of Professional Services

Professional services include **all services** performed by a member while **holding out** as a CPA.

Holding out as a CPA includes any action initiated by a member, whether or not in public practice, that informs others of his or her status as a CPA. For example

- Any oral or written representation to another regarding CPA status.
- Use of the CPA designation on business cards or letterhead.
- Display of a CPA certificate.
- Listing as a CPA in telephone directories.

NOTE: This definition of "holding out" is different from that used in state laws and regulations where it is used to define the practice of public accounting.

Definition of Member

In the context of Rule 102, as opposed to Rule 101 on independence (see Chapter 6), the term "member" is used in the limited sense of a member, associate member, or international associate of the AICPA.

Definition of Conflict of Interest

A conflict of interest may occur if a member performs a professional service for a client or employer, and the member or his or her firm has

- A relationship with another person, entity, product, or service that could, in the member's professional judgment, be viewed by the client, employer, or other appropriate parties as impairing the member's objectivity.

NOTE: The member's professional judgment is subject to the test of reasonableness and appropriateness in the circumstances.

Rationale

To maintain and broaden public confidence, members should perform all professional responsibilities with the highest sense of integrity.

Service and the public trust should not be subordinated to personal gain and advantage.

Regardless of service or capacity, members should protect the integrity of their work, maintain objectivity, and avoid any subordination of their judgment.

Section B: Guidelines for Members in Public Practice

Relationship to Independence

A member should maintain objectivity and be free of conflicts of interest in discharging **all** professional responsibilities.

A member in public practice has an **additional obligation** to be independent in fact and appearance when providing auditing and other attestation services.

Independence in fact presumes the ability and willingness to act with integrity and objectivity and be free of conflicts of interest.

Implications for a Firm's Quality Control

An actual conflict of interest under Rule 102 would also impair independence under Rule 101.

Thus, a firm's quality control system should provide for

- Checking for conflicts of interest in the acceptance or continuance of auditing or other attestation engagements.
- Obtaining written representations from all professional personnel, on hiring and annually thereafter, stating they are familiar with, and are in compliance with, professional standards and the firm's policies and procedures regarding independence, integrity, and objectivity (including freedom from conflicts of interest).

Examples of Conflicts of Interest

In addition to being free from conflicts of interest in auditing and other attestation engagements, a member and the member's firm should be free of conflicts of interest in providing other professional services.

The following situations should cause a member to consider whether others would view the relationship as impairing objectivity:

- Providing litigation services to a plaintiff suing the firm's client.
- Providing tax services to both parties involved in a divorce proceeding who were previously a married couple client.
- Suggesting to a personal financial planning client an investment in a business in which the CPA has a financial interest.
- Providing personal financial planning services to several members of a family who may have opposing interests.
- Providing consulting services to a company that is a major competitor of a company in which the CPA has a position of influence.

- Serving on a city's board of tax appeals which considers matters involving several of the member's clients.
- Providing consulting services related to the acquisition by one client of real estate owned by another client.
- Referring clients to an insurance broker that refers clients to the member under an exclusive arrangement.
- Referring a client to a service bureau in which the member or partners in the member's firm hold material financial interests.

These examples are not all-inclusive and only illustrate situations that could be viewed as impairments.

Consent Permits Performance of Other Services with a Conflict

If a significant relationship that creates a conflict of interest is disclosed to, and consent is obtained from, the client, employer, or other appropriate parties, performance of professional services, other than auditing or other attestation engagements, is permitted.

NOTE: In audit and other attest engagements, it may be impractical or impossible to obtain consent or disclose consent of parties. Auditors' or accountants' reports ordinarily are not restricted as to use. If the report is restricted, it may be practical to make disclosure and obtain consent of all other parties. See AU 532, **Restricting the Use of an Auditor's Report***. When making the disclosure, the member should be mindful of Rule 301 on not disclosing confidential information. This means it may be necessary to obtain specific consent to make the disclosure as well as consent for the conflict of interest.*

Example

A member is approached by a company, for which he or she may or may not perform other professional services, to provide personal financial planning or tax services for its executives. The executives are aware of the company's relationship with the member and have agreed to the arrangement. The member may accept the engagement if the member can perform these investment advisory services with objectivity, since the member may find, in performing these services, that the member may recommend actions to the executives that are unfavorable to the company.

As mentioned above, the member should also consider Rule 301, (Chapter 29) and not disclose confidential information. In this case, the clients are both the company and the executives.

The member should consider informing the company and the executives of possible results of the engagement.

Individual Considers or Accepts Employment with Client	A member may find that an individual participated in an engagement while considering, or after accepting, employment with the client. The member should evaluate whether all work had been performed with objectivity and integrity as required under Rule 102.[1] If the client is a public company, the member should also follow the safeguards set out in ISB Standard 3, *Employment with Audit Clients* (see Chapter 17).

Professional Services Involving Client Advocacy	Some requested professional services involving client advocacy may pose an unacceptable risk of impairing the reputation of a member and his or her firm with respect to independence, integrity, and objectivity because they may

- Stretch the bounds of performance standards.
- Go beyond sound and reasonable professional practice.
- Compromise credibility.

Example

A CPA is asked to advocate, in a meeting with regulators, a client's position on a financial reporting issue that clearly conflicts with an authoritative pronouncement. The CPA should refuse to perform this service.

Service as Director of a Nonclient Bank	The AICPA discourages a member from serving as a director of a non-client bank, if the member has clients (requiring independence or otherwise) that are customers of the bank.

The AICPA discourages bank directorships, to avoid situations in which the member would have

- A conflict of interest under Interpretation 102-2, or
- A problem with confidential client information under Rule 301 (Chapter 29).

NOTE: A more appropriate way for the member to serve the nonclient bank would be as a consultant to the board of directors.

Service as Director of a Consumer Credit Company	A member in public practice may serve as a director or officer of a consumer credit company that purchases installment sales contracts from retailers and receives payments from consumers, as long as he or she does not

---

[1] *The AICPA's Professional Ethics Executive Committee has issued an Exposure Draft, dated June 17, 2002, titled **Omnibus Proposal of Professional Ethics Division Interpretations and Rulings**. The Exposure Draft proposed deleting Ethics Ruling No. 77, **Individual Considering or Accepting Employment with the Client,** because the substance of this Ethics Ruling has been incorporated into the revised Interpretation No. 101-2. Please check for updates to this section on the John Wiley & Sons, Inc. website at www.wiley.com/ethics.*

- Audit the company.
- Participate in matters that might involve a conflict of interest.

Occupational Conflicting Interests

The SEC prohibits auditors from being involved in certain services or occupations. According to the SEC, these services or occupations are either not compatible with the auditor's appearance of complete objectivity, or are fundamentally different from the practice of accountancy.

The SEC prohibits the auditor from

1. Acting as or providing legal counsel to a client.

    Rationale: Serving as legal counsel is concerned with personal rights and interests, a role that is inconsistent with the appearance of independence.

2. Engaging in a commercial business that is directly competitive with the business of a client.

    Rationale: This would appear to a third party as influencing the auditor's objectivity, because the auditor would have access to records, policies, and practices of a business competitor.

    NOTE: There are situations that appear to breach this rule but are acceptable to the SEC. The acceptability by the SEC of a competitive situation is highly dependent on the particular facts. The authors believe that a competitive impairment can be mitigated, but how it can be mitigated depends on the facts and circumstances.

3. Being a broker-dealer.

    Rationale: This activity involves recommending securities, soliciting customers, and the execution of orders that could involve issuer or investor clients. Such activities would cause third parties to question the auditor's ability to be impartial and objective.

Example of conflicts of interest

A consultant to CPA Firm was also a director and member of the audit committee of a client audited by CPA Firm. The consultant's compensation from each of these two relationships was significant in relation to the consultant's total earnings. The SEC concluded that because of the consultant's dual role, CPA Firm's independence was impaired.

Section C: Guidelines for Members Not in Public Practice

Basic Principle

Integrity requires a member to observe both the form and spirit of technical and ethical standards

Circumvention of those standards constitutes subordination of judgment.

In This Section

This section contains the following topics:

Duty Not to Make Knowing Misrepresentations in the Preparation of Financial Statements

A member shall have knowingly misrepresented facts in violation of Rule 102 when a member

- Knowingly makes, or permits or directs another to make, materially false and misleading entries in an entity's financial statements or records.
- Knowingly fails to correct an entity's financial statements or records that are false or misleading when the member has authority to record an entry.
- Knowingly signs, or permits or directs another to sign, a document containing materially false and misleading information.

NOTE: A member who has the authority but fails to correct financial statements or records that are known to be false or misleading violates Rule 102 to the same extent as a member who knowingly makes false or misleading entries.

Duty to Be Candid with Employer's External Accountant

In dealing with his or her employer's external accountant, a member must be candid and not knowingly fail to disclose material facts.

For example, this duty would include being honest and disclosing all relevant facts in responding to oral or written requests for representations made by the employer's external accountant.

NOTE: The duty discussed here applies when a member responds to questions asked by the external accountant. It is not a whistle-blowing responsibility. In situations when the employee/member has a concern about whether the financial statements are presented in accordance with GAAP, the next section governs, not this section.

Steps to Follow for Disagreement with Supervisor on Proper Accounting	The following table leads you through the process for dealing with a disagreement with a supervisor related to the preparation of financial statements or the recording of transactions.

Step	*Description*	*Refer to page*
1	Consider whether there is a material misrepresentation	53
2	Make concerns about potential material misrepresentation known within the entity	54
3	Consider the responsibility for further communication outside the entity.	54

Step 1: Consider Whether There Is a Material Misrepresentation

Is the Supervisor's Proposal an Acceptable Alternative?	Consider whether (1) the entry or failure to record a transaction in the records, or (2) the financial statement presentation or the nature or omission of disclosure in the financial statements, as proposed by the supervisor, represents the use of an acceptable alternative and does not materially misrepresent the facts.
	NOTE: The member should do appropriate research and consult authoritative literature or an independent authoritative source and make a personal judgment. It is a subordination of judgment to simply accept the supervisor's judgment that the matter is not material or has authoritative support. It is appropriate to consult an outside source such as the AICPA's technical information service.
If the Answer Is Clearly Yes	If, after appropriate research or consultation, the member concludes that the matter has authoritative support or does not result in a material misrepresentation, the member need do nothing further.
If the Answer Is No or Is Unclear	If, after appropriate research or consultation, the member concludes there is a material misrepresentation or concludes the answer is unclear, the member should take Step 2.

Step 2: Make Concerns about Potential Material Misrepresentation Known within the Entity

If the Member Concludes Financial Statements or Records Could Be Materially Misstated	Make concerns known to the appropriate higher levels of management within the entity. For example, communicate with the supervisor's immediate superior, senior management, the audit committee or equivalent, the board of directors, or the company's owner. *NOTE: The proper level of communication depends on the nature of the misstatements and the apparent involvement of higher levels in the misstatement. Generally, the communication should be to the next higher level above those who appear to be involved. The authors recommend that when a member of senior management appears to be involved, the communication should be to the audit committee or board of directors or owners.*
Consider Documenting Concerns	Consider documenting the following matters: • Understanding of facts. • Accounting principles involved. • Application of principles to facts. • Parties with whom matters were discussed. *NOTE: The authors recommend that the member make a comprehensive contemporaneous record of these matters.*
If Appropriate Action Is Not Taken	If, after discussing his or her concerns with appropriate persons in the entity, the member concludes that appropriate action was not taken, go to Step 3.

Step 3: Consider The Responsibility for Further Communication Outside the Entity

Consider Need for Legal Counsel	The member may wish to consult with his or her own legal counsel. *NOTE: The authors recommend engaging personal legal counsel before proceeding any further. Legal counsel can help the member understand the member's legal duties in the circumstances as well as provide advice on how to protect against retribution by the entity or potential violation of the law by the member.*

Consider Whether to Continue Relationship with Employer	The member should consider whether the relationship with the employer should continue.
Consider Responsibility to Communicate to Third Parties	The member should consider any responsibility that may exist to communicate to third parties, such as regulatory authorities or the employer's (former employer's) external accountant.
Members Performing Educational Services	Educational services are professional services and Rule 102 applies to those services. Educational services include • Teaching full- or part-time at a university. • Teaching a continuing professional education course. • Engaging in research or scholarship.
Use of the CPA Designation by Member Not in Public Practice	A member not in public practice may use his or her designation on business cards or letterhead, or in connection with financial statements or correspondence. To avoid violating Rule 102, the member should use his or her employment title to indicate that he or she is an employee and not independent of the employer. If the member states in a transmittal that a financial statement is presented in conformity with GAAP, the member must comply with Rule 203, *Accounting Principles* (Chapter 28).

Authoritative Sources

1. Rule 102, *Integrity and Objectivity* (ET 102.01).
2. Interpretation 102-1, *Knowing Misrepresentations in the Preparations of Financial Statements or Records* (ET 102.02).
3. Interpretation 102-2, *Conflicts of Interest* (ET 102.03).
4. Interpretation 102-3, *Obligations of a Member to His or Her Employer's External Accountant* (ET 102.04).
5. Interpretation 102-4, *Subordination of Judgment by a Member* (ET 102.05).
6. Interpretation 102-5, *Applicability of Rule 102 to Members Performing Educational Services* (ET 102.06).
7. Interpretation 102-6, *Professional Services Involving Client Advocacy* (ET 102.07).
8. SEC *Codification of Financial Reporting Policies,* Occupational Conflicting Interests (sec 602.02.e).

9. Ethics Ruling No. 65, *Use of CPA Designation by Member Not in Public Practice* (ET 191.130-.131).
10. Ethics Ruling No. 77, *Individual Considering or Accepting Employment with the Client* (ET 191.154-.155).[2]
11. Ethics Ruling No. 85, *Bank Director,* (ET 191.170-.171).
12. Ethics Ruling No. 99, *Members Providing Services for Company Executives* (ET 191.198-.199).
13. Ethics Ruling No. 101, *Client Advocacy and Expert Witness Services* (ET 191.202-.203).
14. Ethics Ruling No. 117, *Consumer Credit Company Director* (ET 591.233-.234).

---

[2] *The AICPA's Professional Ethics Executive Committee has issued an Exposure Draft, dated June 17, 2002, titled* **Omnibus Proposal of Professional Ethics Division Interpretations and Rulings**. *The Exposure Draft proposed deleting Ethics Ruling No. 77,* **Individual Considering or Accepting Employment with the Client,** *because the substance of this Ethics Ruling has been incorporated into the revised Interpretation No. 101-2. Please check for updates to this section on the John Wiley & Sons, Inc. website at www.wiley.com/ethics.*

PART C

INDEPENDENCE REQUIREMENTS FOR MEMBERS IN PUBLIC PRACTICE

8 ENGAGEMENTS THAT REQUIIRE INDEPENDENCE

Introduction

Rule 101, *Independence* (ET 101.01), requires a covered member, his or her immediate family, and the member's CPA firm (as defined in Chapter 9) to be independent **in the performance of professional services as required by standards**. This chapter identifies those engagements that require independence. The Statements on Auditing Standards (SASs), Statements on Standards for Accounting and Review Services (SSARSs), and the Statements on Standards for Attestation Engagements (SSAEs) are the authoritative standards that require independence.

Some engagements require a covered member, his or her immediate family, and the member's CPA firm as defined in Chapter 9 to be independent; but agreed-upon procedures engagements (Chapter 25) have a less restrictive independence requirement. In this section, you will learn what types of engagements require the more expansive form of independence.

Basic Principle

Independence applies to all audit, examination, and review engagements. A more narrow independence requirement applies to agreed-upon procedures engagements.

Audits

The concept of covered member (immediate family and CPA firm) as defined in Chapter 9 is applied in all audit engagements.

The term "audit" includes engagements to audit

- Financial statements based on GAAP or an other comprehensive basis of accounting.
- Specified elements, accounts, or items of a financial statement.

Examinations

The concept of covered member (immediate family and CPA firm) as defined in Chapter 9 is applied in all examination engagements. Examination is a type of attest engagement that provides the highest level of assurance—reasonable assurance—on the subject matter.

The term "examination" includes engagements to examine

- Prospective financial statements—forecasts and projections.
- Design and operating effectiveness of internal control over financial reporting, or a segment thereof.
- Suitability of design of internal control over financial reporting.
- Specific requirements of an entity's compliance with laws and regulations.
- Management's discussion and analysis.
- Pro forma financial information.
- An entity's written assertion about a defined subject matter.

Reviews

The concept of covered member (immediate family and CPA firm) as defined in Chapter 9 is applied in all review engagements.

A review engagement may include an engagement to review

- Interim financial information of a public entity.
- Annual or interim financial statements of a private entity.
- Annual financial statements of a public entity when that entity does not have its annual financial statements audited.
- Pro forma financial information.
- An entity's written assertion about a defined subject matter.

Comfort Letters Require Independence

Engagements to issue comfort letters for underwriters and certain other requesting parties require the covered member (immediate family and CPA firm) to be independent. If the comfort letter relates to a filing under the Securities Act of 1933, the SEC's additional independence requirements apply.

NOTE: For other requesting parties, such as municipalities, the AICPA independence rules apply.

Compilations

A covered member (immediate family and CPA firm) does not have to be independent to perform a compilation, but the report (or the engagement letter for a management-use-only compilation) has to be modified to recognize the lack of independence. To know when this special report or report language has to be used, you have to apply the definition of covered member (immediate family and CPA firm) to determine independence.

The term "compilation" includes engagements to compile

- Financial statements of a private company.
- Prospective financial statements (forecasts and projections).

Compilation Reports When Not Independent

If a covered member (immediate family and CPA firm) as defined in Chapter 9 is not independent, the compilation report on both private company financial statements and prospective financial statements must be modified to indicate

> We are not independent with respect to XYZ Company.

NOTE: The reason the accountant is not independent should not be described in the report.

Reporting When Not Independent on a Public Company's Financial Statements

A compilation report **cannot** be issued on the financial statements of a public company. Therefore, in this situation, the accountant is required to disclaim an opinion and state that the firm is not independent.

SAS No. 26 (AU 504), *Association with Financial Statements*, requires the following report to be issued:

> We are not independent with respect to XYZ Company, and the accompanying balance sheet as of December 31, 20X1, and the related statements of income and retained earnings and cash flows for the year then ended were not audited by us, and accordingly, we do not express an opinion on them.

NOTE: The reason the accountant is not independent should not be described in the report.

Use of Nonindependent CPA Firm on an Engagement

CPA Firm A is independent with respect to XYZ audit client. CPA Firm A is using CPA Firm B's partners, shareholders, or professional employees on the XYZ audit engagement. CPA Firm B is not independent. In this circumstance, CPA Firm A is also not independent. However, Firm A may use the work of individuals from Firm B in a manner similar to internal auditors. Thus, Firm A would remain independent.

Independence Is Impaired After Member's Report Is Issued

A member was independent when the audit report was initially issued. Afterwards, the member's independence was impaired. The member may resign the report or consent to its use after independence is impaired, provided no "postaudit work" is performed.

*NOTE: Postaudit work does not include the required procedures performed under SAS 58, **Reports on Audited Financial Statements**, paragraphs 71-73.*

Authoritative Sources

1. Rule 101, *Independence* (ET 101.01).
2. *Codification of Statements on Auditing Standards*, which includes the Statements on Standards for Attestation Engagements (2002 edition).

   a. AU 623, *Special Reports*.
   b. AU 634, *Letters for Underwriters and Certain Other Requesting Parties*.
   c. AU 722, *Interim Financial Information*.
   d. AT 100, *Attest Engagements*.
   e. AT 300, *Financial Forecasts and Projections*.
   f. AT 400, *Reporting on Pro Forma Financial Information*.
   g. AT 500, *Reporting on an Entity's Internal Control over Financial Reporting*.
   h. AT 600, *Compliance Attestation*.
   i. AT 700, *Management's Discussion and Analysis*.
3. *Codification of Statements on Standards for Accounting and Review Services* (2001), AR 100, *Compilation and Review of Financial Statements*.
4. Interpretation 101-11, *Modified Application of Rule 101 for Certain Engagements to Issue Restricted-Use Reports under the Statements on Standards for Attestation Engagements* [Revised] (ET 101.13).
5. Ethics Ruling No. 71, *Use of Nonindependent CPA Firm on an Engagement* (ET 191.142-.143).
6. Ethics Ruling No. 74, *Audits, Reviews, or Compilations and a Lack of Independence* (ET 191.148-.149).
7. Ethics Ruling No. 100, *Actions Permitted When Independence Is Impaired* (ET 191.200-.201).

9 DEFINITION OF COVERED MEMBER/PERSON, IMMEDIATE FAMILY MEMBERS, AND CPA FIRM FOR PURPOSES OF INDEPENDENCE REQUIREMENTS

In This Chapter

For information on	*See section*
Who is a covered member/person?	A
Who is an immediate family member?	B
Does the CPA firm have to be independent?	C

Overview

A member in public practice who is deemed to be a covered member/person must be independent when performing services such as audits of financial statements or examinations of prospective financial statements.

Section A defines a covered member/person within the CPA firm.

Section B identifies individuals external to the CPA firm that are deemed to be immediate family members. Generally, investments made by immediate family members and certain employment relationships are ascribed to the covered member/person.

Section C defines the meaning of CPA or accounting firm and the firm-controlled entities.

NOTE: Refer to Chapter 25 for the definition of covered member/ person when engaged to perform an agreed-upon procedures engagement. In those engagements a modified application of Rule 101 is used for restricted-use reports (i.e., agreed-upon procedures reports).

Section A: Who Is a Covered Member/Person?

Introduction

To apply the independence rules (applicable to attest clients), you must be able to define and apply the concept of a covered member/person.

Who Is a Covered Member?

"Covered member" is an AICPA term that applies to any individual that falls into at least one of the following categories:

1. An **individual** on the attest engagement team.

   NOTE: The attest engagement includes audit, review, agreed-upon procedures, and other attest engagements that are covered in the SAS, SSARS, (i.e., review engagements), and the SSAE pronouncement.

2. An **individual** in a position to influence the attest engagement or an individual in the chain of command over the attest engagement.

3. A **partner or manager** who provides nonattest services to the attest client beginning once he or she provides ten hours of nonattest services to the client within any fiscal year and ending on the later of the date (a) the firm signs the report on the financial statements for the fiscal year during which those services were provided, or (b) he or she no longer expects to provide ten or more hours of nonattest services to the attest client on a recurring basis.

   NOTE: The term "partner" includes proprietors, partners, principals, shareholders, or anyone who is equivalent to any of the above.
   The term "manager" means a professional employee who has continuing responsibility for planning and supervision of attest engagements or has authority to determine that an engagement is complete subject to partner approval.

4. A partner in the office in which the lead attest engagement partner primarily practices.

   NOTE: "Office" refers to distinct working subgroups within a CPA firm. Geographic location is not necessarily determinative of a subgroup. Personnel interactions and reporting relationships determine what constitutes an office.

5. The CPA firm, including the firm's employee benefit plans. (See Section C in this chapter.)

6. An entity whose operating, financial, or accounting policies can be controlled (as defined by GAAP for consolidation purposes) by any individual or the CPA firm in 1.

through 5. above or by any combination of 1. through 5. (See Section C in this chapter.)

NOTE: The term "covered member" is not dependent on whether an individual holds a membership in the AICPA.

Who Is a Covered Person?

"Covered person" is an SEC term that describes any individual in a CPA firm that meets the definition of a covered member above. The AICPA and the SEC define "covered member" and "covered person" consistently.

NOTE: The AICPA covers a consultant who consults with the engagement team on technical or industry-specific matters as an "individual in a position to influence the attest team." The SEC covers such individual as an "individual on the attest engagement." Thus, the result of applying the definitions are the same.

Who Is on the Attest Engagement Team?

The attest engagement team consists of

1. Partners, including concurring or second partner reviewers, who work on the engagement.
2. Employees, excluding individuals who perform only routine clerical functions (e.g., word processing or photocopying), who work on the engagement.
3. Contractors, excluding those who perform only routine clerical functions, who work on the engagement.

NOTE: Individuals in items 1., 2., or 3. above are included without regard to whether they are classified as audit, tax, consulting personnel, or some other designation.

SEC Definition of Covered Person

The SEC redefines "member" as the CPA firm and covered persons. "Covered persons" include partners, principals, shareholders, and employees of the CPA firm who

1. Are on the audit engagement team (including concurring partners and all persons who consult with others on the audit, review, or attest engagement).
2. Are in the chain of command, who

   a. Supervise or have direct responsibility for the engagement (including all levels through the CPA firm's chief executive);
   b. Evaluate the performance or recommend the compensation of the engagement partner; or
   c. Provide quality control or oversight of the engagement.

3. Provide ten or more hours of nonaudit services during the fiscal year (beginning on the date the individual performs

the tenth hour of service) through the audit report date or who expect to provide ten or more hours of nonaudit services on a recurring basis (excluding nonmanagerial employees).

NOTE: For example, if the client is on a calendar-year basis and an individual providing nonaudit services has eight hours of service on March 12, and two hours on June 16, the period of being a "member" starts on June 16.

4. Are partners, principals, or shareholders in the office of the CPA firm in which the lead engagement partner practices.

Who Is in a Position to Influence the Attest Engagement?

Individuals in a position to influence the engagement or in the chain of command over the engagement include anyone who

1. Evaluates the performance of the engagement partner.
2. Recommends or determines the compensation of the engagement partner.
3. Supervises or manages the engagement partner.

NOTE: This includes all successive levels above the engagement partner through the CPA firm's chief executive.

4. Consults with the engagement team.
5. Oversees or monitors quality controls of the engagement.

NOTE: Consultants are included in 4. above by the AICPA, whereas they are included as part of the engagement team by the SEC.

Section B: Who is an Immediate Family Member?

Introduction	Now that you can define and apply the meaning of covered member/person based on the individual's role within the CPA firm, you need to recognize that members of your immediate family may impair your independence.

Definition of Immediate Family Member	The term **immediate family member** includes • Spouse, whether or not dependent. • Spousal equivalent, whether or not dependent. • Dependents, whether or not related. *NOTE: A former spouse would not be included in the immediate family provided the covered member/person and the former spouse are legally divorced. A cohabitant is always deemed to be a member of the immediate family when the relationship is equivalent to that of a spouse or partner. Also, other cohabitants may be included in the immediate family. In considering other cohabitants, evaluate the relationship from the perspective of a third party—the appearance of independence—having knowledge of the strength and personal bond between the individuals. Would the third party conclude that there is a threat to independence?*

Exceptions Provided for Immediate Family Members	Generally, investments made in a client and employment relationships with a client by a spouse, spousal equivalent, or dependent, are ascribed to the covered member/person. However, there are two exceptions. 1. If the individual immediate family member is employed by the client in a position that is not a **key** position (AICPA) or in an accounting or financial oversight role (SEC), independence is not impaired (Chapter 19). 2. If in connection with the employment of an immediate family member, such person participates in a retirement, savings, compensation, or similar plan of a client or by an employer that invests in a client, independence is not impaired for **certain** covered members/persons (Chapter 19). *NOTE: The SEC allows the immediate family members of covered persons to acquire an interest in an audit client, if the immediate family member works for the audit client and acquires the interest as an "unavoidable consequence" of participating in an employee compensation program in which employees are granted, for example, stock options in the employer as part of their total compensation package, without impairing the audit firm's independence. The phrase "unavoidable consequence" in this paragraph means that to*

the extent the employee has the ability to participate in the program but has the option to select investments in entities that would not make him or her an investor in an audit client, the employee must choose other investments to avoid an impairment of independence.

Close Relative

The term "immediate family" does not include a parent, sibling, or nondependent child. However, a close relative may impair the independence of **certain** covered members/persons by having a financial interest in a client (Chapter 10) or holding a key position with a client (Chapter 18).

NOTE: The SEC uses the term "close family member" to cover both (1) immediate family members, plus (2) close relatives.

Section C: Does the CPA Firm Have to Be Independent?

Introduction	The CPA firm, including its employee benefit plans, are treated as if they are covered members/persons; therefore, they must be independent. In addition, an entity controlled by a covered member/person or the CPA firm, or any two or more covered members/persons or the CPA firm is treated as if it were a covered member/person.
Definition of CPA Firm	A CPA or accounting firm is an entity that is engaged in the practice of public accounting. The entity may be organized as a sole proprietorship, partnership, corporation, limited liability company, limited liability partnership, or other form of legal organization provided that the characteristics of the CPA firm conform to the resolutions of the Council of the AICPA (ET Appendix B—Council Resolution Concerning Rule 505—*Form of Organization and Name*).
	The definition includes the CPA firm's subsidiaries and controlled associated entities without regard to geographical location. Therefore, the definition includes the CPA firm's pension, retirement, investment and profit-sharing plans, and similar plans.
The CPA Firm's Independence	The CPA firm, including its pension, retirement, and similar plans, must be independent of the client as if the CPA firm were a covered member/person.
Other Entities Treated as a Covered Member/Person	Any entity whose operating, financial, or accounting policies can be controlled (as defined by GAAP for consolidation purposes) by any covered member on the CPA firm or by two or more of any covered members or the CPA firm is treated as if it is a covered member/person.

Authoritative Sources

1. Section 92, "Definitions," in the AICPA's *Code of Professional Conduct*.
2. SEC Regulation S-X, Article 2, *Qualifications and Reports of Accountants*, Reg. 210.2-.01.(a)., and SEC Rule 2-01(f)(11)—

Covered Persons, *Revision of the Commission's Auditor Independence Requirements.*

3. Ethics Ruling No. 106, *Member Has Significant Influence over an Entity That Has Significant Influence over a Client* (ET 191.212-213).

10 DIRECT AND INDIRECT FINANCIAL INTERESTS IN CLIENTS[1]

Introduction

Independence is impaired if (1) during the period of engagement or (2) at the time of expressing an opinion, a covered member/person, including the CPA firm

- Had or was committed to acquire any direct or material indirect financial interest in a client.
- Was a trustee of any trust, or executor or administrator of any estate, that had or was committed to acquire any direct or material indirect financial interest in a client unless the covered member/person has no authority to make investment decisions.

NOTE: A commitment to acquire a financial interest (e.g., agreeing to purchase stock upon issuance) impairs independence at the time of signing the stock subscription contract.

Basic Principle

Direct financial interests are ownership interests held directly in a client. A covered member's/person's direct financial interest in a client impairs independence **without regard to materiality**.

Indirect financial interests are direct ownership interests held in a nonclient entity that itself has a direct financial interest in a client.

---

[1] *The AICPA's Professional Ethics Executive Committee has issued an Exposure Draft, dated June 17, 2002, titled **Omnibus Proposal of Professional Ethics Division Interpretations and Rulings.** The Exposure Draft contains proposed revisions to Interpretation 101-1, **Interpretation of Rule 101**, relating to trustee or executor relationships with a client; Ethics Ruling No. 41, **Member as Auditor of Insurance Company,** and Ethics Ruling No. 70, **Member's Depository Relationship with Client Financial Institution.** The revisions to Interpretation No. 101-1 address those situations in which a covered member serves as a trustee, executor, or administrator of an estate or trust that has a financial interest in an attest client. The committee believes that independence would be considered impaired under such circumstances unless the member has no authority to make investment decisions for the trust or estate. This position is consistent with the new independence rules of the Securities and Exchange Commission, which were released in November 2000. In addition, the committee believes that independence would also be considered impaired if a covered member served as a trustee or executor of a trust or estate that owned more than 10% of the client's securities or when the investment in the attest client represented more than 10% of the trust's or estate's assets, even when the covered member has no authority to make investment decisions.*
Please check for updates to this section on the John Wiley & Sons, Inc. website at www.wiley.com/ethics.

If material, a member's/person's indirect financial interest in a client impairs independence. Materiality is determined primarily by reference to the net worth of the member/person, the CPA firm, and the client.

A member/person may dispose of a disqualifying direct or material indirect financial interest prior to signing an engagement letter or commencing work on the attest engagement and cure the independence problem.

*NOTE: Under existing requirements as of December 1, 2002, the SEC has a less restrictive independence requirement for a foreign accountant who audits a financial statement of a **nonmaterial** division, subsidiary or investee of an international business. The foreign accountant is considered independent if securities of the parent company, subsidiary, or investee are **not** owned by **any member/person** of the foreign accounting firm who is located in the firm's office that audits the division, subsidiary, or investee entity.*

Definitions of Direct and Indirect	Simply stated, a **direct financial interest** is created when a covered member/person invests in a client entity; whereas, an **indirect financial interest** is created when a covered member/person invests in a nonclient entity that has a financial interest in a client.
AICPA Rule on Five Percent Ownership of Client	According to the AICPA, if (1) any partner or professional employee, (2) any immediate family member (spouse, spousal equivalent, or dependent) of anyone in (1) above, or (3) any group of persons in (1) or (2) above owns more than 5% of the equity securities of an audit client, the CPA firm is not independent.
SEC Rule on Five Percent Ownership	The SEC rule is more stringent than the AICPA rule above in that any close family member (parent, nondependent child, or sibling) is included in the ownership control/group, if any such group has filed a Schedule 13D or 13G with the SEC indicating beneficial ownership of more than 5% or control of an audit client. In addition, if a close family member of a partner controls an audit client, the CPA firm is not independent.
Exception for Unsolicited Inheritance and Gift	If any person receives an unsolicited financial interest that would impair independence, such financial interest may be disposed of as soon as practicable and independence is maintained. *NOTE: The SEC specifies that unsolicited financial interests must be disposed of not later than thirty days after having knowledge of and the right to dispose of the interest.*

Examples of Direct Financial Interests

Direct financial interests are investments made by a covered member/person

- In stocks, bonds, notes, options, or other securities of a client.
- As trustee or executor or administrator of an estate in securities of a client if the covered member/person has the authority to make investment decisions.
- As a general partner in a partnership that invests in client securities.
- In an investment club that acquires securities of a client.
- In insurance contracts or retirement plans that invest in a client if the covered member/person has the ability to direct the investments.
- In a client mutual fund or the fund's investment advisor.

Examples of Indirect Financial Interest

Indirect financial interests include

- A covered member's/person's investment as a limited partner in a partnership that invests in a client.
- A covered member's/person's investment in the product of a nonclient financial services company that invests in a client (when the covered member/person cannot direct the investments).
- A financial interest in the client held by a close relative of an individual participating in the engagement.
- A covered member's/person's investments in a nonclient diversified management investment company that invests in client securities.

NOTE: The SEC rules indicate that an investment (aggregated by the covered person and his or her immediate family) of 5% or less in a diversified investment company is not a material indirect investment. In essence, this allows CPA professionals and their family members to invest (up to the 5% cap) in diversified mutual funds that are not audit clients or part of an investment company complex that includes an audit client.

Materiality

Whether an indirect financial interest impairs independence depends on materiality. In determining materiality, the covered member/person should consider the net worth of the

1. Covered member/person (including the net worth of spouse, cohabitant, and dependents).
2. CPA firm.
3. Client.

The covered member/person should select the smallest measure of the above three items.

NOTE: Unless otherwise specified in regulations, a frequently used rule-of-thumb for calculating materiality is 5%. Generally, an indirect financial interest would be considered material when it amounts to 5% or more and would be considered not material if less than 5% of items 1., 2., or 3. above.

Setting up Blind Trusts

A lack of independence concerning a direct or indirect financial interest **cannot** be remedied by placing securities in a blind trust.

To maintain independence, a covered member/person must also ensure that such trusts do not acquire a direct or material indirect financial interest in his or her audit clients.

Trustee of a Trust or Executor/ Administrator of an Estate

If a covered member/person or the CPA firm is a trustee of any trust or executor or administrator of any estate that has or is committed to acquire any direct or material indirect financial interest in a client, the covered member/person is not independent.

NOTE: Mere designation of a member to become a trustee, executor, or administrator does not impair independence, but actual service does. The SEC rule is less stringent in stating that, if the member has no authority to make investment decisions for the trust or estate, independence is not impaired. The more stringent AICPA requirement should be followed.

Financial Interest/ Investment Held by a Close Family Member/Relative

According to AICPA requirements, if an individual participating in the engagement has a close relative that has a financial interest in the client that (1) is material to that relative, and the individual has knowledge of the relative's financial interest, or (2) enables the close relative to exercise significant influence over the client, independence is impaired.

Also, under AICPA requirements, if an individual has the ability to influence or is a partner in the office in which the lead engagement partner practices, independence is impaired if **both** conditions (1) and (2) above are met.

The SEC rule only addresses investments and expands the individuals covered to close family members/relatives of (1) proprietors, partners, or shareholders of the CPA firm, (2) professional employees providing ten or more hours of nonaudit services to the client, (3) spouses, spousal equivalents, and dependents of any person in (1) or (2), and (4) any group of persons in (1), (2), or (3). If such person(s) owns 5% or more of or controls an audit client (as evidenced by filed Schedule 13D or 13G), the CPA firm is not independent.

NOTE: Close family members/relatives are the individual's

- *Nondependent children (including grandchildren and stepchildren).*
- *Brothers and sisters.*
- *Parents.*

Specific Investments/ Financial Interests That Would and Would Not Impair Independence

Type of investment	See subsection
Partnerships	A
Investment clubs	B
Deposits in a client financial institution (savings and checking accounts)	C
Accounts with client broker-dealer and futures commission merchants	D
Financial products of a nonclient financial service company	E
Retirement plan managed by a client insurance company	F
Employee benefit, health and welfare, retirement, savings, or similar plan of clients and nonclients	G
Securities in social clubs	H
Nonclient mutual funds	I
Client mutual funds	J

Subsection A: Partnerships

Definition of Direct vs. Indirect Financial Interest Applied to Partnerships

A general partner/covered member's investment in a partnership that invests in a client is a direct financial interest.

A limited partner/covered member's investment in a partnership that invests in a client is an indirect financial interest.

General Partner

If a covered member has a **direct** financial interest in a partnership that invests in a client, and the covered member is a general partner or functions in a similar manner, independence is impaired.

Limited Partner

If a covered member has a **direct** financial interest in a partnership that invests in a client, and the covered member is a limited partner having a material interest (to the covered member's net worth), independence is impaired.

Subsection B: Investment Clubs

Definition of Investment Club	An investment club is a group of individuals who pool their money, select investments, and invest the pooled funds in the selected investment.
Direct Financial Interest	Any investment made by a covered member/person in an investment club is a direct financial interest. Therefore, if club investments are made in clients, independence is impaired without regard to materiality.

Subsection C: Deposits in a Client Financial Institution

Account Balances Insured	If a covered member/person has checking accounts, savings accounts, certificates of deposit, or money market accounts in a client financial institution, independence is **not** impaired if all such accounts' balances are equal to or less than the state or federal government insurance limits.
Uninsured Account Balances	Independence **is** impaired if the aggregate **uninsured** balances are material to the covered member's/person's net worth. *NOTE: The SEC does not factor in materiality for uninsured accounts. If a covered member/person has any uninsured balance, independence is impaired.*
Exception for CPA Firm Uninsured Balance	According to the SEC, a CPA firm may have an uninsured balance provided that the likelihood of the financial institution experiencing financial difficulty is remote. *NOTE: Under the AICPA requirements, the materiality of the uninsured balance governs, not the likelihood of financial difficulty.*

Subsection D: Accounts with Client Broker-Dealer and Futures Commission Merchants

Broker-Dealer Accounts

Under SEC rules, independence is impaired

1. If the account includes any asset other than cash or securities; and
2. The value of the assets in 1. above exceeds the amount subject to the Securities Investor Protection Corporation (or protection provided by a similar program); or
3. If the broker-dealer extends credit to the covered person (Chapter 16, Loans to and from Clients).

Futures Commission Merchant Accounts

Under SEC rules, independence is impaired if a covered person has a futures, commodity, or similar account with a futures commission merchant audit client.

Subsection E: Financial Products of a Nonclient Financial Services Company

Ability to Direct Investment

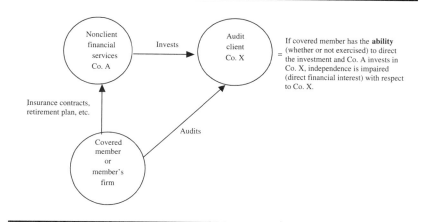

If covered member has the **ability** (whether or not exercised) to direct the investment and Co. A invests in Co. X, independence is impaired (direct financial interest) with respect to Co. X.

Does Not Have Ability to Direct Investment

If the above covered member does **not** have the ability to direct the investments and Co. A invests in a client (but not exclusively in clients), the interest is an indirect financial interest and independence is impaired only if material to the covered member.

Portfolio Is Invested in Clients Only	If Co. A above invests only in clients of the covered member, the interest is a direct financial interest and independence is impaired.

Subsection F: Retirement Plan Managed by a Client Insurance Company

Retirement Funds Maintained in a Pooled Separate Account	A covered member may contribute to a retirement plan that is invested/managed by a client insurance company and be independent with respect to the insurance company. To maintain independence, the retirement funds must be maintained in a pooled separate account, not part of the general assets of the insurance company.

Subsection G: Employee Benefit, Health and Welfare, Retirement, Savings, or Similar Plan of Clients and Nonclients

Covered Member Participates in Client or Nonclient Plan	If a covered member participates in or receives benefits from an employee benefit, health and welfare, retirement, savings, or similar plan **of a client,** independence is impaired with respect to the client and such plans. If a covered member participates in any of the above plans **of clients or nonclients that invest in the client or in other clients,** independence is impaired with respect to the client or those other clients (investees).
Exception for Health and Welfare Plan	If the covered member's participation in a health and welfare plan arises from the covered member's immediate family's permitted employment, independence would not be considered impaired if the plan is normally offered to all employees in equivalent employment positions.

Subsection H: Securities in Social Clubs

Required to Acquire Securities	A covered member who is required by a condition of membership of a social club (e.g., country club or tennis club) to acquire a pro rata share of the club's securities is independent with respect to such club, provided the membership in the club is essentially social.

Subsection I: Nonclient Mutual Funds

Indirect Financial Interest	Investments by a covered member/person in a nonclient nonregulated mutual fund that invests in stock of a client are indirect financial interests. Therefore, if the investments are material to the covered member, independence is impaired. In addition, if any partner or professional employee has significant influence over the fund, independence is impaired.
Specialized Fund	If the mutual fund has a limited number of securities in its portfolio, a covered member's/person's indirect financial interest may be material, causing independence to be impaired.
Audits of Investment Adviser, Sister Funds, or Related Nonfund Entities	If the covered member's/person's investment in a nonclient fund is part of a mutual fund complex that has other funds or nonfund entities that are audited by the member's firm, see Subsection J.

Subsection J: Client Mutual Funds

Audit of Any Fund or Nonfund Entity in the Fund Complex	According to the SEC, to maintain independence, (1) the CPA firm, including the firm's retirement plans (except for self-directed defined contribution plans), (2) any covered person, and (3) or the covered person's immediate family members must be independent of all

- Sister funds (having a common investment adviser).
- Related nonfund entities (e.g., investment adviser, broker-

dealer, bank, or insurance company in the mutual fund complex).

NOTE: In auditing a nonfund entity, the same independence requirements apply to all funds in the investment fund complex.

Subsection K: Insurance Policies

SEC Rule

If a covered person, including a member of his or her immediate family, has an individual insurance policy from an audit client, independence is impaired unless

1. The policy was acquired prior to becoming a covered person, and
2. The likelihood of the insurer becoming insolvent is remote.

NOTE: If the likelihood of the insurance audit client becoming insolvent is not remote, independence is impaired without regard to the member's status at the time the policy was acquired.

A member meeting conditions 1. and 2. above may renew the policy or increase the coverage for preexisting policies without impairing independence.

Authoritative Sources

1. Interpretation 101-1, *Interpretation of Rule 101* (ET 101.02.A.1 and 2).
2. SEC *Codification of Financial Reporting Policies,* Financial Interest in Client Company (sec. 602.02.b.ii.).
3. SEC Rules 2-01(c)(1)(i), Investments in Audit Clients; 2-01(c)(1)(ii)(B), Savings and Checking Accounts; 2-01(c)(1)(ii)(C). Broker-Dealer Accounts; 2-01 (c)(1)(ii)(D), Futures Commission Merchant Accounts; 2-01(c)(1)(ii)(F), Insurance Products; 2-01(c)(1)(ii)(G), Investment Companies; 2-01(c)(1)(iii)(A), Inheritance and Gift; 2-01(c)(1)(iii)(B). New Audit Engagement and; 2-01(c)(1)(iii)(C), Employee Compensation and Benefit Plan. *Revision of the Commission's Auditor Independence Requirements.*
4. Ethics Ruling No. 11, *Member as Executor or Trustee* (ET 191.021-.022).
5. Ethics Ruling No. 17, *Member of Social Club* (ET 191.033-.04).

6. Ethics Ruling No. 35, *Stockholder in Mutual Funds* (ET 191.069-.070).
7. Ethics Ruling No. 36, *Participant in Investment Club* (ET 191.071-.072).
8. Ethics Ruling No. 41, *Member as Auditor of Insurance Company* (ET 191.081-.082).
9. Ethics Ruling No. 66, *Member's Retirement or Savings Plan Has Financial Interest in Client* (Revised)(ET 191.132-.133).
10. Ethics Ruling No. 68, *Blind Trust* (ET 191.136-.137).
11. Ethics Ruling No. 70, *Member's Depository Relationship with Client Financial Institution* (ET 191.140-.141).
12. Ethics Ruling No. 79, *Member's Investment in a Partnership That Invests in Member's Clients* (ET 191.158-.159).
13. Ethics Ruling No. 107, *Participation in Health and Welfare Plan of Client* (ET 191.214-.215).
14. Ethics Ruling No. 109, *Member's Investment in Financial Services Products That Invest in Clients* (ET 191.218-.219).

11 FINANCIAL INTERESTS IN NONCLIENTS THAT HAVE INVESTOR OR INVESTEE RELATIONSHIPS WITH CLIENTS

Introduction

A financial interest in a nonclient that is related in some way to a client may impair independence. This chapter explains and graphically illustrates those investments in nonclients that may impair independence.

Basic Principle

Independence may be impaired because of a covered member's/person's financial interest in a nonclient who is related in various ways to a client. A financial interest in a nonclient may result in a financial interest in a client or place the covered member/person in a capacity equivalent to a member of management.

Important Definitions

To apply the guidance in this chapter, you need to understand the following definitions:

1. Significant influence—According to Accounting Principles Board Opinion No. 18, *The Equity Method of Accounting for Investments in Common Stock*, significant influence exists when the investor owns from 20 to 50% of the investee's voting shares, although circumstances exist when such influence is present with under 20% ownership, or conversely is absent with holdings of 20% or greater.
2. Investor—A partner, general partner, or a natural person or corporation that has the ability to exercise significant influence.
3. Intermediary investor—An entity in which a covered member/person invests that, in turn, invests in a client.
4. Investee—A subsidiary or an entity over which an investor has the ability to exercise significant influence.
5. Common investee—An entity in which both the covered member/person and the client invest.

**Client Has
Material
Investment in
Nonclient**[1]

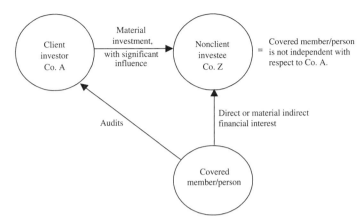

Rationale: Covered member's/person's direct or material indirect financial interest in Co. Z (i.e., common investee) is tantamount to covered member/person having a financial interest in Co. A.

**Client Has
Immaterial
Investment in
Nonclient**[1]

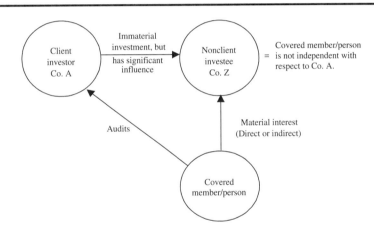

Rationale: Client Co. A's ability to influence Co. Z (i.e., common investee) could enhance or diminish the value of the covered member's/person's financial interest in Co. Z by an amount material to the covered member's/person's net worth without a material effect on its own financial statements. As a result, the covered member/person would not appear to be independent.

NOTE: If the covered member/person had an immaterial (direct or indirect) financial interest in Co. Z, the covered member/person would be independent with respect to Co. A. The SEC quantifies materiality as not exceeding 5% of Co. A's consolidated total assets. In addition, Co. A's equity in Co. Z's income from continuing operations before income taxes cannot exceed 5% of Co. A's consolidated income from continuing operations before income taxes.

---

[1]   *Appendix A to this chapter presents a flowchart of the decision process involved when a covered member/person invests in nonclient entities in which audit clients also invest. This appendix was adapted from www.sec.gov.*

**Nonclient Has
Material
Investment in
Client[2]**

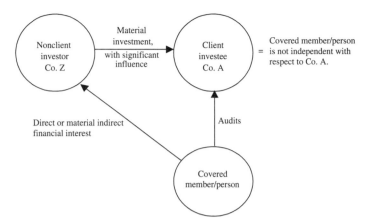

Rationale: Covered member's/person's direct or material indirect interest in Co. Z (i.e., intermediary investor) is tantamount to covered member/person having a financial interest in Co. A.

**Nonclient Has
Immaterial
Investment in
Client[2]**

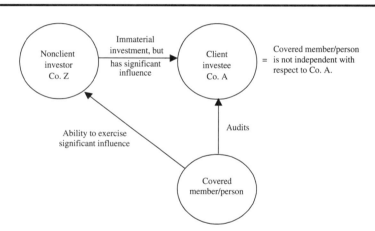

Rationale: A financial interest sufficient to allow the covered member/person to significantly influence the actions of Co. Z (i.e., intermediary investor) could permit the covered member/person to exercise a degree of control over Co. A that would place the covered member/person in a capacity equivalent to a member of management.

---

[2] *Appendix B to this chapter presents a flowchart of the decision process involved when a covered member/ person invests in nonclient entities that invest in audit clients. This appendix was adapted from www.sec.gov.*

Covered Member's/ Person's Investment in Limited Partnership (LP) Having Client General Investor

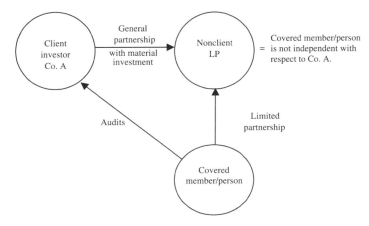

NOTE: However, if (1) Co. A's financial interest in LP is not material and (2) covered member's/person's financial interest in LP is immaterial, covered member's/person's independence with respect to Co. A is not impaired.

Other Relationships

Other relationships, for example, brother-sister entities (under common control) and client-nonclient joint ventures, may affect independence.

To determine if they do

1. Make inquiry(ies) to your client to determine if such relationships exist. (If you **cannot** reasonably obtain information about the relationships, independence is **not** impaired.)

2. If relationships exist, would a reasonable observer conclude that independence is threatened?

Example: Brother-Sister Entities

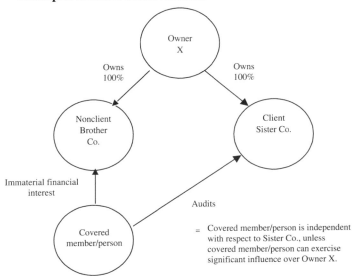

NOTE: If covered member's/person's financial interest in Brother Company is material, covered member/person is not independent with respect to Sister Company.

Example: Joint Ventures

The same logic applied to Brother-Sister above applies to joint ventures. An immaterial financial interest in a nonclient investor would not impair independence, provided the covered member/person could not exercise significant influence over the nonclient investor. For example

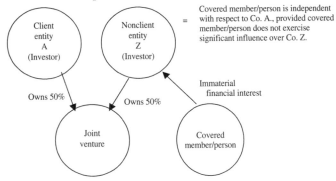

Appendix A
Investing in Entities in Which Audit Clients Invest

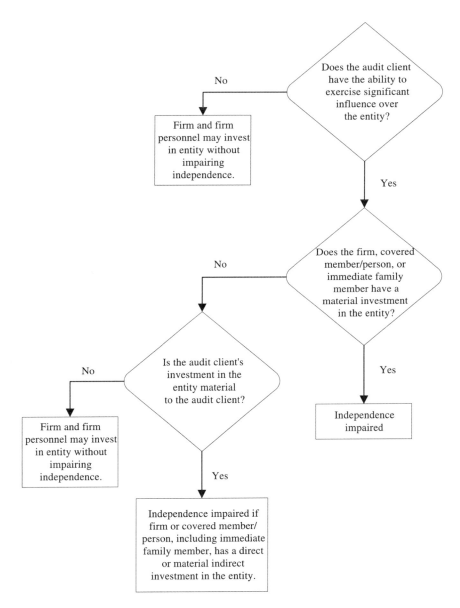

Ethics for CPAs

Appendix B
Investing in Entities That Invest in Audit Clients

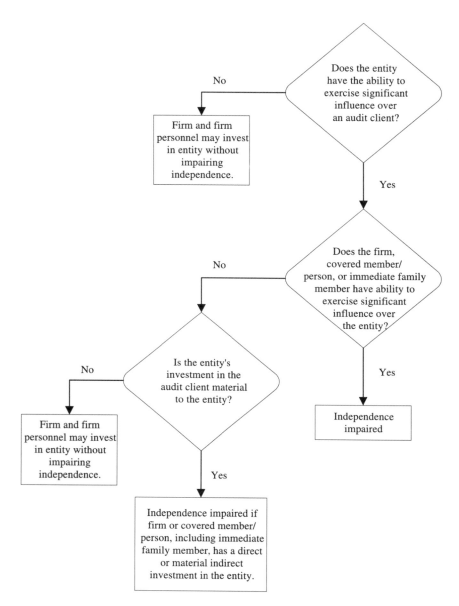

Authoritative Sources

1. Interpretation 101-8, *Effect on Independence of Financial Interests in Nonclients Having Investor or Investee Relationships with a Covered Member's Client* (ET 101.10).
2. SEC *Codification of Financial Reporting Policies,* Interests in Nonclient Affiliates and Investee Companies (Sec. 602.02.b.iii).
3. Ethics Ruling No. 81, *Member's Investment in a Limited Partnership* (ET 191.162-.163).
4. See also Ethics Ruling No. 69, *Invest with a General Partner* (ET 138-.139), which is discussed in Chapter 15, Business Relationships; Cooperative Arrangements; Joint Closely Held Investments; Lease Arrangements; and Investments by Clients in Auditors.
5. See also Ethics Ruling No. 79, *Member's Investment in a Partnership That Invests in Client* (ET .158-.159), which is discussed in Chapter 10, Direct and Indirect Financial Interests in Client.

12 FORMER PRACTITIONERS[1]

Introduction	The independence of a CPA firm might be affected by a former practitioner's financial interest in, or association with, a client.
Definition of Former Practitioner	A proprietor, partner, shareholder or equivalent in a CPA firm, (or professional employee under SEC rules) who leaves by resignation, termination, retirement, or sale of all or part of the practice.
Sarbanes-Oxley Act of 2002	In August 2002, Congress passed the Sarbanes-Oxley Act (known as the Public Accounting Reform and Investor Protection Act). Section 206, "Conflicts of Interest," prohibits a CPA firm from performing any audit service for a public company, if a CEO, CFO, controller, chief accounting officer, or equivalent person was employed by that CPA firm and participated in the audit of the public company during the one-year period preceding the start of the current audit.
Basic Principle (AICPA Rule)	Independence of the CPA firm may be impaired if the former practitioner is considered a member of the CPA firm as a result of the actual, or appearance of, influence or participation in the CPA firm.

---

[1] *The AICPA's Professional Ethics Executive Committee has issued an Exposure Draft, dated June 17, 2002, titled **Omnibus Proposal of Professional Ethics Division Interpretations and Rulings**. The Exposure Draft contains proposed revisions to Interpretations No. 101-2, **Former Practitioners and Firm Independence**. The committee believes that a combination of restrictions and safeguards (i.e., policies and procedures) is the most appropriate and effective manner in which to deal with the threats to independence under such circumstances. Accordingly, the proposed revision includes specific requirements that a firm professional must follow when he or she accepts a **key position** (e.g., having primary responsibility for the preparation of the financial statements or ability to exercise influence over the financial statements) with an attest client. Please check updates to this section on the John Wiley & Sons, Inc. website at www.wiley.com/ethics.*

If a former practitioner who is considered a "member" has a financial interest in or official association with a CPA firm's client, independence may be impaired.

Criteria for Determining CPA Firm's Independence

In determining a CPA firm's compliance with independence requirements, the key is deciding whether a former practitioner is included in the term "a member of the CPA firm."

The criteria for making this determination relate to

- Payments to the former practitioner.
- Participation in the firm's business or professional activities.
- Appearance of participation or association with the CPA firm.

Restrictions on Payments

According to the AICPA, payments of amounts due the former practitioner (1) for his or her capital interest in the firm and (2) for unfunded vested retirement benefits must be

- Subject to a written agreement.
- Not material to the CPA firm.
- Calculated based on an underlying formula that remains fixed during the payout period. (Retirement benefits may be adjusted for inflation.)

NOTE: The SEC imposes additional restrictions on payments as discussed later in this chapter.

Restrictions on Actual Participation

The former practitioner cannot participate in the firm's business or professional activities (whether or not compensated).

NOTE: The AICPA provides an exception to this restriction for a reasonable period of time during the transition period upon leaving the firm for consultations on an advisory basis.

Restrictions on Appearance of Participation or Association

An unacceptable appearance of participation or association would result from actions such as inclusion of the former practitioner's name

- Under the firm's name in an office building directory.
- As a member of the firm in membership lists of business, professional, or civic organizations.
- In the firm's internal directory without being designated as retired.

An unacceptable appearance of participation or association would not be created by the firm providing office amenities such as office space and secretarial and telephone services, except as noted below concerning a position of significant influence with the client.

NOTE: If a former practitioner assumes a position of significant influence with a client, office amenities can no longer be provided.

Additional Restrictions of the SEC

The SEC rule expands the individuals covered above to include any CPA firm professional employees that are employed by audit clients in an accounting role or financial reporting oversight role. Independence will **not** be impaired if a former partner, professional employee, etc., does **not** have an accounting role or financial reporting oversight role with the audit client.

NOTE: The SEC defines accounting role or financial reporting oversight role as a role in which the individual

1. *Exercises influence over accounting records or anyone who prepares them.*
2. *Exercises influence over the contents of the financial statements or anyone who prepares them.*

Individuals included in 2. above include: a member of the board of directors, CEO, president, CFO, COO, general council, chief accounting officer, controller, director of internal audit, director of financial reporting, treasurer, vice president of marketing, or equivalent positions.

If the former partner, principal, or shareholder has an accounting role or financial reporting oversight role at the audit client, independence will **not** be impaired if the individual does not

1. Influence the CPA firm's operations or financial policies;
2. Have a capital balance in the CPA firm; or
3. Have a financial arrangement with the CPA firm other than a fully funded, fixed payment retirement account (not dependent on the CPA firm's financial results).

NOTE: A rabbi trust (or similar arrangement in a jurisdiction not having rabbi trusts) may be used in lieu of a fully funded retirement plan. (A rabbi trust is an irrevocable trust whose assets are not accessible to the CPA firm until all benefit obligations are met. However, a rabbi trust is subject to creditor claims in bankruptcy.)

For a former professional employee of the CPA firm (not a partner, principal, or shareholder) who has **not** been associated with the CPA firm for five or more years, independence is not impaired if the fixed payments are immaterial to the employee when the former employee accepts an accounting or financial reporting oversight role with the audit client.

Accepting Employment— Safeguards Required by the SEC

When a former practitioner (FP) is employed by the client, the SEC also requires that CPA firms implement the following safeguards:

1. The audit engagement team should consider whether the audit plan needs to be modified to reduce the risk of circumvention.
2. If FP will have significant interaction with the audit team, the CPA firm should take steps to ensure that the existing audit team has the stature and objectivity to deal with FP.
3. If FP joins the client (a) within one year of leaving the firm and (b) has significant interaction with the audit team, the next annual audit should be separately reviewed by a professional uninvolved in the audit.

> *NOTE: The purpose of the review is to determine if the audit team exercises appropriate skepticism in evaluating representations and work of FP. The extent of the review depends in part on the position that FP has at the audit client.*
>
> *ISB No. 3, **Employment with Audit Clients,** originally contained an additional safeguard that required prompt liquidation of capital balances, settlement of retirement balances unless immaterial and fixed as to amount and payment, and settlement of immaterial retirement balances under certain circumstances. However, this safeguard has been superseded by the SEC's revised independence rules, discussed under "Additional Restrictions of the SEC."*

Authoritative Sources

1. Interpretation 101-2, *Former Practitioners and Firm Independence* (ET 101.04).
2. SEC Rule 2-01(c)(2)(iii)—*Employment at Audit Client of Former Employee of Accounting Firm. Revision of the Commission's Auditor Independence Requirements.*
3. ISB Standard No. 3, *Employment with Audit Clients.*

13 UNPAID FEES[1]

Introduction	Unpaid fees may impair independence. Both the AICPA and the SEC have rules that govern unpaid fees, and those rules are substantially different. This chapter explains the AICPA and SEC rules and highlights their differences.
Basic Principle	Unpaid fees may impair independence of the CPA firm because they are tantamount to having a financial interest in, or making a loan to, a client.
Definitions of Unpaid Fees	Unpaid fees are fees for (1) audit and (2) other professional services that relate to certain prior periods that are delinquent as of the • Date the current year's audit engagement begins, if the client is an SEC registrant, or • Date the audit report is issued for non-SEC clients (i.e., AICPA rule).
AICPA Rule	Independence is impaired, if when the audit report is issued for the current year, professional fees for (1) billed services, (2) unbilled services, or (3) uncollected notes receivable (arising from professional fees) are delinquent for more than one year prior to the current audit report date. *NOTE: Materiality of the delinquent fees is not considered, and the above rule does not apply to professional fees from a client in bankruptcy.*

---

[1] *Contingent fees and commissions are prohibited for any service performed for a client when the member also performs an audit, certain attestation services, or a compilation for that client. These matters are discussed in Chapter 29, Rule 302—Contingent Fees, and Chapter 32, Rule 503—Commissions and Referral Fees.*

Example:

	Period 1	*Period 2*
Current audit report issued on 2/15/02	Fees for services performed from 2/15/01 to 2/15/02 do not impair independence	Fees for services performed before 2/15/01 do impair independence

---

SEC Rule

The CPA firm's independence is impaired, if unpaid fees for any professional service are material in relation to the fee expected for the current audit at the date the current audit begins.

NOTE: Unpaid fees personally owed by a principal shareholder of a client can also impair independence.

There are two exceptions to the SEC's general rule that apply only to audits of financial statements in filed annual reports. Independence is not impaired, if at the time the current audit begins

1. A definite commitment is made by the client to pay delinquent fees before the current year audit report is issued, or
2. An arrangement is agreed to for periodic payments to pay the delinquent fees, and there is reasonable assurance that such fees will be paid before beginning the audit for the next year.

NOTE: The exceptions above do not apply to a registration of securities under the Securities Act of 1933. Generally, prior year audit and other professional fees should be paid before the current audit begins to avoid independence problems in a registration.

Authoritative Sources

---

1. SEC *Codification of Financial Reporting Policies*, Unpaid Prior Professional Fees (sec 602.02.b.iv).
2. Ethics Ruling No. 52, *Unpaid Fees* (ET 191.103-.104).

14 PERFORMANCE OF OTHER OR NONATTEST SERVICES FOR CLIENTS

Introduction

A member or member's firm may perform services for a client that require independence (attest services) and also perform nonattest services for the same client.

The member must evaluate the effect of the nonattest services on independence.

> **Example:**
>
> A member's firm might perform audit services for a client and also be asked to design an inventory control system for that client. The member must evaluate the nature of the services related to the design of the inventory control system to determine whether the services impair audit independence.

Basic Principle

To avoid an impairment of independence, the member should not perform **management functions** or make **management decisions** for an attest client.

Essential Understanding with Client

The member should establish an understanding with the client regarding

- Objectives of the engagement.
- Services to be performed.
- Management's responsibilities.
- Member's responsibilities.
- Limitations of the engagement.

It should be clear that the member will not make management decisions or perform management functions.

NOTE: It is preferable that the understanding be documented in an engagement letter.

Other Client Responsibilities

The member should be satisfied that the client

- Is in a position to have an **informed judgment** on the results of the nonattest services.

- Understands its responsibility to
  1. Designate a management level individual (or individuals) to be responsible for overseeing the nonattest services provided.
  2. Evaluate the adequacy of the nonattest services performed and the findings reached.
  3. Make management decisions, including accepting responsibility for the results of nonattest services.
  4. Establish and maintain internal controls, including monitoring ongoing activities.

General Examples of Activities That Would Impair Independence

- Authorizing, executing, or consummating a transaction.
- Otherwise having or executing authority on behalf of a client.
- Having custody of client assets.
- Reporting to the board of directors on behalf of management.
- Supervising client employees in the performance of normal recurring activities.
- Determining which of the member's recommendations should be implemented.
- Serving as the client's registrar, stock transfer or escrow agent, or general counsel.
- Preparing source documents or originating data in electronic or other form evidencing the occurrence of a transaction.

> **Example:**
>
> Source documents include purchase orders, payroll time cards, and customer orders. They are the documents on which the evidence of an accounting transaction is initially recorded. Documents created subsequent to the initial transaction record are not source documents.

NOTE: The SEC generally regards bookkeeping services of all types as impairing independence.

SEC versus AICPA on Services to Nonclients Related to the Client

The SEC regards all persons and entities related to the client, such as officers, directors, principal stockholders, affiliates, or an employee benefit plan sponsored by the client, to be the same as the client for purposes of evaluating independence.

The SEC position is that *services that would impair independence if provided to the client would also impair independence if provided to related persons or entities.*

> **Example:**
>
> A partner in a firm is also a lawyer and is engaged to represent the CEO of an audit client in personal litigation. Independence is impaired because legal representation requires advocacy.

The AICPA generally regards these related entities and persons as separate clients, but imposes restrictions on services to employee benefit plans sponsored by the client. (See Subsection M.)

SECPS Restrictions on Consulting Services

SEC Practice Section members should not perform services for clients that are inconsistent with the firm's responsibilities to the public. The SECPS prohibits the following services for audit clients:

- Psychological testing.
- Public opinion polls.
- Merger and acquisition assistance for a finder's fee.
- Executive recruitment (see Subsection H).
- Actuarial services to insurance companies (see Subsections F and G).

The SEC addresses executive recruitment and actuarial services and identifies activities in those areas that impair independence (see Subsections H and G).

Sarbanes-Oxley Act of 2002

In July 2002, Congress passed the Sarbanes-Oxley Act (known as the Public Accounting Reform and Investor Protection Act). Section 201, "Services Outside the Scope of the Practice of Auditors," prohibits CPA firms that audit publicly traded companies under the purview of the SEC from offering the following:

- Bookkeeping or other services related to the accounting records or financial statements of the audit client.
- Financial information systems design and implementation.
- Appraisal or valuation services, fairness opinions, or contribution-in-kind reports.
- Actuarial services.
- Internal audit outsourcing services (Chapter 22).
- Management functions or human resources.
- Broker or dealer investment advisor, or investment banking services.
- Legal services and expert services unrelated to the audit.
- Any other service that the Public Company Accounting Oversight Board determines, by regulations, is impermissible.

NOTE: Section 201 of the Sarbanes-Oxley Act is effective 180 days after the commencement of the operations of the Public Company Accounting Oversight Board. In December 2002, the SEC published proposed rules to implement Section 201 of Sarbanes-Oxley. The proposed rules were published in Release No. 33-8154, "Strengthening the Commission's Requirements Regarding Auditor Independence." The SEC is required to issue final rules by January 26, 2003.

Preapproval for Other Nonaudit Services	The Sarbanes-Oxley Act makes it unlawful for CPA firms to provide other nonaudit services, including tax services, to public company audit clients unless those services are approved in advance by the company's audit committee. In addition, the audit committee approval must be disclosed to investors in periodic reports.

Specific Examples of Activities That Would and Would Not Impair Independence by Type of Service	*Type of service*	*See subsection*
	Bookkeeping	A
	Payroll and other disbursement	B
	Benefit plan administration	C
	Investment advisory or investment management, including broker-dealer and investment banking services	D
	Corporate finance—consulting or advisory	E
	Appraisal and valuation, including fairness opinions	F
	Actuarial services for insurance companies and related accounts for audit clients	G
	Executive or employee search and human resource services	H
	Business risk consulting	I
	Information systems design, installation, or integration	J
	Management advisory services	K
	Representative of creditor's committee	L
	Employee benefit plan sponsored by client	M
	Assisting clients in implementing SFAS 133 (Derivatives)	N
	Legal services	O
	Tax services	P

Subsection A: Bookkeeping

Example Activities That Would *Not* Impair Independence	• Record transactions for which management has determined or approved the appropriate account classification, or post coded transactions to a client's general ledger. • Prepare financial statements based on information in the trial balance. • Post client-approved entries to a client's trial balance. • Propose standard, adjusting, or correcting journal entries or other changes affecting the financial statements to the client.

- Provide data-processing services.

NOTE: The GAO considers maintaining or preparing the entity's general ledger or posting coded transactions to the general ledger to be a performance of management function, which impairs independence (see Chapter 23).

Example Activities That Would Impair Independence

- Determine or change journal entries, account codings or classification for transactions, or other accounting records without obtaining client approval.
- Authorize or approve transactions.
- Prepare source documents or originate data.
- Make changes to source documents or entries without client approval.

SEC Position on Bookkeeping Services

Under rules existing as of December 31, 2002, with two exceptions, the SEC considers an auditor to not be independent if the auditor

1. Maintains or prepares client accounting records.
2. Prepares financial statements (or the basis of such statements) that are filed with the SEC.
3. Prepares source data underlying financial statements.

NOTE: The Sarbanes-Oxley Act makes it unlawful for an auditor of a public company to provide bookkeeping or other services related to the accounting records or financial statements of the audit client. (See proposed rule Release No. 33-8154.)

Exceptions to the SEC's Position on Bookkeeping Services

The SEC will not deem independence to have been impaired in the following circumstances:

- In rare emergency/unusual situations when the auditor **does not** undertake managerial actions or make managerial decisions.

  NOTE: The registrant and auditor should contact the SEC relative to the application of the emergency exception.

- Accounting services for a foreign component of a domestic client, provided **all** of the following six conditions are met:

  1. The services are limited, routine, or ministerial bookkeeping services.
  2. It is impractical to make other arrangements.
  3. The foreign entity is not material to the consolidated financial statements.
  4. The foreign entity does not have employees capable or competent to perform the services.

5. The services are consistent with the professional ethics rules in the foreign location.
6. Total fees for the bookkeeping services for all foreign entities collectively do not exceed the greater of one percent of the consolidated audit fee or $10,000.

Subsection B: Payroll and Other Disbursement

Example Activities That Would *Not* Impair Independence

- Using payroll time records provided and approved by the client, generate unsigned checks, or process client's payroll.
- Transmit client-approved payroll or other disbursement information to a financial institution provided the client has authorized the member to make the transmission and has made arrangements for the financial institution to limit the corresponding individual payments as to amount and payee. In addition, once transmitted, the client must authorize the financial institution to process the information.
- Make electronic payroll tax payments in accordance with US Treasury Department or comparable guidelines provided the client has made arrangements with the financial institution to limit such payments to a named payee.

NOTE: The SEC takes a much more restrictive position on bookkeeping services than the AICPA. See Subsection A in this chapter for a discussion of the SEC's position.

Example Activities That Would Impair Independence

- Accept responsibility to authorize payment of client funds, electronically or otherwise, except as specifically provided for with respect to electronic payroll tax payments.
- Accept responsibility to sign or cosign client checks, even if only in emergency situations.
- Maintain a client's bank account or otherwise have custody of a client's funds or make credit or banking decisions for the client.
- Sign the payroll tax return on behalf of client management.
- Approve vendor invoices for payment.

Subsection C: Benefit Plan Administration

Example Activities That Would *Not* **Impair Independence**	• Communicate summary plan data to plan trustee. • Advise client management regarding the application or impact of provisions of the plan document. • Process transactions (e.g., investment/benefit elections or increase/decrease contributions to the plan; data entry; participant confirmations; and processing of distributions and loans) initiated by plan participants through the member's electronic medium, such as an interactive voice response system or Internet connection or other media. • Prepare account valuations for plan participants using data collected through the member's electronic or other medium.
Example Activities That Would Impair Independence	• Make policy decisions on behalf of client management. • When dealing with plan participants, interpret the plan document on behalf of management without first obtaining management's concurrence. • Make disbursements on behalf of the plan. • Have custody of assets of a plan. • Serve a plan as a fiduciary as defined by ERISA. *NOTE: See Subsection M for a discussion of the effect of providing services to a benefit plan on independence with respect to the sponsor.*

Subsection D: Investment Advisory or Investment Management, Including Broker-Dealer and Investment Banking Services

Example Activities That Would *Not* **Impair Independence**	• Recommend the allocation of funds that a client should invest in various asset classes, depending upon the client's desired rate of return, risk tolerance, etc. • Perform recordkeeping and reporting of client's portfolio balances including providing a comparative analysis of the client's investments to third-party benchmarks. • Review the manner in which a client's portfolio is being managed by investment account managers, including determining whether the managers are (1) following the guidelines of the client's investment policy statement; (2) meeting the client's investment objectives; and (3) conforming to the client's stated investment styles.

- Transmit a client's investment selection to a broker-dealer or equivalent provided the client has authorized the broker-dealer or equivalent to execute the transaction.

Example Activities That Would Impair Independence

- Act as a broker-dealer, promoter, or underwriter for a client.
- Make investment decisions on behalf of client management or otherwise have discretionary authority over a client's investments.
- Execute a transaction to buy or sell a client's investment.
- Have custody of client assets, such as taking temporary possession of securities purchased by a client.
- Recommend an audit client's securities to anyone.

NOTE: Section 201 of the Sarbanes-Oxley Act makes it unlawful for an auditor of a public company to provide

1. *Broker or dealer services,*
2. *Investment advisor services, and*
3. *Investment banking services.*

Subsection E: Corporate Finance—Consulting or Advisory

Example Activities That Would *Not* Impair Independence

- Assist in developing corporate strategies.
- Assist in identifying or introducing the client to possible sources of capital that meet the client's specifications or criteria.
- Assist in analyzing the effects of proposed transactions including providing advice to a client during negotiations with potential buyers, sellers, or capital sources.
- Assist in drafting an offering document or memorandum.
- Participate in transaction negotiations in an advisory capacity.
- Be named as a financial advisor in a client's private placement memoranda or offering document.

Example Activities That Would Impair Independence

- Commit the client to the terms of a transaction or consummate a transaction on behalf of the client.
- Act as a promoter, underwriter, broker dealer, or guarantor of client securities, or distributor of private placement memoranda or offering documents.
- Maintain custody of client securities.

Subsection F: Appraisal and Valuation (Including Fairness Opinions)

Example Activities That Would *Not* Impair Independence

- Test the reasonableness of the value placed on an asset or liability included in a client's financial statements by preparing a separate valuation of that asset or liability.
- Perform a valuation of a client's business when all significant matters of judgment are approved by the client and the client is in a position to have an informed judgment on the results of the valuation.

*NOTE: The GAO limits appraisal and valuation services to **reviewing** the work of the entity or a specialist employed by the entity (see Chapter 23).*

Example Activities That Would Impair Independence

- Prepare a valuation of an employer's securities contained in an employee stock ownership plan (ESOP) to support transactions with participants, and allocations within the ESOP, when the client is not in a position to have an informed judgment on the results of this valuation.
- Prepare an appraisal, valuation, or actuarial report using assumptions determined by the member and not approved by the client.

With four exceptions consistent with the above AICPA requirement, the CPA firm is not independent if it provides any of these services and the results are material to the financial statements or will be audited by the CPA firm. The four exceptions are

1. The client or specialist employed by the client provides primary support for the recorded balances.
2. For pensions, other postemployment benefit, or similar liabilities, the client takes responsibility for all significant assumptions and data.
3. The valuation is performed in the context of a tax engagement.
4. The valuation does not affect the financial statements.

NOTE: The listed exceptions above do not include an exception for purchase price allocation in an acquisition.

Fairness opinions are opinions on the adequacy of consideration in a transaction. In foreign jurisdictions, contribution-in-kind reports may be required. Auditors should contact the SEC with questions involving such reports.

Section 201 of the Sarbanes-Oxley Act prohibits the performance of appraisal and valuation services.

Subsection G: Actuarial Services for Insurance Companies and Related Accounts for Audit Clients

Example Activities That Would *Not* Impair Independence	According to the SEC, independence is not impaired if the auditor • Assists management in developing methods, assumptions, and amounts for policy, loss reserves, and other actuarial items in the financial statements. • Assists management in converting the financial statements from a statutory basis to a GAAP basis. • Analyzes actuarial alternatives for federal tax planning purposes. • Assists management in the financial analysis of various matters (e.g., proposed new policies, new markets, acquisitions, reinsurance needs)
Example Activities That Would Impair Independence	According to the SEC, independence would be impaired if • The auditor provides the client with its actuarial capabilities. • Management does not accept responsibility for significant actuarial methods and assumptions. • The auditor's involvement is continuous. *NOTE: Section 201 of the Sarbanes-Oxley Act makes it unlawful for an auditor of a public company to provide actuarial services to that company.*

Subsection H: Executive or Employee Search and Human Resource Services

Example Activities That Would *Not* Impair Independence under AICPA Requirements	• Recommend a position description or candidate specifications. • Solicit and perform screening of candidates and recommend qualified candidates to a client based on the client-approved criteria (e.g., required skills and experience). • Participate in employee hiring or compensation discussions in an advisory capacity. *NOTE: The GAO prohibits the CPA firm from performing executive search and recruiting activities for the audit client (see Chapter 23).*

Example Activities That Would Impair Independence under AICPA Requirements	• Commit the client to employee compensation or benefits arrangements. • Hire or terminate client employees.

SEC Rule	The SEC (consistent with SECPS requirements) is more stringent and explicit than the AICPA requirements above in that the auditor may not

1. Search for, seek out, or perform reference check of prospective candidates for managerial, executive, or director positions.
2. Engage in psychological testing or other formal evaluations.
3. Act as negotiator on the client's behalf.
4. Recommend a specific candidate for a specific job.

NOTE: The auditor may interview candidates or advise the client, at the client's request, on a candidate's competence for accounting-related positions.

Section 201 of the Sarbanes-Oxley Act makes it unlawful for an auditor of a public company to provide human resources services to that company.

Subsection I: Business Risk Consulting

Example Activities That Would *Not* Impair Independence	• Provide assistance in assessing the client's business risks and control processes. • Recommend a plan for making improvements to a client's control processes and assist in implementing these improvements.

Example Activities That Would Impair Independence	• Make or approve business risk decisions. • Present business risk considerations to the board or others on behalf of management.

Subsection J: Information Systems—Design, Installation, or Integration

Example Activities That Would *Not* Impair Independence	• Design, install or integrate a client's information system, provided the client makes all management decisions. • Customize a prepackaged accounting or information system, provided the client makes all management decisions. • Provide the initial training and instruction to client employees on a newly implemented information and control system.
Example Activities That Would Impair Independence	• Supervise client personnel in the daily operation of a client's information system. • Operate or manage a client's information system or local area network (LAN).

Explicit SEC Requirements Relating to Hardware or Software Underlying Financial Statements	When designing or implementing hardware/software related to a client's financial statements, the SEC explicitly requires that the following five requirements be followed. Management must
	
	1. Acknowledge in writing to the CPA firm and the client's audit committee (or its board of directors) the company's responsibility for controls over financial reporting.
	2. Designate a competent employee or employees, preferably within senior management, to make all management decisions.
	3. Make all decisions about
	
	   a. Systems to be evaluated/selected.
	   b. Controls to be implemented.
	   c. Scope and timetable for implementation.
	   d. Testing.
	   e. Training.
	   f. Conversions.
	   g. Other matters.
	
	4. Evaluate the adequacy of design and results of implementation.
	5. Not rely on the auditor's work as the primary basis for determining the adequacy of internal controls over financial reporting.
	
	NOTE: The management does not perform all of the five requirements above, the auditor's independence is impaired.
	
	   Section 201 of the Sarbanes-Oxley Act makes it unlawful for an auditor of a public company to provide financial information systems design and implementation to that company.

| **SEC's Proxy Disclosure Requirements** | Under SEC rules, a company must disclose, in all annual proxy statements filed after February 5, 2001, the aggregate fees billed for information technology services, as well as other nonaudit services, during the most recent fiscal year. Such information technology fees should be disclosed under the caption "Financial Information Systems Design and Implementation Fees." |

Subsection K: Management Advisory Services

| **Example Activities That Would *Not* Impair Independence** | As long as the member's role is advisory in nature, independence would not be considered to be impaired even if the services are very extensive. |

> **Example:**
> A member has attended board meetings; interpreted financial statements, forecasts and other analyses; counseled on expansion plans; and counseled on banking relationships. Even though the member's involvement has been extensive, independence is not impaired because the services have been limited to providing advice in all these areas.

| **SEC Rule** | According to the SEC, independence is impaired if the auditor acts, temporarily or permanently, as a director, officer, or employee, or performs any decision-making, supervisory, or ongoing management function (see Chapter 13). |

NOTE: Section 201 of the Sarbanes-Oxley Act identifies performing "management functions" as a prohibited service, which is consistent with existing SEC rule.

Subsection L: Representative of Creditor's Committee

| **Examples of Activities That Would Impair Independence with Respect to the Debtor Corporation** | • Sign or cosign checks issued by the debtor corporation.
• Sign or cosign purchase orders in excess of established amounts.
• Exercise general supervision to insure compliance with budgetary controls and pricing formulas established by management, with the consent of creditors, as part of an overall program aimed at the liquidation of deferred indebtedness. |

NOTE: All of the activities are management functions and would impair independence with respect to the debtor.

Subsection M: Employee Benefit Plan Sponsored by Client

Nature of Services Provided to Employee Benefit Plan	Asset management or investment services that may include having custody of assets, performing management functions, or making management decisions are provided to an employee benefit plan sponsored by an audit client or other attest service client. *NOTE: Independence would be impaired for the plan—the issue is independence with respect to the sponsor. (See Chapter 24, Independence Requirements for Audits of Employee Benefit Plans, for a discussion of plan-related independence issues.)*
AICPA Position on Defined Benefit Plan	If the assets under management or in the custody of the member are material to the plan or the client sponsor, independence is impaired with respect to the sponsor.
AICPA Position on Defined Contribution Plan	Impairment of independence with respect to the sponsor would occur if the member makes management decisions or performs management functions on behalf of the sponsor or has custody of the sponsor's assets. *NOTE: The AICPA views the plan and its participants as separate clients from the sponsor.*
Position of the SEC and Other Regulatory Agencies	Government regulatory agencies such as the SEC and DOL do not accept the AICPA position that the plan and its participants are separate clients. Services that would impair independence for the plan would generally have the same effect with respect to the sponsor.

Subsection N: Assisting Clients in Implementing SFAS 133 (Derivatives)

Introduction	Statement of Financial Accounting Standards (SFAS) 133, *Accounting for Derivative Instruments and Hedging Activities*, is complex and clients may need assistance in implementation. ISB Interpretation 99-1 provides guidance on the effect of assistance on (1) accounting application and (2) valuation consulting on the auditor's independence.

Basic Principle	Independence is impaired by acting in a capacity equivalent to that of management or auditing the results of the auditor's own work or the work of someone else in the auditor's firm.

Rationale	The auditor cannot be placed in the position of making professional judgments about the results of the auditor's own work (or that of others in the firm) because a "self-review" cannot be sufficiently objective. The auditor also cannot be in the position of accepting responsibility for the choices and judgments inherent in the preparation of financial statements to the extent that the auditor is acting as a member of management.

Examples of Accounting Application Assistance That Would *Not* Impair Independence	• Discuss the requirements of SFAS 133 and the related concepts, terminology and implementation issues. • Provide sample journal entries used to apply SFAS 133. • Provide guidance on compiling an inventory of derivatives. • Provide guidance in determining whether specific derivatives meet the criteria as hedges. • Provide examples and discuss factors to be considered in formally documenting hedging relationships and the client's risk management objective and hedging strategies. • Discuss factors to be considered in making critical judgments such as separation of the intrinsic value of instruments from their time value. • Provide guidance in determining the accounting for hedged items. • Provide guidance or assist management in developing and adapting systems to account for derivatives and hedged items.

Examples of Accounting Application Assistance That Would Impair Independence	Perform services that would be subject to audit procedures such as the following:
	
	    • Compiling the inventory of derivatives.
	    • Creating the initial journal entries to be recorded.
	    • Initially determining whether specific derivatives meet the relevant criteria as hedges.
	    • Making management decisions concerning the implementation of SFAS 133.

Examples of Valuation Consulting Assistance That Would *Not* Impair Independence	• Provide guidance or assist in developing the client's own valuation model. • Provide guidance on the nature or relevant model inputs (volatility, yield curves, etc.). • Validate client or third-party models used. • Validate reasonableness of inputs to models (client assumptions). • Provide a generic or standardized model (similar to a Black-Scholes or binomial software model).
Examples of Valuation Consulting Assistance That Would Impair Independence	• Compute derivative values (using either auditor- or client-approved assumptions and an auditor-developed or third-party model approved by the client). • Develop or be responsible for key assumptions or inputs (for use in any valuation model or product). • Provide an auditor-developed nonstandardized model for the client's use to value derivatives.

Subsection O: Legal Services

Conflict between Role of Auditor and Attorney	According to the SEC, if a CPA firm provides any service to an audit client when the person providing the service must be admitted to practice before a US court, the firm is not independent. *NOTE: The SEC has a long-standing position that there is a fundamental conflict between the role of the auditor and attorney. However, persons with foreign affiliates of US CPA firms who are not required to be admitted to a US bar may provide legal services if* *1. Local law does not preclude the services.* *2. The services relate to nonmaterial matters.* *3. The services are routine and ministerial.* *Section 201 of the Sarbanes-Oxley Act makes it unlawful for an auditor of a public company to provide legal services and expert services unrelated to the audit.*

Subsection P: Tax Services

SEC Proposed Restriction on Certain Tax Services

In proposing rules to implement Section 201 of the Sarbanes-Oxley Act, the SEC is considering certain tax services as impairing independence. Such prohibited tax services would include representing a client before a tax court and formulating tax strategies designed to minimize a company's tax obligations.

Authoritative Sources

1. Interpretation 101-3, *Performance of Other Services* (ET 101.05).
2. SEC Rule 2-01(c)(4)(i), Bookkeeping or other services related to the audit client's accounting records or financial statements; 2-01(c)(4)(ii), Financial information systems design and implementation; 2-01(c)(4)(iii), Appraisal or valuation services or fairness opinions; 2-01(c)(4)(iv), Actuarial services; 2-01(c)(4)(v), Internal Audit Services; 2-01(c)(4)(vi), Management functions; 2-01(c)(4)(vii), Human resources; 2-01(c)(4)(viii), Broker-dealer services; and 2-01(c)(4)(ix), Legal services. *Revision of the Commission's Auditor Independence Requirements.*
3. Title II, "Auditor Independence," Sec. 201, "Service Outside the Scope of Practice of Auditors," Sarbanes-Oxley Act of 2002.
4. Ethics Ruling No. 8, *Member Providing Advisory Services* (ET 191.015-.016).
5. Ethics Ruling No. 9, *Member as Representative of Creditor's Committee* (ET 191.017-.018).
6. Ethics Ruling No. 111, *Employee Benefit Plan Sponsored by a Client* (ET 191.222-.223).
7. ISB Interpretation 99-1, *Impact on Auditor Independence of Assisting Clients in the Implementation of SFAS 133 (Derivatives).*

15 BUSINESS RELATIONSHIPS; COOPERATIVE ARRANGEMENTS; JOINT CLOSELY HELD INVESTMENTS; LEASE ARRANGEMENTS; AND INVESTMENTS BY CLIENTS IN AUDITORS

In This Chapter

For information on	*See section*
SEC position on business relationships	A
Cooperative arrangements	B
Joint closely held investments	C
Lease arrangements	D
Investments in and underwriting by audit client in CPA firm and its securities	E

Overview

The SEC considers all direct and material indirect business relationships with clients as impairing independence. Section A discusses the SEC's position on business relationships.

The AICPA prohibits members and CPA firms from having cooperative arrangements with the client. The AICPA provides some relief for arrangements that are not material. Section B discusses cooperative arrangements, including the SEC position on such arrangements.

Covered members are prohibited from having a joint closely held investment with the client if along with the client the member controls the joint investment. Section C discusses joint closely held investments.

Section D explains the AICPA and SEC requirements on lease arrangements with clients.

Finally, Section E indicates that the CPA firm's independence is impaired if the audit client invests in the CPA firm. Similarly, independence may be impaired if the audit client's directors or officers invest in the equity securities of the CPA firm.

Section A: SEC Position on Business Relationships

Introduction

The SEC prohibits business relationships with clients and does not specifically address or recognize the AICPA's cooperative arrangements concept. This prohibition applies (1) during the period of the professional engagement,[1] and (2) at the time of expressing an opinion.

Basic Principle

Direct and material indirect business relationships, **other than a consumer in the normal course of business,** with persons associated with an audit client in a decision-making capacity (such as officers, directors, or substantial stockholders), impair independence.

NOTE: A "consumer" is defined in the seventh edition of Black's Law Dictionary as "a person who buys goods or services for personal, family, or household use with no intention of resale." Therefore, the authors believe that for a CPA firm, being the consumer in a business relationship means that the CPA firm buys goods or services for internal use within the firm with no intention of reselling those goods or services.

Specifically Prohibited Relationships

The SEC explicitly prohibits

- Joint business ventures.
- Limited partnership agreements.
- Investments in supplier or customer companies.
- Sales by the member of items other than professional services.

NOTE: Other relationships might also impair independence. See section D for SEC restrictions on leasing arrangements with clients.

Decision Criteria

When making decisions on independence matters involving business relationships, the member should consider

- Whether a mutuality or identity of interest with the client exists, that
- Would cause the member to lose the appearance of objectivity and impartiality.

---

[1] *See Appendix A for the definition of "period of professional engagement."*

Section B: Cooperative Arrangements

Introduction	If during the period of the professional engagement,[2] a member or the CPA firm had any cooperative arrangement with the client that is **material** to the firm or the client, independence is impaired.
Basic Principle	If a member or CPA firm has a material cooperative arrangement with a client, independence is impaired, because advancement of the member's/CPA firm's interest would, to some extent, be dependent upon advancement of the client's interest. *NOTE: The SEC prohibits direct business relationships, such as cooperative arrangements, without regard to materiality.*
What Is a Cooperative Arrangement?	A cooperative arrangement may exist when the member or CPA firm and the client join together to conduct a mutual business activity. The following examples illustrate cooperative arrangements that impair independence. • Prime/subcontractor relationships to provide services/products to third parties. • Joint ventures to develop or market services or products. • Combining arrangements in which the member or CPA firm and the client bundle services/products and market those to third parties with reference to both parties. • Arrangements under which the member or CPA firm acts as a distributor/marketer of the client's services/products or vice versa.
Joint Participations	Joint participation in a business activity with a client does not constitute a cooperative arrangement, **if all of the following conditions are met:** 1. The member or CPA firm and the client have separate contracts with the third party. 2. The member or CPA firm does not assume any responsibility for activities or results of the client. 3. Neither the member or CPA firm nor the client has the authority to act as a representative or agent for the other.

---

[2] *See Appendix A for the definition of "period of professional engagement."*

*NOTE: Many business arrangements with clients will not generate an
independence problem from an AICPA perspective, because they can be
structured as a joint participation, not a cooperative arrangement.
However, the SEC considers whether, in the particular circumstances,
the member and the client have a mutuality or identity of interest that to
a reasonable observer would impair independence.*

A Reminder about Contingent Fees in Joint Participations	Rule 302, *Contingent Fees* (ET 302.01) (see Chapter 30), prohibits contingent fees for any professional service for a client when the member performs for that client

1. Audits or reviews of financial statements,
2. Compilations of financial statements (when a third party is expected to use the report and the report does not disclose a lack of independence), and
3. Examinations of prospective financial statements.

A Reminder about Commissions in Joint Participations	Rule 503, *Commissions and Referral Fees* (ET 503.01) (see Chapter 33), prohibits the receipt of a commission for recommending or referring

1. Any product/service to a client, or
2. Any product/service supplied by a client

when any audit, review, or compilation (without lack of independence paragraph) of a financial statement or examination of prospective financial statements is performed for the client.

Section C: Joint Closely Held Investments

Introduction	If (1) during the period of the professional engagement,[3] or (2) at the time of expressing an opinion, a covered member, including the member's firm, had a joint closely held investment with any client or officer, director, or any owner (e.g., a principal stockholder) who has the ability to exercise significant influence over the client, independence may be impaired.
Basic Principle	If a covered member has a joint closely held investment with a client, the mutuality of interest with that client may cause independence to be impaired. Independence is impaired if the joint investors have the ability to control the investment (i.e., entity or property).
What Is a Joint Closely Held Investment?	A joint closely held investment is an investment in an entity or a property by the covered member and the client (or the client's officers, directors, or owners who have the ability to exercise significant influence over the client) that enables them to control (as defined in FASB Statement No. 57, *Related-Party Disclosures*) the entity or property.
	NOTE: Materiality used to be included in the SEC's definition of a joint closely held investment. It was deleted in the revision of the definition in November 2001. Therefore, the SEC does not consider materiality or the existence of control. The AICPA, however, prohibits joint investments where control exists and the investment is material to the covered member's net worth.

---

[3] *See Appendix A for the definition of "period of professional engagement."*

Joint Interest in Vacation Home

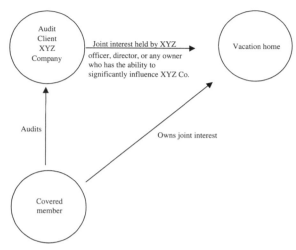

If XYZ Company and the covered member control the vacation home, the CPA firm is not independent with respect to XYZ Company **(even if the vacation home is used solely for the personal interests of the owners)**.

Investment with General Partner of Private Entity

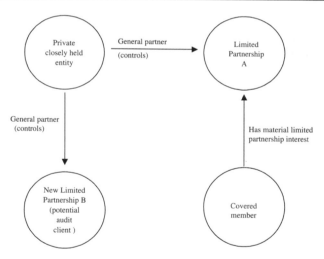

The general partner has control over Limited Partnership A and New Limited Partnership B. This constitutes a joint closely held investment. Therefore, if the covered member's investment **is material,** independence is impaired.

NOTE: According to the AICPA ruling, if the covered member's investment in Limited Partnership A was not material, independence would not be impaired with respect to Limited Partnership B. Under SEC rules, if Limited Partnership B was an SEC registrant, CPA firm would not be independent with respect to Limited Partnership B without regard to the materiality of the covered member's investment.

Section D: Lease Arrangements

Introduction	The AICPA and SEC have different requirements concerning lease arrangements between a member or a member's firm and a client.
Basic Principle	A lease arrangement with a client will impair independence if the lease is a capital lease (AICPA) or if the lease is material to the member or the member's firm (SEC).
AICPA Position	According to the AICPA, a covered member or a member's firm that leases property to or from a client

1. Impairs its independence if the lease meets the criteria for a capital lease (FASB Statement No. 13, Accounting for Leases, paragraph 6.a.i), unless the lease is considered a loan from a financial institution (Chapter 16, Loans to and from Clients).
2. Does not impair its independence if the lease meets the criteria for an operating lease (FASB Statement No. 13, paragraph 6.a.ii), the terms and conditions of the lease are comparable with similar leases, and all amounts are paid in accordance with lease terms.

SEC Position	The SEC does not apply the above decision criteria. Instead, the SEC considers a lease to or from a client that is **material** to the CPA firm as impairing independence.

Example of a material lease

CPA Firm had its office in a building that was owned by XYZ Company, an audit client. The CPA Firm was the only tenant other than the client and occupied approximately 25% of the available office space. According to the SEC, independence was impaired because a reasonable third party would question the CPA Firm's objectivity.

Rental of Block Computer Time	The SEC also addresses other rental relationships with clients. For example, the SEC considers a CPA firm's rental of block computer time to a client, except in emergency or temporary situations, to be a business relationship beyond the customary professional relationship. Therefore, independence is impaired.

Section E: Investments in and Underwriting by Audit Client in CPA Firm and Its Securities

---

SEC Rule   Under SEC rules, an auditor's independence would be impaired if the audit client or an affiliate of the client has, or agrees to acquire, any direct investment in the CPA firm. In addition, if the audit client's officers or directors own more than 5% of the equity securities of the CPA firm, the CPA firm is not independent.

NOTE: The SEC rule also covers subsidiaries and associated entities of the CPA firm.

Engaging Audit Client to Underwrite CPA Firm's Securities

The SEC also indicates that independence is impaired if a CPA firm **engages** an audit client to

1.   Underwrite any security issued by the CPA firm.
2.   Act as a broker-dealer, market maker, promoter, or analyst for any security issued by the CPA firm.

Authoritative Sources

---

1.   Interpretation 101-1, *Interpretation of Rule 101* (ET 101.02.A.3).
2.   Interpretation 101-12, *Independence and Cooperative Arrangements with Clients* (ET 101.14).
3.   SEC's Rule 2-01(c)(3)—Business Relationships, *Revision of the Commission's Auditor Independence Requirements* (effective February 2, 2001), and SEC *Codification of Financial Reporting Policies*, Business Relationships (Sec. 602.02.g), as amended.
4.   SEC's Rule 2-01(c)(1)(iv)(B)—Underwriting, *Revision of the Commission's Auditor Independence Requirements.*
5.   SEC's Rule 2-01(c)(1)(iv)(A)—Investments by the Audit Client in the Accounting Firm, *Revision of the Commission's Auditor Independence Requirements.*
6.   Ethics Ruling No. 69, *Investment with a General Partner* (ET 191.138-.139).
7.   Ethics Ruling No. 91, *Member Leasing Property to or from a Client* (ET 191.182-.183).
8.   Ethics Ruling No. 92, *Joint Interest in Vacation Home* (ET 191.184-.185).

16 LOANS TO AND FROM CLIENTS

Introduction

Independence is impaired, if (1) during the period of the engagement,[1] or (2) at the time of expressing an opinion, a covered member or person (including immediate family members or the CPA firm) had

1. Any loan (e.g., including any margin loan, loan commitment, loan guarantee, letter of credit, or a line of credit),
2. To or from any client, or
3. Any officer, director, principal stockholder (record or beneficial owner of more than 10% of the client's equity securities), or other individual owner of 10% or more of the client's equity or ownership interests.

This chapter focuses primarily on the exceptions to the rule above.

Basic Principle

All loans to or from clients **without regard to materiality** (unless the loan is from a financial institution and meets certain conditions), impair independence.

Exceptions

Exceptions relate **only** to financial institutions. There are two categories of financial institution loan exceptions

1. Grandfathered loans, and
2. Other permitted loans.

*NOTE: The mere servicing of a loan by a client financial institution does **not** impair independence.*

Definition of Grandfathered Loans

Grandfathered loans must be

1. From a financial institution, **and**
2. Made under normal lending procedures, terms, and requirements.

---

[1] *See Appendix A for the definition of "period of professional engagement."*

NOTE: For purposes of applying the grandfathered loan provisions, if the covered member/person is a partner in a partnership (not the CPA firm), loans are ascribed to that individual when

1. *For a limited partnership, the individual's interest (individually or combined with other covered members/persons) exceeds 50%.*
2. *For a general partnership, the individual (individually or together with other covered members/persons) can control the partnership.*

"Normal lending procedures, terms, and requirements" is defined as procedures, terms, and requirements that are reasonably comparable to those relating to loans of a similar character made to other borrowers during the loan commitment period. In making comparisons with other loans, the member should consider all loan provisions, including

* *Amount of loan in relation to collateral.*
* *Repayment terms.*
* *Interest rate, including points.*
* *Closing costs.*
* *General availability of loans to the public.*

Conditions for Grandfathered Loans

A grandfathered loan must meet **one** of the following conditions. The loan was

1. In existence as of January 1, 1992.
2. Obtained from a client financial institution before independence was required.
3. Obtained from a nonclient financial institution that was later sold to a client.
4. Obtained prior to February 5, 2001 and met the requirements of the prior provisions of Interpretation 101-5.
5. Obtained between February 5, 2001 and May 31, 2002 and met the requirements of the SEC during that period.
6. Obtained after May 31, 2002 from a client financial institution by the borrower prior to his or her becoming a covered member/person (as defined in Chapter 9).

NOTE: In applying the grandfathered loan exemptions, the date of the loan commitment or line of credit extension is used, not the closing date or date funds were obtained. If subsequent to the relevant date in 1. through 6. above, any of the terms (e.g., maturity date, interest rate, revised collateral or covenants) are changed from the original loan agreement, the loan is no longer grandfathered.

Other Requirements for Grandfathered Loans

To avoid a loss of independence, grandfathered loans must be current at all times, and fall into one of the following categories:

1. A home mortgage, including a home equity loan.
2. A secured loan having

    a. Collateral value greater than or equal to the loan balance, or

    b. If collateral value is less than the loan balance, the unsecured portion must not be material to the covered member's/person's net worth.

  3. An unsecured loan that is not material to the member's/person's net worth.

NOTE: The only grandfathered exception for mortgage loans recognized by the SEC is a mortgage loan collateralized by the borrower's primary residence (provided the loan was not obtained while the covered person in the CPA firm was a covered person). In other words, the SEC does not grant an exception for mortgages for vacation homes, secured loans (other than permitted loan discussed below), or unsecured loans that are not material.

Other Permitted Loans

Other than grandfathered loans, a covered member/person may have other permitted loans from a financial institution that will not impair independence.

Other permitted loans must be obtained under the financial institution's normal lending procedures, terms, and requirements, and be kept current as to all terms.

Types of Other Permitted Loans

Other permitted loans must fall within one of the following categories:

  1. Automobile loans.
  2. Lease collateralized by an automobile.
  3. Loans fully secured by the cash surrender value of a life insurance policy.
  4. Loans fully collateralized by cash deposits at the same financial institution (e.g., passbook loans).
  5. Credit cards and cash advances where the aggregate outstanding balance is reduced to $5,000 or less by the payment due date.

    NOTE: The SEC increases the credit card balance to $10,000. However, the more stringent AICPA requirement should be followed.

Loan from a Nonclient Subsidiary of Client

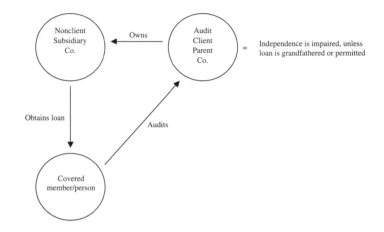

Loan from a Nonclient Parent of a Client Subsidiary

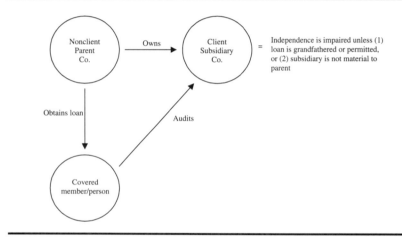

Covered Member/Person Connected with Entity Having a Loan to or from Client

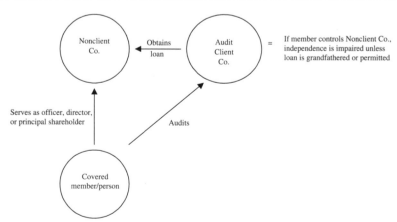

NOTE: The member may be independent under the rule on loans to and from clients, but have a conflict of interest under Interpretation 102-2, **Conflicts of Interest** *(ET 102.03). See Chapter 6.*

Authoritative Sources

1. Interpretation 101-1, *Interpretation of Rule 101* (ET 101.02.A.4).
2. Interpretation 101-5, *Loans from Financial Institution Clients and Related Terminology* (ET 101.07).
3. SEC Rule 2-01(c)(1)(ii)(A), Loans/Debtor-Creditor Relationship, and 2-01(c)(1)(ii)(E), Credit Cards. *Revision of the Commission's Auditor Independence Requirements.*
4. Ethics Ruling No. 67, *Servicing of Loan* (ET 191.134-.135).
5. Ethics Ruling No. 98, *Member's Loan from a Nonclient Subsidiary or Parent of an Attest Client* (ET 191.196-.197).
6. Ethics Ruling No. 110, *Member Is Connected with an Entity That Has a Loan to or from a Client* (ET 191.220-.221).

17 EMPLOYMENT BY AND CONNECTIONS WITH CLIENTS[1]

	For information on	*See section*
In This Chapter	General principles, prohibitions, and exceptions	A
	Specialized industry clients	B

Overview

Section A discusses how independence is impaired when a partner or professional employee of a CPA firm is employed by or connected with a client and presents two exceptions to the general principles when independence may not be impaired. Section A also discusses the effect on independence (1) when a partner or professional employee considers or accepts employment with a client, and (2) when a client employee becomes a partner or professional employee in the CPA firm.

Section B discusses how a covered member can maintain independence when joining a credit union or trade association client. Also, Section B discusses how a covered member who is an owner or lessee in a common interest realty association can maintain independence with respect to that association.

NOTE: The term "partner" includes a current partner, principal, shareholder, or owner of the CPA firm.

---

[1] *The AICPA's Professional Ethics Executive Committee has issued an Exposure Draft, dated June 17, 2002, titled **Omnibus Proposal of Professional Ethics Division Interpretations and Rulings**. The Exposure Draft proposes revisions to Interpretation 101-2, Former Practitioners and Firm Independence, to ensure that independence is maintained when a firm professional is considering or has accepted employment with an attest client. The proposed revision also includes specific requirements that a CPA firm professional must follow when he or she accepts a **key position** with an attest client, and specific policies and procedures related to individual and firm responsibilities when firm professionals are considering employment with, or have become employed by, an attest client. The Exposure Draft incorporates the guidance in Ethics Ruling No. 77, "Individual Considering or Accepting Employment with the Client," and therefore that ruling is being proposed for deletion. In addition, the Exposure Draft incorporates many of the safeguards described in ISB Standard No. 3, **Employment with Audit Clients**. Please check for updates to this section on the John Wiley & Sons, Inc. website at www.wiley.com/ethics.*

Section A: General Principles, Prohibitions, and Exceptions

Introduction	A CPA firm is not independent if a partner or professional employee of the CPA firm (1) is employed by a client as a director, officer, or an employee, (2) is associated with a client as a promoter, underwriter, or voting trustee, or (3) functions as a trustee for any pension or profit-sharing trust of the client.

Section A also discusses the effect on independence when

- A partner or professional employee considers or accepts employment with the client during the engagement
- A client officer, director, or employee becomes a partner or professional employee in the CPA firm.

Basic Principle	Independence is impaired whenever the partner or professional employee

- Is virtually a part of the client's management or under management's control.
- Performs management functions as an employee or makes management decisions.
- Is connected with the client as a promoter, underwriter, voting trustee, director, or officer.

Prohibited Relationships	Prohibited relationships apply to (1) the period covered by the financial statements, (2) the period of the professional engagement, and (3) at the time of expressing an opinion.[2]

Connection with the client as promoter, underwriter, or voting trustee is prohibited.

Employment by the client as director, officer, employee, or in any management position is prohibited. The SEC expressly states that acting, temporarily or permanently, as a director, officer, or employee, or performing any decision-making, supervisory, or ongoing monitoring function impairs independence.

In addition, the partner, professional employee, or CPA firm cannot serve as a trustee of the client's (1) pension trust, or (2) profit-sharing trust, without losing independence with respect to the client and the trust.

---

[2]   *See Appendix A for the definition of "period of professional engagement."*

NOTE: If a partner or professional employee serves on a client's deferred compensation committee, the CPA firm's independence is impaired because this constitutes performance of a management function.

Exceptions for Advisory Boards and for Certain Not-for-Profit Organizations

A partner or professional employee may serve on an advisory board of a client without impairing independence provided **all** of the following conditions are met:

1. The responsibilities are in fact advisory,
2. The advisory board neither makes, nor appears to make, management decisions, and
3. The advisory board and the client's board of directors (or those having equivalent authority to make decisions) are distinct groups, with minimal, if any, common membership.

Example

A partner or professional employee serving on a curricula advisory board of a college that is an audit client of the firm may not impair independence.

A partner or professional employee may also be a purely **honorary** director or trustee of a charitable, religious, civic, or similar organization and remain independent with respect to such organization.

To remain independent, the partner or professional employee must

1. Hold a directorship or trusteeship that is purely **honorary,**
2. Not vote on board matters,
3. Not otherwise participate in board or management functions, and
4. If named in letterheads and externally circulated materials of the organization, be identified as an honorary director or honorary trustee.

NOTE: A partner or professional employee serving on the board of directors of a nonprofit social club (e.g., a golf or tennis club) is not independent, because the organization is not a charitable, religious, civic, or similar organization.

Members on Board of a Federated Fund-Raising Organization

A partner or professional employee may serve as a director or officer of a local United Way (or similar organization) and be independent with respect to those charities that receive funds from the federated organization. However, if the federated organization exercises managerial control over a given charity, the CPA firm is not independent.

*NOTE: If the partner or professional employee concludes that a conflict of interest exists under Interpretation 102-2, **Conflicts of Interest** (ET 102.03), independence is impaired. See Chapter 7.*

Considering or Accepting Employment with a Client (AICPA Rule)

During the performance of an engagement, a partner or professional employee participating in the engagement may (1) be offered employment by the client, or (2) seek employment with the client.

In this situation, to avoid any appearance that integrity or objectivity has been impaired, the partner or professional employee must remove himself or herself from the engagement until the offer is rejected, or employment is no longer being sought.

If a CPA firm becomes aware that a partner or professional employee participated in the engagement (1) while employment was being considered, or (2) after it had been accepted, the CPA firm should consider what additional procedures, if any, should be performed. Additional procedures required may involve reperformance of work done or other procedures.

NOTE: Once a partner or professional employee is asked to consider employment with the client during the engagement, it is not sufficient to ask the client to defer discussion until the report is issued. Moreover, if a partner or professional employee has no interest in pursuing employment opportunities with the client, the individual should promptly notify the client. There would be no impairment of independence. A CPA firm should have explicit policies requiring the partner or professional employee to immediately notify the CPA firm, if asked by a client to consider employment.

Considering or Accepting Employment with a Client (SEC Rule)

A CPA firm may not be independent if a partner or professional employee is employed by an audit client or serves as a member of the client's board or similar management body. According to ISB Standard No. 3, *Employment with Audit Clients*, if such individual has

1. Knowledge of, and
2. Relationships with the client,

that could adversely influence the audit, independence is impaired unless the CPA firm implements the safeguards discussed below.

NOTE: As discussed in Chapter 12, Former Practitioners, Section 206 of the Sarbanes-Oxley Act of 2002 makes it unlawful for a CPA firm to perform an audit of a public company if that company's CEO, CFO, controller, chief accounting officer, or equivalent position was

1. Previously employed by the CPA firm, and
2. Participated in the audit of the company during the one-year period preceding the start of the current year's audit.

On December 2, 2002, the SEC issued proposed rules, Release No. 33-8154, "Strengthening the Commissions Requirements Regarding Auditor Independence" to address Section 206 of Sarbanes-Oxley.

Considering Employment— Safeguards	1. The CPA firm requires the partner or professional employee to promptly notify the CPA firm of the conversations about possible employment with the client. 2. If employment negotiations are in process, the CPA firm immediately removes the partner or professional employee from the audit. 3. The CPA firm reviews the partner's or professional employee's work on the audit to determine its adequacy.
Accepting Employment— Safeguards	1. The audit engagement team considers whether the audit plan needs to be modified to reduce the risk of circumvention. 2. If the partner or professional employee will have significant interaction with the audit team, the CPA firm takes steps to ensure that the existing audit team has the stature and objectivity to deal with the partner or professional employee. 3. If the partner or professional employee (a) joins the client within one year of leaving the CPA firm and (b) has significant interaction with the audit team, the next annual audit is separately reviewed by a professional uninvolved in the audit. The purpose of the review is to determine if the audit team exercises appropriate skepticism in evaluating representations and work of the former partner or professional employee. The extent of the review depends in part on the position that individual has at the audit client.
Accepting Employment— Safeguards (SEC Rule)	The SEC superseded paragraph 2.b.iv of ISB Standard No. 3 and created certain revised safeguards for former partners or professional employees. The former partner or professional employee must not: (1) influence the firm's operations or financial policies; (2) have a capital balance in the firm, or (3) have a financial arrangement, other than one providing for regular payment of a fixed dollar amount through a fully funded retirement plan, rabbi trust, or similar vehicle. If a former professional employee was not a partner and has been disassociated from the accounting firm for more than five years, the fixed payments made to that employee must be immaterial to him or her.

Client, Director, Officer, or Employee Is Employed by CPA Firm	According to both the SEC and the AICPA, independence will not be impaired when a former officer, director, or employee of the client becomes a partner or professional employee in the CPA firm, **provided**
	    1. Such individual completely disassociates himself or herself from the client (including its affiliates), and
	    2. Does not participate in auditing the client's financial statements that cover any of the employment period.

NOTE: The AICPA uses the term "disassociates," which is explained in the next section. The SEC does not use the term but requires that the individual (1) not participate in the engagement, and (2) is not in a position to influence the audit.

The requirements above also cover former audit client employees.

Steps Involved in Disassociating from Client

To completely disassociate from the client, according to the AICPA, the partner or professional employee should

- Terminate the relationship with the client.
- Dispose of any direct or material indirect financial interest in the client.
- Collect or repay any client loans unless permitted or grandfathered as defined in Chapter 16, Loans to and from Clients.
- Withdraw from a client-sponsored health or welfare plan, unless the client is legally required to let the member participate (e.g., a COBRA plan) and the individual pays 100% of the premiums on a current basis.
- Stop contributing to client-sponsored benefit plans or stop any management/trustee relationship with the client's benefit plan.
- Liquidate or transfer all vested pension benefits as soon as possible.

NOTE: The partner or professional employee may not be able to liquidate or transfer pension benefits on a timely basis because

- *A significant penalty is imposed, or*
- *The administrative requirements of the plan do not permit timely liquidation or transfer.*

If either of these conditions prevent liquidation or transfer, independence would not be considered impaired as long as the individual does not participate in the engagement.

Service on the Board of Directors of a Nonclient Bank

The AICPA discourages a partner or professional employee from serving as a director of a nonclient bank, if the individual has clients (requiring independence or otherwise) that are customers of the bank.

The AICPA discourages bank directorships to avoid situations in which the individual would have

- A conflict of interest under Interpretation 102-2 (ET 102.03), as discussed in Chapter 7, or
- A problem with confidential client information under Rule 301 (ET 301.01), as discussed in Chapter 29.

NOTE: A more appropriate way for the partner or professional employee to serve the nonclient bank would be as a consultant to the board of directors.

Faculty Member as Auditor of a Student Fund

A full- or part-time faculty member is not independent with respect to the university's student fund when that fund requires the university to perform management functions such as

- Acting as a collection agent for student fees.
- Approving and signing checks.

Section B: Specialized Industry Clients

Introduction

A covered member (Chapter 9) may join a client credit union, own or lease in a common interest realty association, become a member of a client trade association, or be a cofiduciary with a client bank and maintain independence if certain conditions are followed.

Membership in a Client Credit Union

A membership in a client credit union does not impair independence provided that all of the following conditions are met:

1. The covered member must individually qualify to join the credit union, other than by qualifying because of the services provided by the CPA firm.
2. Any loans from the credit union must meet the conditions discussed in Chapter 16.
3. Any deposits must be fully insured and any uninsured deposits must be immaterial to the covered member.

Association with a Common Interest Realty Association (CIRA)

A covered member, including his or her CPA firm, may be associated (e.g., owner or lessee) of a CIRA (e.g., cooperatives, condominiums, time-share developments, homeowner associations) and be independent with respect to the CIRA if **all** of the following conditions are met:

1. The CIRA performs functions similar to local governments (e.g., road maintenance).
2. The covered member's annual assessment is not material to the covered member or the CPA firm or the CIRA's operating budgeted assessments.
3. The liquidation of the CIRA or sale of its assets would not result in a distribution to the covered member.
4. Creditors, in the event of insolvency, would not have recourse to the covered member.

Membership in a Client Trade Association

If a partner or professional employee joins a trade association that is a client, independence is not impaired provided the individual does not serve the association as an officer, director, or in any capacity equivalent to a member of management.

**Trustee of a
Charitable
Foundation That
Is Sole Beneficiary
of Estate**

A partner or professional employee becomes a trustee of a charitable foundation that is the sole beneficiary of the foundation's deceased organizer. The individual is not independent with respect to the foundation or the estate.

**Co-Fiduciary with
Client Bank**

A partner or professional employee, along with a client bank, serves as a cofiduciary for an estate or trust. If the estate or trust assets are not material to the total assets of the bank or its trust department, independence is not impaired with respect to the bank.

Authoritative Sources

1. Interpretation 101-1, *Interpretation of Rule 101* (ET 101.02.B.1 and 2).
2. Interpretation 101-4, *Honorary Directorships and Trusteeships of Not-for-Profit Organization* (ET 101.06).
3. SEC Rule 2-01(c)(2)(i), *Employment at Audit Client of Accountant* and Rule 2-01(c)(2)(iv), *Employment at Accounting Firm of Former Employee of Audit Client. Revision of the Commission's Auditor Independence Requirements.*
4. SEC Rule 2-01(c)(4)(vi), *Management Functions.*
5. ISB Standard No. 3, *Employment with Audit Clients.*
6. Ethics Ruling No. 2, *Association Membership* (ET 191.003-.004).
7. Ethics Ruling No. 11, *Member as Executor or Trustee of a Charitable Foundation* (ET 191.021-.022).
8. Ethics Ruling No. 12, *Member as Trustee of a Charitable Foundation* (ET 191.023-.024).
9. Ethics Ruling No. 14, *Member on Board of Federated Fund-Raising Organization* (ET 191.027-.028).
10. Ethics Ruling No. 16, *Member on Board of Directors of Nonprofit Social Club* (ET 191.031-.032).
11. Ethics Ruling No. 19, *Member on Deferred Compensation Committee* (ET 191.037-.038).
12. Ethics Ruling No. 31, *Performance of Services for Common Interest Realty Associations (CIRAs), Including Cooperatives, Condominium Associations, Planned Unit Developments, Homeowners Associations, and Timeshare Developments* (ET 191.061-.062).
13. Ethics Ruling No. 38, *Member as Cofiduciary with Client Bank* (ET 191.075-.076).
14. Ethics Ruling No. 48, *Faculty Member as Auditor of a Student Fund* (ET 191.095-.096).
15. Ethics Ruling No. 64, *Member Serves on Board of Or-*

ganization for Which Client Raises Funds (ET 191.128-.129).

16. Ethics Ruling No. 72, *Member on Advisory Board of Client* (ET 191.144-.145).
17. Ethics Ruling No. 75, *Membership in Client Credit Union* (ET 191.150-.151).
18. Ethics Ruling No. 77, *Individual Considering or Accepting Employment with the Client* (ET 191.154-.155).
19. Ethics Ruling No. 82, *Campaign Treasurer* (ET 191.164-.165).
20. Ethics Ruling No. 85, *Bank Director* (ET 191.170-.171).
21. Ethics Ruling No. 93, *Service on Board of Directors of Federated Fund-Raising Organization* (ET 191.186-.187).

18 EMPLOYMENT OF A SPOUSE, DEPENDENT, OR CLOSE RELATIVE BY A CLIENT

Introduction

If (1) during the period of the professional engagement, or (2) at the time of expressing an opinion

- An individual participating on the engagement team,
- An individual in a position to influence the engagement,
- A partner in the office in which the lead engagement partner primarily practices, or
- Any other partner or manager who has provided ten or more hours of nonaudit services to the client

has an immediate family member (spouse, spousal equivalent, or dependent without regard to relationship) or a close relative (parent, nondependent child, or sibling) that is employed by the client, the CPA firm may not be independent.

NOTE: The SEC combines "immediate family member" and "close relative" into a single category—"close family member."

Basic Principle

With one exception under AICPA requirements, if an individual as defined above has an immediate family member or a close relative as defined above who is employed by a client in a key position as defined by the AICPA or in an accounting role or financial reporting oversight role as defined by the SEC, independence is impaired.

NOTE: Under the AICPA rules, if a partner or manager providing only nonaudit services has a close relative in a key position with a client, independence is not impaired.

AICPA Definition of Key Position

According to the AICPA, an immediate family member or close relative has a key position with a client when that person has

1. Primary responsibility for **significant** accounting functions that support **material** financial statement components, or

2. Primary responsibility for the preparation of financial statements, or
3. The ability to exercise influence over the contents of the financial statements.

NOTE: For an attest engagement, as compared to an audit engagement, a key position is one in which the immediate family member or close relative is primarily responsible or able to influence the subject matter of the engagement.

SEC Definition of Accounting Role or Financial Reporting Oversight Role

The SEC definition includes any immediate family member or close relative in the AICPA definition above plus any individual who either exercises

1. More than minimal influence over the contents of the accounting records or over anyone who prepares such records or,
2. Influence over anyone who prepares financial statements.

Individual Having the Ability to Exercise Significant Influence

The following individuals have the ability to exercise significant influence under the AICPA and SEC definitions above.

- Director (or similar position)
- CEO
- President
- CFO
- COO
- General Counsel
- Chief Accounting Officer
- Controller
- Director of Internal Audit
- Director of Financial Reporting
- Treasurer

NOTE: The SEC includes a vice president of marketing in its list of individuals having the ability to exercise significant influence, but the AICPA does not.

Authoritative Sources

1. Interpretation 101, *Interpretation of Rule 101* (ET 101.02-03, as revised July 2002).
2. SEC Rule 2-01(c)(2)(11)—Employment at Audit Client of Certain Relatives of Accountant, *Revision of the Commission's Auditor Independence Requirements*.

19 GIFTS AND PRIVILEGES

Introduction

If a covered member accepts (1) more than a token gift or (2) other unusual consideration from a client, even with the firm's knowledge, the appearance of independence may be impaired.

Basic Principle

The receipt of gifts or other unusual consideration from clients leaves the recipient open to allegations that they are obligated to the client; thus, the appearance of independence may be impaired.

Prohibited Transfers

A covered member should not accept more than a token gift from a client. Also, a member should not accept lavish entertainment from a client. Likewise, a member should not purchase client products or services at discounts that are not available to the general public.

NOTE: An individual recipient cannot mitigate the appearance of a lack of independence by disclosing the gift or privilege to the CPA firm. Therefore, CPA firms should have a policy that prohibits acceptance of gifts greater than a defined token amount (e.g., $100).

Exercise Caution in Accepting or Returning Gifts

In practice, the prohibition against accepting gifts has to be interpreted sensibly and, if returned, handled diplomatically. Clients could be offended by the sudden rejection of, for example, a wedding present given to an individual in an act of friendship and without an ulterior motive.

Authoritative Source

1. Ethics Ruling No. 1, *Acceptance of a Gift* (ET 191.001-.002).

20 ACTUAL OR THREATENED LITIGATION

Introduction

In some circumstances, independence may be considered to be impaired as a result of litigation or the expressed intention to bring litigation.

The litigation may be between a client and the covered member/person or between third parties (such as investors or creditors) and the client company and its management or the member.

Basic Principle

Independence may be impaired whenever the covered member/person and the client company or its management are in threatened or actual positions of *material adverse interests* by reason of threatened or actual litigation.

Litigation impairs independence whenever it would reasonably be expected to *alter substantially the normal relationship* between the client's management and the covered member/person.

Rationale

To render an informed, objective conclusion on a client's financial statements, the relationship between management and the covered member/person must be characterized by complete candor and full disclosure regarding all aspects of the client's operations.

The covered member/person must be able to exercise unbiased professional judgments on financial reporting decisions made by management.

When the covered member/person and the client management are placed in adversarial positions, the covered member's/person's objectivity may be affected by self-interest or management's candor and willingness to make disclosure may be impaired.

Litigation between Client and Member

Independence would be considered to be impaired in the following circumstances:

- Present management brings litigation alleging deficiencies in the covered member's/person's audit work.

- The covered member/person brings litigation against present management alleging management's fraud or deceit.
- Present management expresses an intent to bring litigation alleging deficiencies in audit work and the auditor concludes it is probable a claim will be filed.

Independence would not generally be considered to be impaired when litigation (threatened or actual) relates to a nonattest engagement and the alleged damages are not material to the member's firm or the client company.

NOTE: Examples of such claims that would not impair independence include disputes concerning overbillings for services, and disputes relating to tax, consulting, or other nonattest services.

Litigation by Third Parties

A covered member/person may become involved in litigation (primary litigation) in which the covered member/person and the client company or its management and others are mutual defendants, such as a class-action suit on behalf of stockholders against management, the auditors, and underwriters in a securities offering.

Independence would not ordinarily be considered impaired in the following circumstances:

- The client, its management, or its directors file cross-claims against the auditor to protect a right to legal redress in the event of an adverse decision in the primary litigation. (Except when there is a significant risk of settlement of the cross-claim in an amount material to the CPA firm or the client.)
- Underwriters or others assert cross-claims against the covered member/person, but the company and present management do not.

If a person who files cross-claims against a covered member/person is also an officer or director of other clients of the covered member/person, independence would not usually be impaired for those other clients.

Example

A class-action suit is filed against the auditor and Company A and its directors and management. The directors of Company A file cross-claims against the auditor. One of the directors is also a member of the board of Company B, which is also an audit client of the auditor. The auditor's independence with respect to Company B is not impaired.

Litigation by Third Parties in the Name of the Client	A third-party litigant, such as an insurance company, may bring litigation against the covered member/person in the name of the client under subrogation rights.

Litigation by Third Parties in the Name of the Client

A third-party litigant, such as an insurance company, may bring litigation against the covered member/person in the name of the client under subrogation rights.

When the client is only the nominal plaintiff, the covered member's/person's independence would not normally be affected.

However, adverse interests, and hence impaired independence, may exist if the covered member's/person's defense alleges fraud or deceit by present management.

NOTE: If the insurance company is also a client of the covered member/person, independence with respect to the insurance company may be impaired if a settlement or judgment would be material to the CPA firm or the insurance company.

SEC Position on Impairment of Appearance of Independence

The SEC considers whether the particular circumstances of the situation, including the nature of the claims and defenses made, may impair independence.

The naming of auditors and clients as codefendants in a civil suit would not in and of itself impair independence.

The appearance of independence, however, could be adversely affected by situations in which management and the auditor are bound closely together by common allegations against them.

Example

In one situation, management and the auditors were charged with agreeing together to withhold information from stockholders and the SEC staff.

This situation creates such a commonality of legal interest with the client that it is doubtful whether the auditors could be considered independent.

Effect of ADR Techniques

Alternative dispute resolution (ADR) techniques are used to resolve disputes without litigation.

An agreement to use ADR techniques signed in advance of a dispute, or the start of an ADR proceeding under such an agreement, would not ordinarily impair independence because such a proceeding is normally designed to facilitate negotiation.

If an ADR proceeding is started that is similar to an adversarial action, such as binding arbitration, independence would be impaired.

Termination of Impairment

An impairment of independence arising from threatened or actual litigation is usually eliminated when a final resolution is reached and there are no longer matters at issue between the member and the client.

Authoritative Sources

---

1. Interpretation 101-6, *The Effect of Actual or Threatened Litigation on Independence* (ET 101.08).
2. SEC *Codification of Financial Reporting Policies,* Litigation (Sec 602.f.ii).
3. Ethics Ruling No. 95, *Agreement with Attest Client to Use ADR Techniques* (ET191.190-.191).
4. Ethics Ruling No. 96, *Commencement of ADR Proceedings* (ET 191.192-.193).

21 INDEMNIFICATION AGREEMENTS

Introduction

Indemnification agreements between the member and client may

1. Indemnify the member from certain damages, losses, or costs resulting from client acts or misrepresentations, or
2. Indemnify the client from certain liabilities and costs resulting from acts of the member.

The first situation impairs independence from an SEC perspective and may also impair independence based on AICPA rules. The second situation impairs independence from both an SEC and an AICPA perspective. This section defines and discusses indemnification agreements.

Basic Principle

Indemnification agreements reduce a member's objectivity and thereby impair independence. With one limited exception (discussed below), they impair independence.

Definition of Indemnification

An indemnification agreement is a contract between two parties whereby one party agrees to compensate or reimburse a second party for certain losses or expenses incurred.

Indemnification of the Member by the Client

The AICPA permits a member to include an indemnification clause in an engagement letter without impairing independence **provided** the indemnification is **restricted to knowing misrepresentations made by the client's management**.

The SEC considers indemnification to be against public policy. Therefore, the CPA firm, inserting such a clause in an engagement letter, would not be independent. According to the SEC, indemnity agreements remove one of the major stimuli to objective and unbiased consideration of problems encountered in an engagement. Existence of such an agreement may result in the use of less extensive procedures or a failure to carefully appraise information disclosed during the engagement.

Indemnification of the Client by the Member   If a member (e.g., as a condition of obtaining or retaining a client), agrees that the member or the member's firm will indemnify the client for damages, losses, or claims arising from litigation, or claims, or settlements that relate to client acts, the member is not independent under AICPA or SEC rules.

Authoritative Sources

1. SEC *Codification of Financial Reporting Policies,* Indemnification by Client, (sec 602.02.f.i).
2. Ethics Ruling No. 94, *Indemnification Clause in Engagement Letters* (ET 191.188-.189).
3. Ethics Ruling No. 102, *Member's Indemnification of a Client* (ET 191.204-.205).

22 OUTSOURCING OF THE INTERNAL AUDIT FUNCTION AND OTHER EXTENDED AUDIT SERVICES

Introduction

A member or CPA firm may be asked to assist in performance of a client's internal audit function or to otherwise extend audit services beyond the requirements of GAAS.

Definition of Extended Audit Services

Extended audit services involve performing audit procedures that are generally of the type considered to be extensions of audit scope applied in the audit of financial statements.

Examples

Extended audit services might include confirming receivables, analyzing fluctuations in account balances, and testing and evaluating the effectiveness of controls.

Sarbanes-Oxley Act of 2002

In July 2002, Congress passed the Sarbanes-Oxley Act (known as the Public Accounting Reform and Investor Protection Act). Section 201, "Services Outside the Scope of the Practice of Auditors," prohibits CPA firms that audit publicly traded companies under the purview of the SEC from providing internal audit outsourcing to audit clients.

On December 2, 2002, the SEC issued proposed rules, Release No. 33-8154 "Strengthening the Commission's Requirements Regarding Auditor Interpretations" to address internal audit outsourcing. The SEC is required to issue final rules by January 26, 2003.

Basic Principle

Subject to SEC limits (described in detail later and revised SEC rules to be published by January 26, 2003), independence would not be considered to be impaired provided that the member does not act or appear to act in a capacity equivalent to a member of client management or as an employee.

NOTE: The discussion in this chapter is based on SEC rules in effect as of December 31, 2002, not the revised rules to be issued by January 26, 2003.

The GAO prohibits the CPA firm from performing internal audit services. The audit organization would be prohibited from performing internal audit services because these services are considered to be a management function.

Essential Understanding with Client

A member should be satisfied that the client's management, board of directors, and audit committee understand

- The member may not perform management functions or make management decisions.
- The member may not act or appear to act in a capacity equivalent to that of an employee.
- Client management is responsible for establishing and maintaining internal control, including responsibility for ongoing monitoring.
- Client management is responsible for directing the internal audit function.

NOTE: It is preferable that the understanding be documented in an engagement letter.

Requirements for Responsibilities of the Client's Management

The client should be responsible for

- Designating a competent individual (or individuals), preferably within senior management, to be responsible for the internal audit function.
- Determining the scope, risk and frequency of internal audit activities.
- Evaluating the findings and results arising from internal audit activities.
- Evaluating the adequacy of the audit procedures performed and audit findings by obtaining reports from the member and other means.

NOTE: These requirements can normally be met by the client appointing an employee as director of internal audit who is, or reports to, a senior member of management. The director of internal audit would then establish audit scope and report on audit results to the board or audit committee.

In addition, under SEC requirements, if the CPA firm performs internal audit services related to accounting, the client's management must

- Acknowledge in writing to the CPA firm and the company's audit committee (or board of directors) the company's responsibility for internal control over financial reporting, and
- Not rely on the auditor's work as the primary basis for determining the adequacy of its internal controls.

Other Responsibilities of the Member

The member should

- Direct, review and supervise day-to-day performance of the audit procedures.
- Report to the individual responsible for the internal audit function information that allows the individual to evaluate audit scope and findings.
- Assist that individual, as requested, in
  - Performing preliminary audit risk assessments.
  - Preparing audit plans.
  - Recommending audit priorities.

Examples of Activities That Would Impair Independence

- Performing ongoing monitoring activities or control activities that
  - Affect the execution of transactions (such as assistance in authorization of transactions).
  - Ensure that transactions are properly executed or accounted for.
- Performing routine activities in operating or production processes equivalent to an ongoing compliance or quality control function.
- Determining which recommendations for improving controls should be implemented.
- Reporting to the board or audit committee on behalf of management or the individual responsible for internal audit.
- Authorizing, executing, or consummating transactions.
- Otherwise exercising authority on behalf of the client.
- Preparing source documents of transactions.
- Having custody of assets.
- Approving or being responsible for the overall internal audit work plan.
- Being connected with the client in any capacity that is or appears to be equivalent to a member of management or employee.

  Examples

  The appearance of an unacceptable connection with the client would be created by

  - Being listed as an employee in directories or other client publications.
  - Permitting oneself to be referred to by title or description as supervising or being in charge of the internal audit function.
  - Using the client's letterhead or internal correspondence forms in communications.

Examples of Permissible Related Activities

- Performing separate evaluations of the effectiveness of a client's internal control, including separate evaluations of the client's ongoing monitoring activities.

- Performing an attestation engagement to report on the client's assertion regarding the effectiveness of its internal control over financial reporting as long as management does not rely on the member's work as the primary basis for its assertion.
- Providing operational auditing services to review business processes, as selected by the client, and assess their efficiency and effectiveness.
- Performing very frequent, but separate, evaluations of the effectiveness of the ongoing control and monitoring activities built in to the client's normal recurring activities.

NOTE: In all of these examples, the member would need to observe the previously explained requirements relating to responsibilities of client management versus the member's responsibilities and communicate an understanding of these matters to the client's management, board, and audit committee.

SEC Limits

The CPA firm must limit internal audit services related to accounting systems, controls over such systems, and financial statements to 40% of the total hours expended by a registrant on such services (in a given fiscal year).

NOTE: The 40% rule does not apply to companies with less than $200 million in assets.

If the CPA firm performs internal audit services related to accounting, the client's management must

1. *Acknowledge in writing to the CPA firm and the company's audit committee (or board of directors) the company's responsibility for internal control over financial reporting.*
2. *Not rely on the auditor's work as the primary basis for determining the adequacy of its internal controls.*

The client's management must also meet the other four requirements listed under **Requirements for Responsibilities of the Client's Management**.

Authoritative Sources

1. Interpretation 101-13, *Extended Audit Services* (ET 101.15).
2. SEC Rule 2-01(c)(4)(v), Internal Audit Services, *Revision of the Commissioner's Auditor Independence Requirement.*
3. Ethics Ruling No. 103, *Attest Report on Internal Controls* (ET 191.206-.207).
4. Ethics Ruling No. 104, *Operational Auditing Services* (ET 191.208-.209).
5. Ethics Ruling No. 105, *Frequency of Performance of Extended Audit Procedures* (ET 191.210-.211).

23 INDEPENDENCE REQUIREMENTS FOR GOVERNMENTAL AUDITS AND NONPROFIT ORGANIZATIONS SUBJECT TO YELLOW BOOK REQUIREMENTS[1]

Introduction

Auditors of governmental units and certain nonprofit organizations have additional ethics considerations. For example, governmental audits are more likely to involve a principal auditor and other auditors than audits of commercial entities. Federal circulars and state and local statutes frequently require participation by small and minority-owned CPA firms in the audit of entities and units that are part of the government's general-purpose financial statements. This chapter provides guidance on the independence requirements for different auditors that may be involved in the audit of the general-purpose financial statements of a state or local government or other governmental audits.

The chapter also discusses the General Accounting Office's independence requirements and the AICPA ethics rulings that address governmental audits.

Finally, the chapter discusses independence requirements of the Housing and Urban Development (HUD)–assisted programs.

NOTE: This chapter assumes that you have a knowledge of GAAP for governmental entities.

---

[1] *The AICPA's Professional Ethics Executive Committee has issued an Exposure Draft, dated June 17, 2002, titled* **Omnibus Proposal of Professional Ethics Division Interpretations and Rulings.** *The Exposure Draft contains proposed revisions to Interpretation 101-10,* **The Effect on Independence of Relationships with Entities Included in the Governmental Financial Statements,** *as a result of recent changes to the governmental reporting model due to the issuance of Government Accounting Standards Board (GASB) Statement No. 34,* **Basic Financial Statements—and Management's Discussion and Analysis—for State and Local Governments,** *and the anticipated release of revisions to the Audit and Accounting Guide,* **Audits of State and Local Governments,** *in September 2002. In addition, certain changes were made to the Interpretation to conform to the AICPA's new independence rules. Please check for updates to this section on the John Wiley & Sons, Inc. website at www.wiley.com/ethics.*

In This Chapter   This chapter contains the following sections:

For information on	*See section*
Independence requirements for auditors of state and local governments	A
General Accounting Office (GAO) independence requirements	B
AICPA Ethics Rulings on governmental audits	C
HUD requirements	D

Section A: Independence Requirements for Auditors of State and Local Governments

Categories of Auditors

There are four categories of auditors that may be involved in the audit of a state or local government's general-purpose financial statement.

1. Principal auditor.
2. Other auditor of a **material** fund type, fund, account group, component unit, or related (disclosed or footnoted) organization.
3. Other auditor of **immaterial** fund type(s), account group(s), component unit(s), or related (disclosed) organization(s) that are **material** in the aggregate.
4. Other auditor of **immaterial** fund type(s), account group(s), component unit(s), or related (disclosed) organization(s) that are **immaterial** in the aggregate.

Principal Auditor of the General-Purpose Financial Statements

The principal auditor (category 1) of the government's general-purpose financial statements must be independent of

1. The primary government (including all of its fund types, funds, and account groups).
2. All component units of the reporting entity.
3. All other entities that are required to be disclosed in notes to the general-purpose financial statements under GASB Statement No. 14, *The Financial Reporting Entity,* except for disclosed organizations for which the primary government is not financially accountable, and where the required financial statement note does not include financial information.

Other Auditor of a *Material* Fund Type, Fund, Account Group, Component Unit, or Disclosed Organization

The category 2. other auditor must be independent of

1. The fund type, fund, account group, component unit, or disclosed organization being audited.
2. The primary government.
3. Any other fund type, fund, account group, component unit, or disclosed organization of the financial reporting entity that is financially accountable to such entity or unit, or can significantly influence the entity or unit audited.

Other Auditor of *Immaterial* **Fund Type(s), Account Group(s), Component Unit(s), or Related Organization(s) That Are** *Material* **When Aggregated**	The category 3. other auditor must be independent of the 1. Entities/units being audited, and 2. The primary government.
Other Auditor of *Immaterial* **Fund Type(s), Account Group(s), Component Unit(s), or Disclosed Organization(s) That Are** *Immaterial* **in the Aggregate**	The category 4. other auditor must be independent of the 1. Entities/units being audited, and 2. Must not be associated with the primary government in any capacity as a • Promoter, underwriter, or voting trustee. • Director, officer, employee, or member of management. • Trustee of any pension fund.

Section B: GAO Independence Requirements

Introduction to GAO Independence Requirements	In January 2002, the GAO established new requirements for auditor independence under Government Auditing Standards (i.e., the Yellow Book). The new standard applies to all Yellow Book audits for periods beginning on or after January 1, 2003, with earlier implementation encouraged. The new standard is available on the GAO's website at http://www.gao.gov/govaud/agagas3.pdf.

NOTE: The revised independence requirements were originally scheduled to be applicable to all audits for periods beginning on or after October 1, 2002. However, the GAO has extended the date to January 1, 2003.

The old GAO standards required that public accountants follow the AICPA's independence requirements and the requirements of the relevant state board of accountancy. The revisions contain some differences from current AICPA independence rules. In some cases, the new GAO rules are more restrictive than the AICPA's standards.

Applicability	The new standards apply to CPAs, non-CPAs, government financial auditors, and performance auditors. More specifically, they apply to auditors of

- Federal, state, and local governments,
- Not-for-profit and for-profit recipients of federal (and some state) grant and loan assistance, such as

  - Colleges, universities, and trade schools,
  - Hospitals,
  - Charitable organizations,
  - Cities, counties, and school and utility districts,
  - Small businesses with SBA loans,
  - HUD projects and lenders,
  - Public housing authorities,
  - Many state-administered programs and contracts.

Nongovernment auditors should also follow the AICPA *Code of Professional Conduct* and the ethical requirements of the state board and state society of CPAs with jurisdiction over the practice of the public accountant and audit organization.

GAO's Frequently Asked Questions	In July 2002, the GAO issued a document that answers frequently asked questions regarding the auditor independence change. These frequently asked questions may help to clarify some provisions of the new requirements and can be found at www.gao.govaud/d02870g.pdf.

Using Specialists   Auditors using the work of specialists should

- Assess the specialist's ability to perform the work and report results impartially.
- Provide the specialist with the GAO independence requirements.
- Obtain representations about independence from the specialist.

If the independence of the specialist is impaired, the audit should not use the specialist's work.

Categories of Impairments

The new standards state that auditors must consider three categories of impairments.

- **Personal impairments.**
- **External impairments.**
- **Organizational impairments.**

NOTE: Organizational impairments apply to government auditors and do not apply to CPAs in a CPA firm.

If any of these impairments affect the auditor's capability to perform the work and report the results impartially, the auditor should decline to perform the work. If the auditor, because of a legislative requirement or other reasons, cannot decline to perform the work, the auditor should report the impairment(s) in the scope section of the auditor report.

This section contains the following subsections:

For information on	*See subsection*
Personal impairments to independence	1
External impairments to independence	2
Organizational impairments to independence	3

Subsection 1: Personal Impairments to Independence

Definitions of Personal Impairments

These impairments result from relationships and beliefs that might cause an auditor to limit inquiries or disclosure, or weaken or slant audit findings.

Examples of Personal Impairments

Examples of personal impairments include

- An **immediate** or **close** family member of the auditor is a director or officer of the audited entity, or an employee of the audited entity, and can directly and significantly influence the entity or the program under audit.

NOTE: An immediate family member is a spouse, spousal equivalent, or dependent (whether or not related). A close family member is a parent, sibling, or nondependent child.

- The auditor has a direct or material indirect financial interest in the audited entity or program.
- The auditor is responsible for managing an entity or making decisions that could affect the entity's operations or the program being audited.
- The auditor concurrently or subsequently performs an audit and maintains the official accounting records when such services involved

  - Preparing source documents or originating data, in electronic or other form.
  - Posting transactions (whether coded by management or not coded).
  - Authorizing, executing, or consummating transactions.
  - Maintaining an entity's bank account or otherwise having custody of the audited entity's funds.
  - Otherwise exercising authority on behalf of the entity, or having authority to do so.

- The auditor has preconceived ideas toward individuals, groups, organizations, or objectives of a particular program that could bias the audit, or the auditor has biases resulting from social and political convictions and/or employment in or loyalty to a group, organization, or level of government that could affect the audit.
- The auditor seeks employment with an audited organization during the performance of the audit.

Quality Control System Requirements

Audit organizations should include requirements to identify personal impairments and determine compliance with independence requirements as part of their internal quality control systems. At a minimum, audit organizations should

- Establish policies and procedures to identify personal impairments, including whether performing nonaudit services affects the subject matter of audits, and apply safeguards to appropriately reduce the impairment risk.
- Communicate the audit organization's policies and procedures to all auditors in the organization and ensure understanding of requirements through training, periodic acknowledgment of auditors of their understanding, or other means.

- Establish internal policies and procedures to monitor compliance, and a disciplinary mechanism to promote compliance, with the organization's policies and procedures.
- Stress the importance of independence and the expectation that auditors will always act in the public interest.

Responding to an Identified Personal Impairment

Auditors should notify the appropriate officials within their organizations if they have any personal impairment to independence. When a personal impairment is identified, it should be resolved on a timely basis by

- Requiring the auditor to eliminate the personal impairment (for example, selling a financial interest in situations where the personal impairment is unique to an individual auditor).
- Withdrawing from the audit in situations when the impairment cannot be mitigated.
- Reporting the impairment in the scope section of the audit report in situations when government auditors cannot withdraw from the audit.

Nonaudit Services

Audit organizations that provide nonaudit services should consider whether providing these services creates a personal impairment. Nonaudit services, which may or many not involve a report, involve performing tasks that directly support the entity's operations, such as developing or implementing accounting systems or designing or implementing information technology or other systems; or providing information or data to a requesting party without providing verification, analysis, or evaluation of the information or data.

Overarching Principles for Nonaudit Services

The GAO independence standard for nonaudit services is based on two overarching principles.

1. Auditors should not provide nonaudit services that involve performing management functions or making management decisions. Examples of prohibited activities include

   - Serving as members of an entity's management committee or board of directors.
   - Making policy decisions that affect future direction and operation of an entity's programs.
   - Supervising entity employees.
   - Developing policy for programs.
   - Authorizing an entity's transactions.
   - Maintaining custody of an entity's assets.

2. Auditors should not audit their own work or provide nonaudit services in situations where the amounts or services involved are significant/material to the subject matter of the audit.

NOTE: When evaluating whether the amounts or services are significant or material, audit organizations should consider (1) ongoing audits, (2) planned audits, (3) requirements and commitments for providing audits, which includes laws, regulations, rules, contracts, and other agreements, and (4) policies placing responsibilities on the audit organizations for providing audit services. (Since government auditors generally have broad audit responsibilities that may extend to a level of government or a particular entity within a level of government, government auditors need to be especially careful when providing nonaudit services that their independence is not impaired because of their full range of audit responsibilities.)

Seven Safeguards

To perform nonaudit services that do not violate the preceding principles, the audit organization must comply with all of the following *seven safeguards*. The audit organization should

1. Prevent personnel who provided the nonaudit services from planning, conducting, or reviewing audit work related to the nonaudit service.

NOTE: If a CPA firm provides no more than forty hours of nonaudit services in relation to a specific audit engagement, this safeguard would not be required.

2. Be prevented from reducing the scope and extent of the audit work beyond the level that would be appropriate if the nonaudit work were performed by another unrelated party.
3. Document its consideration of the nonaudit service, and its rationale that providing the nonaudit service does not violate the two overarching principles.
4. Before performing nonaudit services, establish and document an understanding with the audited entity regarding the objectives, scope of work, and product or deliverables of the nonaudit service. Also establish and document an understanding with management that management is responsible for the substantive outcomes of the work and complies with the following:

    •   Designates a management level individual to be responsible for the nonaudit service.
    •   Establishes and monitors the performance of the nonaudit service according to management's objectives.
    •   Makes management-level decisions related to the nonaudit service.
    •   Evaluates the services performed and any resulting findings.

5. Make sure that its quality control systems for compliance
    with independence requirements include (a) policies and
    procedures to assure consideration of the effect on the on-
    going, planned, and future audits when deciding whether
    to provide nonaudit services and (b) a requirement to have
    the understanding with management of the audited entity
    documented. The understanding should be communicated
    to management in writing and specify management's abil-
    ity to conduct the required oversight, and that manage-
    ment's responsibilities were performed.
6. In cases where certain nonaudit services impair the audit
    organization's ability to meet the overarching principles
    for certain types of audit work, communicate to manage-
    ment of the audited entity that the audit organization
    would not be able to perform subsequent audit work re-
    lated to the subject matter of the nonaudit service.
7. For audits selected for peer review, identify all related
    nonaudit services to the audit organization's peer reviewer
    and ensure that the audit documentation described in these
    safeguards is made available for peer review.

Prohibited and Permitted Services

The standard includes an express prohibition on auditors providing
certain bookkeeping/recordkeeping services, and limits payroll
processing and certain other services, all of which are presently
permitted under the AICPA rules. These prohibited and permitted
services are described in more detail as follows.

*NOTE: The services described in the following sections are permitted as
long as the two overarching principles are met and the audit organization complies with the seven safeguards.*

Basic Accounting Assistance

Permitted services

- Preparing draft financial statements based on management's
  chart of accounts and trial balance and any adjusting, cor-
  recting, and closing entries that have been approved by
  management;
- Preparing draft notes to the financial statements using information determined and approved by management;
- Preparing a trial balance using management's chart of accounts;
- Maintaining depreciation schedules when management has
  determined the method of depreciation, rate of depreciation,
  and salvage value of the asset;

Prohibited services

- Maintaining or preparing the audited entity's basic accounting records;

- Taking responsibility for basic financial or other records that will be audited by the audit organization;
- Posting transactions (whether coded or not coded) to the entity's financial records or to other records that subsequently provide data to the entity's financial records.

Payroll Services

Permitted services

- Computing employee pay amounts based on entity-maintained and -approved time records, salaries or pay rates, and deductions from pay;
- Generating unsigned payroll checks;
- Transmitting client-approved payroll to a financial institution, provided management has approved the transmission and limited the financial institution to make payments only to previously approved individuals.
- Processing the entity's entire payroll when payroll was material to the audit.

Appraisal or Valuation Services

Permitted services

- Reviewing the work of the entity or a specialist employed by the entity where the entity or specialist provides the primary support for the balances recorded in financial statements or other information that will be audited;
- Valuing an entity's pension, other postemployment benefit, or similar liabilities, provided management has determined and taken responsibility for all significant assumptions and data.

Indirect Cost Proposal or Cost Allocation Plan

Permitted services

- Preparing an entity's indirect cost proposal or cost allocation plan, provided management has taken responsibility for all significant assumptions and data.

Prohibited services

- Conducting the required audit when the auditors also prepared the entity's indirect cost proposal and indirect costs recovered by the entity during the prior year exceeded $1 million. (This is a prohibition under Office of Management and Budget policy.).

Tax Filings

Permitted services

- Preparing routine tax filings in accordance with applicable laws, rules, and regulations.

Human Resource Services	*Permitted services* • Participating on an evaluation panel to review applications; • Interviewing candidates to provide input to management in arriving at a listing of best qualified applicants to be provided to management. *Prohibited services* • Recommending a single individual for a specific position; • Conducting an executive search or a recruiting program for the audited entity.

Information Technology Services	*Permitted services*
	
	 • Advising on system design, system installation, and system security if management acknowledges responsibility for the design, installation, and internal control over the entity's system and does not rely on the auditor's work as the primary basis for determining
	
	     • Whether to implement a new system,
	     • The adequacy of the new system design,
	     • The adequacy of major design changes to an existing system, and
	     • The adequacy of the system to comply with regulatory or other requirements.
	
	 Prohibited services
	
	 • Operating or supervising the operation of the entity's information technology system.

Legislative and Administrative Decision Making	*Permitted services* • Gathering and reporting unverified external or third-party data to aid legislative and administrative decision making.
Internal Control Self-Assessments	*Permitted services* • Advising an entity regarding its performance of internal control self-assessments.
Assisting Legislative Bodies	*Permitted services* • Assisting a legislative body by developing questions for use at a hearing.

Other Permitted Services	The new standard does recognize that auditors can participate on committees or task forces in a purely advisory capacity, provide routine advice, answer technical questions, provide training, and provide tools such as best-practice guides without violating these two overarching principles or having to comply with the safeguards previously discussed.

Subsection 2: External Impairments to Independence

Definition of External Impairments	External impairments to independence occur when an auditor is deterred from acting objectively and exercising professional skepticism by actual or perceived pressures from management and employees of the audited entity or oversight organizations.
Examples of External Impairments	An auditor may not be able to make an independent and objective judgment when management and employees of the audited entity or oversight organizations

  • Interfere with the scope of an audit, including pressure to reduce costs by inappropriately reducing the extent of work performed.
  • Interfere with the choice or application of audit procedures or selection of transactions to be examined.
  • Unreasonably restrict the time for completing an audit or issuing the report.
  • Interfere in assigning, appointing, and promoting audit personnel.
  • Restrict funds or resources provided to the audit organization in such a way as to adversely affect the organization's ability to carry out its responsibilities.
  • Have authority to overrule or to inappropriately influence the content of the audit report.
  • Threaten to replace the auditor over disagreements with the contents of an audit report, the auditor's conclusions, or the application of an accounting principle or other criteria.
  • Jeopardize the auditor's continued employment for reasons other than incompetence, misconduct, or the need for audit services.

Resolving Impairments	An audit organization's internal quality control system should include internal policies and procedures for reporting and resolving external impairments.

Subsection 3: Organizational Impairments to Independence

Definition of Organizational Impairments

Organizational impairments relate to the fact that the government audit organization's ability to perform the work and report the results impartially can be affected by its place within the government and the structure of the government entity that the audit organization is assigned to audit.

NOTE: This section does not apply to CPAs in a CPA firm (e.g., in the public practice of accountancy).

Considerations When Reporting Externally to Third Parties

There is a presumption that government auditors are free from organizational impairments to independence when reporting externally to third parties if their audit organization is organizationally independent from the audited entity. The government audit organization can be considered organizationally independent in a number of ways.

1. The audit organization is assigned to a different level of government from the one to which the audited entity is assigned.

   Example

   A federal auditor audits a state government program.

2. The audit organization is assigned to a different branch of government in the same level as the audited entity.

   Example

   A legislative auditor audits an executive branch program.

3. The audit organization's head meets any of the following criteria:

   a. Is directly elected by voters of the audited jurisdiction.
   b. Is elected or appointed by a legislative body subject to removal by a legislative body, and reports and is accountable to a legislative body.
   c. Is appointed by someone other than a legislative body, but the appointment is confirmed by the legislative body and the legislative body has oversight and approval power and can remove the individual from the position.
   d. Is appointed by, accountable to, reports to, and can be removed only by a statutorily created governing body, the majority of whose members are independently elected or appointed, and come from outside the organization being audited.

Other Organizational Structures' Independence

Other organizational structures may also be considered independent for external reporting as long as they have all of the following statutory protections to:

1. Prevent the audited entity from abolishing the audit organization.
2. Require that if the head of the audit organization is removed from office, the agency's head reports this fact and the reasons for the removal to the legislative body.
3. Prevent interference by the audited entity with the initiation, scope, timing, and completion of any audit.
4. Prevent interference by the audited entity with the audit report.
5. Require reporting by the audit organization to a legislative body or other independent governing body on a recurring basis.
6. Give sole authority over selecting, retaining, advancing, and dismissing staff to the audit organization.
7. Provide statutory access to records and documents concerning the agency, program, or function being audited.

Requirement to Document Statutory Safeguards

Statutory provisions that allow the audit organization to meet these safeguards should be documented and reviewed during the external quality assurance review.

Considerations When Reporting Internally to Management

A government internal audit organization can be presumed to be free from organizational impairments to independence when reporting internally to management if the head of the organization is

- Accountable to the head or deputy head of the government entity,
- Required to report the results of the audit organization's work to the head or deputy head of the government entity, and
- Located organizationally outside of the staff or line management function of the audited unit.

Distribution of Reports Outside the Organization

Further distribution of reports outside the organization should be made only according to law, rule, regulation, or policy. The fact that auditors are auditing their employers should be clearly reflected in the audit reports.

Additional   In addition, the audit organization should
Considerations

- Have personnel systems based on merit and avoid political
  pressures on auditors.
- Report regularly to the audit committee or appropriate oversight body.
- Document the conditions that allow it to be considered free
  of organizational impairments to independence to report internally. (Such conditions should be reviewed during peer
  reviews.)

Section C: AICPA Ethics Rulings on Governmental Audits

Serving as an Elected Legislator	If any partner or professional employee of a firm served as an elected legislator for a city at the same time his or her firm was engaged to perform an attest engagement for the city, independence would be considered to be impaired even though the city manager is an elected official rather than an appointee of the legislature.
Serving on Advisory Unit	A member's independence with respect to a county is not impaired as a result of serving on a citizens' committee that is studying • Possible changes in the form of county government, or • The financial status of the state when the client is a county in that state.
Member as a Bondholder	A member who owns an immaterial amount of municipal bonds is not independent with respect to the municipality. Such ownership is considered a loan to that client.

Section D: HUD Requirements

**Housing and
Urban
Development
(HUD)
Requirements**

Auditors of HUD–assisted programs should be aware that the
HUD Handbook contains additional independence requirements.
For example, the Handbook states, in 4370.2 REV-1 (Chapter 3),
that an independent public accountant who performs bookkeeping
services for a HUD project is prohibited from performing audits of
the project. Auditors performing audits subject to HUD's guidelines should review these requirements. The HUD Handbook can
be found at www.hud.gov.

Authoritative Sources

1. Interpretation 101-10, *The Effect on Independence of Relation-
    ships with Entities Included in the Governmental Financial
    Statements* (ET 101.12).
2. Amendment No. 3, *Independence,* to the *Government Auditing
    Standards: Standards for Audit of Governmental Organiza-
    tions Programs, Activities, and Functions (the Yellow Book).*
    Issued in January 2002.
3. Ethics Ruling No. 10, *Member as Legislator* (ET 191.019-
    .020).
4. Ethics Ruling No. 20, *Member Serving on Governmental Ad-
    visory Unit* (ET 191.039-.040).
5. Ethics Ruling No. 29, *Member as Bondholder* (ET 191.057-
    .058).
6. The HUD Handbook, 4370.2 REV-1. The Handbook can be
    found at www.hud.gov.

24 INDEPENDENCE REQUIREMENTS FOR AUDITS OF EMPLOYEE BENEFIT PLANS

Introduction

This chapter explains the independence requirements established by the Department of Labor (DOL) Regulation 2509.75-9, *Interpretive Bulletin Relating to Guidelines on Independence of Accountant Retained by Employee Benefit Plan*. The DOL has independence requirements that are stricter than AICPA rules. This chapter also presents the AICPA ethics rulings that address audits of employee benefit plans and highlights differences between the DOL and those rulings.

Basic Principle

An auditor's independence with respect to an employee benefit plan is impaired whenever the auditor has a financial interest in or relationship with the **plan** or **plan sponsor**.

DOL's Definition of "Member"

According to the DOL, member includes

1. All owners, partners, or shareholders in the CPA firm.
2. All professional employees participating in the audit.
3. All professional employees located in an office of the CPA firm participating in a significant portion of the audit.

When a Member Is Not Independent

DOL indicates that a member is not independent if (1) during the period covered by the financial statements, (2) during the period of engagement,[1] or (3) at the date of the audit report, the member or the member's firm

1. Had, or was committed to acquire a direct or material indirect financial interest in the plan or plan sponsor,
2. Was connected with the plan or plan sponsor as a promoter, underwriter, or investment advisor, or

---

[1] *See Appendix A for the definition of "period of professional engagement."*

3. Was employed by the plan or plan sponsor as a voting trustee, director, or employee.

If the member maintains financial records for the plan, DOL regulations also state that the member is not independent.

NOTE: The meaning of "maintenance of financial records" is unclear. Some DOL officials maintain that posting a general ledger from client-prepared underlying records and preparing participant account balances (i.e., bookkeeping) for a defined benefit plan impairs independence. The AICPA rules allow members to provide bookkeeping services, which is not equivalent to maintaining financial records, and remain independent (See Chapter 14). The DOL has not clarified what maintenance of financial records means.

Member Provides Appraisal or Valuation Services

DOL regulations do not discuss whether providing appraisal or valuation services (relating to real estate or securities that do not have a market price) impairs independence. DOL officials have publicly expressed concern about members providing such services to benefit plans.

NOTE: A member, if asked to provide appraisal or valuation services to a plan, should consider obtaining DOL's opinion on the matter in advance. Chapter 37 provides information on how to contact the DOL about independence questions.

Member Serves As Director of Plan Sponsor

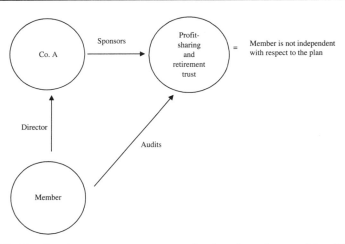

NOTE: Member (i.e., any partner or professional employee of the CPA firm) would be involved in management functions that affect the plan; therefore, independence is impaired.

Member Provides Asset Management or Investment Services to Plan

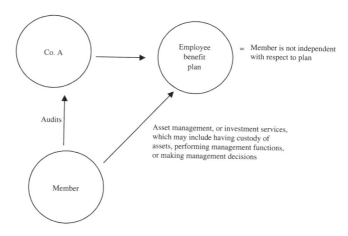

NOTE: *Independence is also impaired with respect to Co. A if the plan is a defined benefit plan and if the assets of the plan are material to the plan or Co. A. However, if the plan is a defined contribution plan and the member does not make management decisions or perform management functions on behalf of Co. A or have custody of Co. A's assets, independence is not impaired.*

Member's Relationships with Participating Employer(s) in a Multiemployer Benefit Plan

Member's independence is not impaired with respect to a multiemployer benefit plan unless the member

1. Had significant influence over a participating employer,
2. Was in a key position with such employer, or
3. Was associated with such employer as a promoter, underwriter, or voting trustee.

NOTE: *The DOL does not permit any direct or material indirect financial interest in any plan sponsor of a multiemployer plan.*

Member, Spouse, or Cohabitant Participates in Health and Welfare Plan of Client

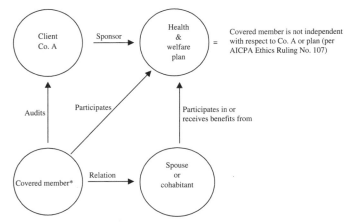

* *Covered member in this context excludes: (1) a partner or manager who provides ten or more hours of nonattest services to the client, or (2) any partner in the office where the lead attest engagement partner practices.*

NOTE: However, if covered member's spouse or cohabitant participates in the Plan by being employed by Co. A, the covered member would be independent provided that

1. *The covered member is independent with respect to Co. A, given the spouse's or cohabitant's position (Chapter 18), and*
2. *The Plan is normally offered to all employees of Co. A that are in equivalent positions.*

Authoritative Sources

1. Department of Labor, *Interpretive Bulletin Relating to Guidelines on Independence of Accountant Retained by Employee Benefit Plan* (Reg. 2509.75-9).
2. Interpretation 101-1, *Interpretation of Rule 101* (ET 101.02).
3. Ethics Ruling No. 21, *Member as Director and Auditor of the Entity's Profit Sharing Trust* (ET 191.041-.042).
4. Ethics Ruling No. 60, *Employee Benefit Plans—Member's Relationships with Participating Employers* (ET 191.119-.120).
5. Ethics Ruling No. 107, *Participation in Health and Welfare Plan of Client* (ET 191.214-.215).
6. Ethics Ruling No. 111, *Employee Benefit Plan Sponsored by Client* (ET 191.222-.223).

25 INDEPENDENCE REQUIREMENTS FOR AGREED-UPON PROCEDURES (AUP) ENGAGEMENTS

The definitions of covered members as presented in Chapter 9 do not apply to agreed-upon procedures engagements performed under the Statements on Standards for Attestation Engagements (SSAEs).

If an agreed-upon procedures report issued under the SSAEs states that (1) its use is restricted to identified parties, and (2) the member (as defined below) believes that the report will be restricted to those parties, a modified definition of "covered member" applies.

Basic Principle

The concept of independence differs in an AUP engagement as compared to an audit engagement. In an AUP engagement, independence applies to a reduced subset of covered members, which is less inclusive than covered members in other attest services.

Restricted-Use AUP Reports

A modified notion of independence applies to agreed-upon procedures reports issued under the SSAEs for

1. Prospective financial statements.
2. Compliance with specified requirements of laws and regulations.
3. Effectiveness of internal control over compliance.
4. Reports issued under SSAE No. 10, *Agreed-Upon Procedures Engagements* (as modified by SSAE No. 11).

The SSAE reports have to contain the following paragraph:

This report is intended solely for the information and use of (list or refer to specified parties) and is not intended to be and should not be used by anyone other than these specified parties.

NOTE: Restricted-use reports under the SSAEs continue to be restricted even if they are made a matter of public record.

Meaning of "Member" on an AUP Engagement	The following individuals and their immediate families (spouse, spousal equivalent, and dependent) are required to be independent of the responsible party in an AUP engagement:

- Individuals participating on the attest engagement team.
- Individuals who directly supervise or manage the attest engagement partner.
- Individuals who consult with the attest engagement team on technical or industry issues.

NOTE: The responsible party is the person(s) that represents the client who is responsible for the subject matter of the engagement. If the nature of the subject matter is such that no such party exists, a party that has a reasonable basis for making a written assertion about the subject matter becomes the responsible party.

Prohibited Financial Relationships at the CPA Firm Level

If the CPA firm has any of the illustrative prohibited relationships listed below (1) during the period of the AUP engagement or (2) at the time report is issued, the CPA firm is not independent.

Prohibited relationships

1. Had or was committed to acquire a direct or material indirect financial interest (Chapter 10).
2. Was a trustee or executor/administrator of any trust/estate that had or was committed to acquire a direct or material indirect financial interest (Chapter 10).
3. Had any joint closely held investment with the client or any officer, director, or principal stockholder (Chapter 15).
4. Had any loan (except those exempted) to or from the client or any officer, director, or principal stockholder (Chapter 16).

Applicability of Rule 101 and Interpretations of Rule 101

Rule 101, *Independence*, and its interpretations, except as discussed above, applies to all AUP engagements.

NOTE: If the CPA firm provides nonattest services under 101-3 (Chapter 14) that are proscribed and that do not directly relate to the subject matter of the attest engagement, independence is not impaired by the performance of those services.

Authoritative Source

1. Interpretation 101-11, *Modified Application of Rule 101 for Certain Engagements to Issue Restricted-Use Reports under the Statements on Standards for Attestation Engagements.*

26 ALTERNATIVE PRACTICE STRUCTURES

Overview

A traditional CPA firm engaged in auditing and other attestation services might be closely aligned with another organization, public or private, that performs other professional services (e.g., tax and consulting).

These types of alliances are sometimes called *Alternative Practice Structures* (APS)—a nontraditional structure for the practice of public accounting.

Section A: Model of an APS

Diagram of a Possible APS

The following diagram depicts typical relationships among a CPA firm providing attest services and an allied public company and its subsidiaries:

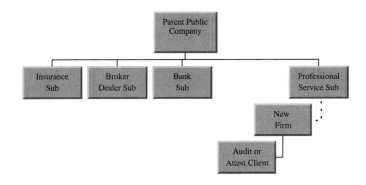

Background of Possible APS Model

An existing CPA firm is sold by its owners to another entity shown in the diagram as **Parent Public Co**.

Parent Public Co. has several existing subsidiaries shown as **Insurance Sub, Broker-Dealer Sub,** and **Bank Sub**. It also has formed a new subsidiary, **Professional Services Sub,** that provides **nonattest** professional services, such as tax, personal financial planning, and consulting.

The former owners and employees of the CPA firm that has been sold to Parent Public Co. became employees of Professional Service Sub, and provide nonattest services through that entity.

The owners separately form a new CPA firm shown as **New Firm** in the diagram that they own and control. New Firm provides audit and attest services to clients.

New Firm leases employees, office space and equipment and back-office functions, such as billing and advertising, from Parent Public Co. (In the diagram, a dotted line from New Firm to Professional Services Sub indicates this alliance between the entities.)

Section B: APS Independence Rules for Members

Definition of Member or Member's Firm in APS	**Member** in an APS includes any person (whether leased or employed) or entity that is defined as a member in Chapter 9 (Interpretation 101-9). New Firm is the **firm** in that definition.
Applicability of Independence Requirements	All the members and the firm (New Firm) are subject to all of the independence requirements (Rule 101 and its interpretations and rulings). *NOTE: This means that the independence requirements are applied in the traditional manner to the owners and employees of New Firm. The determination of whether an employee of New Firm is a member is not affected by whether the individual is leased from Professional Services Sub or employed directly by New Firm.*
Existence of More Than One New Firm	If there is more than one New Firm, then the owners of one New Firm generally would not be considered members with respect to audit or attest clients of Other New Firms. However, if owners of one New Firm **perform services** for Other New Firms or **have shared economic interests** with them, they would be considered members. **Example** If owners of New Firm perform services in Other New Firm, such owners are considered owners of both CPA firms for purposes of applying the independence requirements. Individuals with a managerial position (leased or otherwise) in one office of a New Firm might at times be considered to have a managerial position in another office of that or Other New Firms if work is done in more than one office. **Example** An audit manager leased from Professional Services Sub works on audits in two offices—one in each of two New firms. The audit manager is a member of both New Firms and has to be independent of audit and attest clients of both New Firms.

Section C: APS Independence Rules for Other-Than-Members

Introduction

Independence requirements normally extend only to those persons and entities included in the term "member or member's firm." In the case of an APS, that would be limited to New Firm and persons who own or are employed by New Firm, or who are controlled by one or more of those persons.

To ensure the protection of the public interest, additional restrictions are required for an APS.

Basic Principle

Persons or entities who can immediately and directly exert significant influence over New Firm owners and managerial employees are subject to all of the same independence requirements as a member.

NOTE: These persons and entities are called direct superiors and are defined more precisely later.

Other persons and entities in the APS that are not connected with a member or member's firm through direct reporting relationships are subject to some, but not all, independence requirements.

Definition of Direct Superiors and Applicable Independence Requirements

Persons subject to the same independence requirements as a member are persons so closely associated with

- An owner of New Firm, or
- A person with a managerial position in New Firm located in an office participating in a significant portion of the audit or attest engagement (whether leased or employed directly by New Firm)

that such *persons* can directly control the activities of the owner or managerial employee.

A person who can *directly control* is the immediate superior of the owner or managerial employee who has the power to direct activities of that person so as to be able to directly or indirectly derive a benefit from that person's activities.

Example

The chief executive of the office of Professional Service Sub where the owners and managerial employees of New Firm are employed is a *direct superior*. The chief executive has day-to-day responsibility for the activities of the owners and managerial employees of New Firm, and can recommend their promotions and compensation levels.

The chief executive is subject to all of the independence requirements with respect to New Firm's audit and attest services clients.

Definition of Indirect Superiors and Other Public Co. Entities

Indirect superiors are persons one or more levels above persons included in the definition of *direct superior*. (Members do not directly report to indirect superiors.)

Generally, indirect superiors start with persons in the organization structure to whom direct superiors report and go upline from that point.

Indirect superiors also include spouses, cohabitants, and dependent persons of those persons.

Example

The chief executive of Professional Services Sub reports to the senior vice president of Public Co. The senior vice president is an indirect superior. So is the senior vice president's spouse.

Other Public Co. Entities are Public Co. itself and all entities consolidated in Public Co.'s financial statements that are not included in the definition of member or subject to the same rules as a member.

Example

Broker-Dealer Sub and its officers are Other Public Co. Entities.

Applicability of Independence Requirements to Indirect Superiors and Other Public Co. Entities

Indirect superiors and other Public Co. entities may not have a relationship contemplated by Interpretation 101-1.A (ET Section 101.2) with an audit or attest client of New Firm that is *material* to those persons or entities.

Interpretation 101.1.A is concerned with investments, loans, and similar matters (See Chapters 10, 11, and 16).

Materiality is based on the aggregate amount of financial relationships with the attest client assessed in relation to the person's net worth.

Example

The senior vice president of Public Co., to whom the CEO of Professional Services Sub reports, owns equity and debt securities of one of New Firm's audit clients. If the combined amount of the senior VP's interest is material to that person's net worth, New Firm's independence is impaired.

If the financial relationships with New Firm's client are held by an Other Public Co. entity, then materiality is based on the amount of the aggregate interest in relation to the consolidated financial statements of Public Co.

Other Restrictions Applicable to Indirect Superiors and Other Public Co. Entities

Independence of New Firm for an audit or attest client would also be impaired by the following relationships:

- Indirect superiors or other Public Co. entities have financial relationships that permit them to exert significant influence over the client.
- Other Public Co. entities or their employees are connected with the client as a promoter, underwriter, voting trustee, director or officer.

Except as noted above, services may be provided to a New Firm client without impairing independence that *would* impair independence if performed by a member.

Example

Bank Sub provides trustee and asset custodial services to an audit client of New Firm. If New Firm provided these services, its independence would be impaired. However, provision of the services by Bank Sub does not impair New Firm's independence.

Other Restrictions Applicable to New Firm

New Firm (and its owners and employees) may not perform a service requiring independence for Public Co. or any of its subsidiaries or divisions.

Example

New firm could not audit the consolidated financial statements of Public Co. or the individual financial statements of a subsidiary or division.

If an audit or attest client of New Firm holds an investment in Public Co. that is material to the client or allows the client to exercise significant influence, New Firm is not independent with respect to that client.

Example

Company A, an audit client of New Firm, acquires a 25% interest in Public Co. New Firm is not independent of Company A.

When making referrals of services among New Firm and any of the entities within Public Co., a member should consider Rule 102 on integrity, objectivity, and conflicts of interest and the related interpretations (see Chapter 7).

Example

An owner of New Firm is assisting an audit client in obtaining financing. Before referring that client to Bank Sub, the owner should consider the provisions of Interpretation 102-2, *Conflicts of Interest.*

Authoritative Source

1. Interpretation 101-14, *The Effect of Alternative Practice Structures on the Applicability of Independence Rules* (ET Section 101.16).

NOTE: At this time, some individual regulators have issued positions on APS, and the SEC has commented on APS issues to CPA firms involved, and to the AICPA and the APS. However, the AICPA guidelines provide the only general guidance.

The SEC requires public companies to disclose in their proxy statements the percentage of audit hours (in relation to total audit hours) performed by leased employees when that percentage is greater than fifty percent.

27 QUALITY CONTROL SYSTEMS FOR INDEPENDENCE

	For information on	See section
In This Chapter	A firm's quality control responsibilities	A
	A member's related quality control responsibilities	B

Overview

A firm has a responsibility to ensure that its personnel comply with professional standards applicable to its accounting and auditing/attest practice.

To meet this responsibility, a firm designs and implements a system of quality control policies and procedures, including those related to maintaining independence, integrity, and objectivity.

A member has a responsibility to comply with professional standards and with the firm's policies and procedures related to ensuring compliance with professional standards.

Applicability

CPA firms or individual members that are enrolled in an AICPA-approved practice-monitoring program are obligated to adhere to quality control standards. In addition, the Principles of Professional Conduct (see Chapter 2) indicate that members should practice in firms that have in place quality control procedures to provide reasonable assurance that services are competently delivered and adequately supervised.

The Statements on Quality Control apply to a CPA firm's accounting, auditing, and attest practice.

Section A: A Firm's Quality Control Responsibilities

Element of Quality Control	A firm should establish policies and procedures to provide reasonable assurance that • Personnel maintain independence (in fact and appearance) in all required circumstances. • All professional responsibilities are performed with integrity. • Personnel maintain objectivity in discharging professional responsibilities.
Requirement to Adhere to Applicable Rules	A firm should require that all professional personnel adhere to the applicable independence rules, regulations, interpretations, and rulings of the • SEC • AICPA • State CPA society • State board of accountancy • State statute • Other regulatory agencies (such as DOL and GAO)
Inform Personnel of Requirements and Specific Prohibitions and Restrictions	A firm should inform personnel of applicable requirements and of the following: • Investments that are not to be held. • Relationships that must not exist. • Transactions prohibited by firm policy. **Example** A firm can inform personnel of requirements through training, and of prohibited investments through maintaining and communicating a list of clients that require maintenance of independence (e.g., a restricted client list). A firm needs to keep the list current and communicate changes in it on a timely basis.
Affirmation of Compliance	A firm should periodically obtain written independence representations from all professional personnel that affirm that the individual • Is familiar with the firm's policies and procedures related to independence, integrity, and objectivity. • Held no prohibited investments during the period.

- Engaged in no prohibited relationships, activities, or transactions during the period.

Resolution and Documentation of Independence Questions	A firm should designate a competent person, or group, as responsible for resolving questions that arise on independence. A firm should establish requirements for documentation of the resolution of independence questions, including sources consulted in and outside the firm.
Confirmation of Independence of Other Auditors	A firm when acting as principal auditor should confirm the independence of another firm engaged to perform segments of an engagement.
SECPS Independence Quality Control Requirements	The SECPS's membership requirements obligate each CPA firm to ensure that the firm has policies and procedures in place to comply with independence requirements of the AICPA and SEC. Such policies and procedures should cover relationships between (1) the CPA firm, its benefit plans, and its professionals, and (2) restricted entities of the firm.
SEC Rules on a Firm's Quality Control Relating to Independence	The SEC permits an auditor to remedy certain inadvertent violations (e.g., a family member makes an investment of which the member is not aware) of the independence requirements if <ul><li>The auditor did not know about the violation.</li><li>The violation was promptly corrected once it became known.</li><li>The firm has quality controls in place that provide reasonable assurance that the firm and its personnel maintain independence.</li><li>For firms that provide audit, review, or attest services to more than 500 public companies, their quality controls should include<ul><li>Written independence policies and procedures</li><li>Automated systems to track investments in securities by partners and managerial employees that may impair independence.</li><li>A system that provides timely notification to all professionals about entities from which independence is required.</li><li>Annual or ongoing training on independence.</li><li>Annual internal inspection and testing of the firm's independence system.</li><li>Notice to all firm personnel of the names and titles of</li></ul></li></ul>

senior management responsible for independence matters.

- Written policies and procedures to require firm partners and covered persons (see Chapter 9) to report promptly to the firm employment negotiations with an audit client.

NOTE: The firm is required to immediately remove such professionals from the audit engagement and to promptly review all audit work that those professionals performed.

- Disciplinary measures to ensure compliance.

NOTE: The SEC encourages all firms to adopt the above elements of quality controls over independence, but notes that smaller CPA firms may not need all of them.

The elements of quality control in 4. above apply to professionals participating in the audit in offices of accounting firms located outside the US starting January 1, 2003.

Section B: A Member's Related Quality Control Responsibilities

Requirement to Be Informed	A member has a personal responsibility to be well-informed about applicable requirements as well as about firm policies and procedures.

> **Examples**
>
> A member can become well-informed by attending firm training, studying authoritative sources, and educational materials, such as this book.

Requirement to Be Sensitive to Potential Impairment of Independence	A member has a responsibility to be sensitive to activities and relationships that might create a mutuality of interests with clients or conflicts of interest that might impair independence in fact or be seen by a reasonable observer as impairing independence in appearance.

Responsibility for Self-Assessment	A member has a responsibility to review continuously activities and relationships to assess whether the member has fulfilled

- The obligation to users of audit or attest work to apply objective judgment.
- The obligation to the firm to adhere to its established policies and procedures.
- The obligation to fellow professionals to avoid activities and relationships that would appear to a reasonable observer to impair independence.

Responsibility for Affirming Adherence to Requirements	A member has a responsibility to affirm honestly, in accordance with firm policies, adherence to requirements on independence, integrity, and objectivity after reviewing personal investments, relationships, and transactions.

Responsibility for Resolving Independence Issues	A member may determine the need to act to avoid or cure a departure from professional standards or firm policies and procedures. The member should act promptly and notify appropriate firm personnel designated with responsibility for resolving independence questions.

> **Example**
>
> A member should dispose of a financial interest in a new client promptly. On learning a prohibited interest or relation with a client exists, a member should notify appropriate firm personnel.

Authoritative Sources

---

1. Statement on Quality Control Standards (SQCS) No. 2, *System of Quality Control for a CPA Firm's Accounting and Auditing Practice* (QC Section 20).
2. AICPA *Guide for Establishing and Maintaining a System for Quality Control for a CPA Firm's Accounting and Auditing Practice.*
3. SEC's Rule 2-01(d)—Quality Controls. *Revision of the Commission's Auditor Independence Requirements.*

*NOTE: The AICPA **Guide** contains examples of independence quality control policies and procedures for four hypothetical firms—a national firm, a regional firm, a local, one-office firm, and a sole practitioner. The **Guide** is available at www.aicpa.org/members/div/secps/refmanual.htm.*

PART D

AICPA RULES OTHER THAN INDEPENDENCE, INTEGRITY, AND OBJECTIVITY

28 RULES 201, 202, AND 203—GENERAL STANDARDS, COMPLIANCE WITH STANDARDS, AND ACCOUNTING PRINCIPLES

	For information on	*See section*
In This Chapter	General standards applicable to all members	A
	Compliance with standards for members in public practice	B
	Representations about accounting principles applicable to members in public practice	C
	Representations about accounting principles applicable to members not in public practice	D

Overview

Section A discusses the general standards of professional competence, due professional care, planning and supervision, and sufficient relevant data that apply to all AICPA members.

Section B discusses the standards promulgated by bodies designated by Council for members in public practice.

Section C discusses representations by member in public practice when departures from generally accepted accounting principles exist.

Section D discusses representations in letters or other communications by members not in public practice when departures from generally accepted accounting principles exist.

NOTE: In the context of Rules 201, 202, and 203, as opposed to Rule 101 on independence (see Chapters 6 and 9), the term "member" is used in the limited sense of a member, associate member, or international associate of the AICPA.

Section A: General Standards Applicable to All Members

Rule 201

Rule 201 states that a member shall comply with the following standards and any interpretations issued by bodies designated by Council:

1. **Professional Competence.** A member must only perform services that the member or the member's firm can complete with professional competence.
2. **Due Professional Care.** A member must exercise due professional care when performing professional services.
3. **Planning and Supervision.** A member must adequately plan and supervise the performance of professional services.
4. **Sufficient Relevant Data.** The member must obtain sufficient relevant data to provide a reasonable basis for conclusions or recommendations when performing professional services.

When Rule 201 Applies

This rule applies to any professional service provided by an AICPA member, whether or not in public practice.

When the member in public practice performs an engagement governed by the Statements on Auditing Standards, the Statements on Standards for Attestation Engagements, Statements on Standards for Accounting and Review Services, the Statements on Standards for Consulting Services, or the Statements on Standards for Tax Services, Rule 201 does not apply because the provisions of the rule are already incorporated in those standards. When a member in public practice performs a professional service not governed by these standards, Rule 201 applies.

Work involving any professional service, including consulting services, tax services, personal financial planning, or bookkeeping, is covered by Rule 201 when performed by a member not in public practice.

The Meaning of Competence

When a member performs services or work covered by Rule 201, he or she must

- Have or obtain the requisite technical qualifications and knowledge.
- Apply knowledge and skill with reasonable care and diligence.

- Have the ability to supervise and evaluate the quality of the work (when applicable).
- Exercise sound judgment.

NOTE: If a member does not have the necessary competence (even with additional research or consultation), the member should suggest that someone else perform the work.

Retaining a Subcontractor to Assist a Member with a Consulting Service Engagement	When retaining a subcontractor, a member has a responsibility to ensure that the subcontractor has the - Professional qualification, - Technical skills, and - Other resources required. *NOTE: The member may want to obtain references regarding the sub-contractor's competency and reputation from other CPAs and other customers of the subcontractor.*
Supervision of a Technical Specialist on a Consulting Engagement	A member must be qualified to supervise and evaluate the work of specialists that he or she employs. *NOTE: Supervision does not require that the member be qualified to perform each of the specialist's tasks. The member should be able to define the tasks and evaluate the end product.*

Section B: Compliance with Standards for Members in Public Practice

Rule 202	Rule 202 states that a member who performs auditing, review, compilation, consulting services, tax, or other professional services shall comply with standards promulgated by bodies designated by Council.

Bodies Designated to Issue Standards

	Designated body	*Standards*
1.	Accounting and Review Services Committee (ARSC)	Statements on Standards for Accounting and Review Services (SSARS)
2.	Auditing Standards Board	• Statements on Auditing Standards (SAS) • Statements on Standards for Attestation Engagements (SSAE) • Statements on Quality Control Standards (SQCS)
3.	Consulting Services Executive Committee (CSEC)	Statements on Standards for Consulting Services (SSCS)
4.	Tax Executive Committee	Statements on Standards for Tax Services (SSTS)

NOTE: Council resolutions give the first three bodies the authority to promulgate SSAE in their respective areas of responsibility.

Section C: Representations about Accounting Principles Applicable to Members in Public Practice

Rule 203	If the audited or reviewed financial statements or data contain any departure from an established accounting principle that has material effect on the statements or data taken as a whole, a member should not 1. Express an opinion or state that the entity's financial statements or other financial data are presented in conformity with generally accepted accounting principles. 2. State that he or she is not aware of any material modifications that should be made to such statements or data in order for them to be in conformity with generally accepted accounting principles. The only exception to the rule is: If the statements or data contain a departure needed to prevent the statements from being misleading, the member will still be in compliance with Rule 203 if the member describes • The departure, • The approximate effects, if possible, and • The reasons why compliance with the principle would result in a misleading statement.

Bodies Designated to Issue Established Accounting Principles	*Designated body*	*Standards*
	1. Financial Accounting Standards Board (FASB)	• Statements of Financial Accounting Standards and Interpretations • Accounting Principles Board Opinions • AICPA Accounting Research Bulletins
	2. Governmental Accounting Standards Board (GASB)	• Statements of Governmental Accounting Standards (issued in July 1984, and thereafter) • GASB Interpretations
	3. Federal Accounting Standards Advisory Board (FASAB)	• Statements of Federal Accounting Standards

Rule 203
  Departures from
  Established
  Accounting
  Principles—
  Audit
  Engagements
	An auditor is permitted to express an unqualified audit opinion on financial statements that contain a material departure from pronouncements covered by Rule 203 in those unusual circumstances when literal application of that pronouncement would result in misleading financial statements.
	
	NOTE: The authors believe circumstances that could cause adherence to a Rule 203 pronouncement to produce misleading financial statements would be extremely rare. Only a handful of such reports have ever been issued.

Rule 203
  Departures from
  Established
  Accounting
  Principles—
  Review
  Engagements
	An accountant is permitted to indicate that he or she is not aware of any material modifications when the reviewed financial statements contain a material departure from a pronouncement covered by Rule 203 in those unusual circumstances when literal application of that pronouncement would result in misleading financial statements.
	
	NOTE: The authors believe circumstances that could cause adherence to a Rule 203 pronouncement to produce misleading financial statements would be extremely rare.

Submission of **Financial** **Statements**	If a member is a stockholder, partner, director, officer, or employee for an entity other than his or her CPA firm and the member submits financial statements for distribution to third parties, the member should clearly communicate, preferably in writing, the member's relationship with the other entity, and should not imply the member is independent. Rule 203 applies if the member states that the financial statements are prepared in conformity with GAAP. *NOTE: Although the **Code of Professional Conduct** does not require that the communication be in writing, the authors recommend that such communications be in writing.*

Example

> XYZ Company
> 123 Santa Fe Way
> Anytown, US
>
> I have prepared the attached XYZ Company balance sheet for the period ending December 31, 20X1. Please call me if you have any questions.
>
> Sincerely,
>
> *Dan M. Guy*
>
> Dan M. Guy, CPA
> Controller

> *NOTE: The authors believe that the member should not use his or her CPA firm letterhead (or other firm identification) in any such transmittal document. However, the member is not precluded from using CPA firm letterhead provided he or she complies with applicable standards, including the disclosure of a lack of independence.*

Applicability of Rule 203 to Litigation Support Services

Rule 203 applies to a member performing litigation support services.

Section D: Representations about Accounting Principles Applicable to Members Not in Public Practice

Representations about GAAP	Rule 203 (see Section C) applies to members not in public practice when they represent in a letter or other communication that financial statements are in conformity with GAAP.

Types of Representations Covered	Letters, reports or other communication about financial statements include • A client entity's representations and reports to its auditor. • Reports to regulatory agencies and creditors.

Authoritative Sources

1. Appendix A, *Council Resolution Designating Bodies to Promulgate Technical Standards.*
2. Rule 201, *General Standards* (ET 201.01).
3. Rule 202, *Compliance with Standards* (ET 202.01).
4. Rule 203, *Accounting Principles* (ET 203.01).
5. Interpretation 201-1, *Competence* (ET 201.02).
6. Interpretation 203-1, *Departures from Established Accounting Principles* (ET 203.02).
7. Interpretation 203-2, *Status of FASB, GASB, and FASAB Interpretations* (ET 203.03).
8. Interpretation 203-4, *Responsibility of Employees for the Preparation of Financial Statements in Conformity with GAAP* (ET 203.05).
9. Ethics Ruling No. 8, *Subcontractor Selection for Management Consulting Services Engagements* (ET 291.015-.016).
10. Ethics Ruling No. 9, *Supervision of Technical Specialists on Management Consulting Services Engagements* (ET 291.017-.018).
11. Ethics Ruling No. 10, *Submission of Financial Statements by a Member in Public Practice* (ET 291.019-.020). (Revised, effective July 31, 2002.)
12. Ethics Ruling No. 11, *Applicability of Rule 203 to Member Performing Litigation Support Services* (ET 291.021-.022).

29 RULE 301—CONFIDENTIAL CLIENT INFORMATION

Basic Rule

Rule 301 prohibits a member in public practice from disclosing confidential client information without the client's specific consent.

What Is Not Prohibited by the Rule

Rule 301 does not

1. Release a member from his or her professional obligations under Rule 202, *Compliance with Standards*, and Rule 203, *Accounting Principles* (see Chapter 28).
2. Affect compliance with

    a. A subpoena or summons.
    b. Applicable laws and regulations.

    NOTE: Confidentiality of client information is a professional rule but must be distinguished from privileged communication. Therefore a member may be compelled by subpoena or summons to disclose confidential client information. However, certain communications between CPAs and their tax clients are protected by a privilege of confidentiality under Section 7525 of the Internal Revenue Code. In addition, some states statutes may include a privilege of confidentiality for accountant/client communications.

3. Prohibit professional practice reviews under the authority of

    a. The AICPA.
    b. A state society.
    c. A state board of accountancy.

4. Prevent a member from initiating an ethics complaint or responding to an ethics inquiry from

    a. The AICPA's Professional Ethics Division.
    b. The AICPA's Trial Board.
    c. A state society or state board investigative or disciplinary body.

Applicability to Purchase or Merger of an Accounting Practice

This rule applies to a review of a practice for a purchase, merger or sale. The member must take precautions, such as obtaining a confidentiality agreement from the prospective purchaser, to protect the confidential information.

Members Shall Not Use Client Information for Their Own Advantage

Members

- Involved in professional practice reviews.
- Involved in ethics complaints or ethics inquiries.
- Reviewing a practice in connection with a prospective purchase or merger.

May not

- Disclose confidential client information obtained during these reviews or investigations
- Use such information for their own benefit.

Members involved in professional practice or investigative or disciplinary hearings, however, are not restricted from appropriately exchanging information in connection with these reviews or investigations.

Changing CPAs to Hide Information

Rule 301 is not intended to help an unscrupulous client hide illegal acts or other information by changing CPAs.

Example

A member withdraws from an engagement after discovering irregularities in the client's tax return. If the successor accountant contacts the member, the member should, at a minimum, suggest that the successor ask the client to allow the member and successor to talk freely. This notifies the successor of some conflict. *The member withdrawing from the engagement should seek legal advice as to his or her status and obligations in this situation.*

SEC Rules on Insider Trading

The SEC prohibits illegal insider trading under the Securities Exchange Act of 1934.

Illegal insider trading can occur when

- Buying or selling a security while possessing material, non-public information about the security, or
- Communicating (tipping) such information to others who trade the securities.

Insider trading violates the law if the person who trades or communicates the information violates his or her fiduciary duty or other relationship of trust and confidence.

Examples of Insider Trading Cases Brought by the SEC

The SEC has brought insider cases against

- Corporate officers, directors and employees who traded the corporation's securities after learning significant confidential corporate information.
- Friends, business associates and family members who traded securities after receiving information from corporate officers, directors or employees.
- Law, banking, brokerage, and printing firm employees who were given confidential information to provide services to the corporation whose securities they traded.
- Government employees who had access to confidential information.
- Others who took advantage of confidential information from their employers.

FTC Privacy Disclosure Rules

Accountants who provide tax planning, financial planning, or tax preparation services to individual nonbusiness clients should be aware of the new FTC privacy disclosure rules that as of July 1, 2001, require accountants doing tax returns to provide notice of their privacy policies and practices to clients. The new rules also limit the disclosure of personal client information to nonaffiliated parties.

Additional information on these rules can be found at www.ftc.gov/privacy/glbact/index.htm.

Specific Activities That Would and Would Not Violate Client Confidentiality

Type of activity	*See section*
Permitted Use of Outside Bureaus or Agencies	A
Distribution of, or Revealing, Information to Others	B
Investment Advisory or Management Consulting Services	C
Service on the Board of a Nonclient Bank	D

Section A: Use of Outside Bureaus or Agencies

Use of Outside Bureaus or Agencies	A member may use • Outside services to process clients' tax returns (i.e., perform calculations and print the return). • A records retention agency to store clients' records, working papers, etc.
Member Must Take Precautions to Preserve Confidentiality	Whether using an outside service bureau or a records retention agency, the member is responsible for taking all necessary precautions to preserve the confidentiality of client information.

Section B: Distribution of, or Revealing Information

Disclosure to Insurance Carrier or Attorney Permitted	A member may give confidential client information, without the client's permission, to • A professional liability insurance carrier solely to help defend the member against actual or potential claims. • The member's attorney or a court to initiate, pursue, or defend himself or herself in legal or alternative dispute resolution proceedings.
Revealing Names of Clients	A member may disclose the names of clients without the client's specific consent unless disclosing the client's name would reveal confidential information. **Example** A member's practice is limited to bankruptcy matters. Disclosing a client's name may suggest that client is experiencing financial difficulties. This may be confidential client information and therefore disclosing the name of the client is prohibited. *NOTE: The ethical responsibility for confidentiality does not override the legal duty imposed by law or regulation to report matters to government authorities. Therefore, the member must comply with applicable federal or state laws.*
Revealing Client Information to Competitors	A client may be engaged to perform services that involve examining confidential information about competitors. The member would be prohibited under Rule 301 from revealing confidential information. **Example** A municipality in a state enforces a personal property tax on business inventories, fixtures and equipment, and machinery. The municipality uses CPA Firm A to examine the books and records of businesses to verify the amount declared. CPA Firm A will examine sales, purchases, gross profit percentages, and inventories as well as fixed asset accounts. Company Z is one of the companies examined, and retains CPA Firm B as its CPA. Firm B objects to Firm A's examination on the grounds that information gathered on Company Z, the client, could be inadvertently conveyed to Company Z's competitors by Firm A. Firm A would be allowed to perform the engagement, as long as all parties complied with the prohibition against revealing client information.

**Request from
Trade
Association**

A trade association is compiling a report containing profit or loss per-
centages of companies for distribution to its members. The trade association requests such information from the member about his or her
clients. If the member has the clients' permission, he or she may comply with this request.

**Disclosure of
Confidential
Client
Information
in a Divorce**

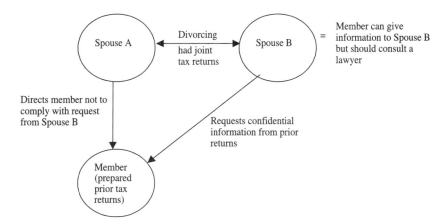

Rationale: Since Spouse B is a client with respect to prior tax returns,
the member is not prohibited by Rule 301 from giving information to
Spouse B. The member, however, should review the legal implications
with an attorney.

**FTC Privacy
Disclosure
Rules**

The Federal Trade Commission (FTC) has requirements that are designed to protect the privacy of broadly defined financial services, including tax planning, financial planning, or tax return preparation services. The FTC privacy disclosure rules require accountants that are
"significantly engaged" in providing these services to consumer (as
opposed to business) clients to provide notice of their privacy policies
and practices to clients. There are onetime disclosures to new clients
and annual disclosures to all clients. The new rules also limit the disclosure of personal client information to nonaffiliated parties.

An appendix to the FTC rule provides sample clauses related to the
required disclosures. This appendix is on the FTC's website at
www.ftc.gov/privacy/glbact/index.htm.

Section C: Investment Advisory or Management Consulting Services

Member Providing Investment Advisory Services to Company Executives	A member may accept an engagement in which the member is retained by a company to provide personal financial planning or tax services for its executives if the member can perform these investment advisory services with objectivity. (The executives are aware of the company's relationship with the member and have agreed to the arrangement.) The member must carefully consider

- Rule 102, *Integrity and Objectivity* (ET 102.01) (Chapter 7) since the member may find, in performing these services, that the member may recommend actions to the executives that are unfavorable to the company.
- Rule 301, *Confidential Client Information* (ET 301.01) since the member has a responsibility to keep client information confidential. In this case, the clients are both the company and the executives.

The member should consider informing the company and the executives of possible results of the engagement.

Disclosing Information Obtained from Nonclient Sources	A member performing management consulting services may not reveal information from outside nonclient sources without permission when the nonclient source conveyed the information with the understanding that it would not be disclosed. Rule 301 prohibits disclosing confidential information from clients, and therefore does not directly apply. However, Rule 501, Acts Discreditable, does apply. See Chapter 31 on Rule 501 for related guidance.
Disclosing Knowledge Obtained from a Different Client Engagement	A member who has knowledge and expertise gained from previous client engagements, which results in special competence in a particular field, can provide that knowledge and expertise to another client as long as the details of a previous client's engagement are not disclosed.

Example

A prospective client, Company B, has asked a member's firm to study the desirability of its using a newly developed electronic ticketing system for his business. The member has performed a recent study for another client, Company A, that leads the member to believe that the ticketing system would not be desirable for Company B. The member should communicate reservations about the ticketing system provided that the details of Company A's engagement are not disclosed. If, however, Company B would clearly know the origin of the information and such information is sensitive, the member should not accept the engagement without the approval of Company A.

Section D: Service on the Board of Directors of a Nonclient Bank

Service on the Board of Directors of a Nonclient Bank

The AICPA discourages a member from serving as a director of a non-client bank, if the member has clients (requiring independence or otherwise) that are customers of the bank.

The AICPA discourages bank directorships to avoid situations in which the member would have

- A conflict of interest under Interpretation 102-2 (ET102.03) as discussed in Chapter 7, or
- A problem with confidential client information under Rule 301 (ET 301.01) as discussed in Chapter 29.

NOTE: A more appropriate way for the member to serve the nonclient bank would be as a consultant to the board of directors.

Authoritative Sources

1. Rule 301, *Confidential Client Information* (ET 301.01).
2. Interpretation 301-3, *Confidential Information and the Purchase, Sale or Merger of a Practice* (ET 301.04).
3. The Securities Exchange Act of 1934, *Insider Trading*, Section 21 (d) (2).
4. Ethics Ruling No. 1, *Computer Processing of Clients' Returns* (ET 391.001-.002).
5. Ethics Ruling No. 2, *Distribution of Client Information to Trade Associations* (ET 391.003-.004).
6. Ethics Ruling No. 3, *Information to Successor Accountant about Tax Return Irregularities* (ET 391.005-.006).
7. Ethics Ruling No 5, *Records Retention Agency* (ET 391.009-.010).
8. Ethics Ruling No. 6, *Revealing Client Information to Competitors* (ET 391.011-012).
9. Ethics Ruling No. 7, *Revealing Names of Clients* (ET 391.013-.014).
10. Ethics Ruling No. 14, *Use of Confidential Information on Management Consulting Service Engagements* (ET 391.027-.028).
11. Ethics Ruling No. 15, *Earlier Similar Management Consulting Service Study with Negative Outcome* (ET 391.029-.030)
12. Ethics Ruling No. 16, *Disclosure of Confidential Client Information* (ET 391.031-.032).

13. Ethics Ruling No. 18, *Bank Director* (ET 391.035-.036).
14. Ethics Ruling No. 20, *Disclosure of Confidential Client Information to Professional Liability Insurance Carrier* (ET 391.039-.040).
15. Ethics Ruling No. 21, *Member Providing Services for Company Executives* (ET 391.041-.042).
16. Ethics Ruling No. 23, *Disclosure of Confidential Client Information in Legal or Alternative Dispute Resolution Proceedings* (ET 391.045-.046).

30 RULE 302—CONTINGENT FEES

In This Chapter   This chapter applies only to members in public practice. It contains the following sections:

For information on	See section
AICPA requirements	A
State requirements	B

Overview   The AICPA once prohibited contingent fees for all professional services. The AICPA, similar to the SEC, has retained the prohibition for any professional service when the CPA also provides audit, certain attestation services, or compilation services to the client as described in Section A.

Some state boards still prohibit contingent fees (see Section B). Other organizations, such as the SEC, generally have not taken exception to the AICPA rules except for its application to affiliates of audit clients (see page 211).

Section A: AICPA

Basic Rule	Rule 302 prohibits contingent fees **for any professional service performed for a client** when the member in public practice (or member's firm) also performs for that client

1. An audit or a review of a financial statement.
2. An examination of prospective financial information.
3. A compilation of a financial statement expected to be used by third parties, except when the compilation report discloses a lack of independence.

These services are referred to in this chapter as disqualifying services.

NOTE: The guidance on contingent fees is similar to that for commissions and referral fees. The reader may also want to consider the guidance in Chapter 33, Rule 503—Commissions and Referral Fees.

Rationale	The basic purpose of this rule and Rule 503 on commissions is to ensure the member's objectivity and to avoid a conflict of interest in performing the service, (i.e., a contingent fee impairs independence).

Period of Applicability	This prohibition applies during

- The period in which the member is engaged to perform any of these disqualifying services, and
- The period covered by any historical financial statements involved in these services.

Basic Rule— Prohibition on Tax Return Preparation or Claim for Refund for a Contingent Fee	Rule 302 also prohibits a member in public practice from preparing for a contingent fee

- An original or amended tax return, or
- A claim for a tax refund.

This includes giving advice on determining some portion of a return or claim for refund for events that have occurred at the time the advice is given.

Definition of a Contingent Fee	A contingent fee is a fee for performing any service in which the amount of the fee (or whether a fee will be paid) depends on the results of the service.

NOTE: A member's fees may vary depending on the complexity of services rendered.

Exceptions to Definition

Solely for applying this rule, fees are not considered contingent if they are

- Fixed by the courts or other public authorities.
- In tax matters, determined based on the results of judicial proceedings or the findings of governmental agencies.

Example

A member performs services for a client in bankruptcy. The judge awards a fee to the member. Such fee is not considered a contingent fee.

A fee is considered to be based on the findings of governmental agencies if the member can demonstrate, at the time that fees are set, that the member's client reasonably expects substantive consideration from an agency. The expectation is not reasonable when original tax returns are being prepared.

Definition of the Receipt of a Contingent Fee

A contingent fee is deemed to be received when

- The performance of the related services is complete, and
- The contingent fee is determined.

NOTE: This means that the contingent fee does not have to have been paid by the client to be deemed to have been received by the member's firm.

Examples of Permitted Contingent Fees

The following are some examples of tax services for which contingent fees would be permitted

- Representing a client

  - In a tax return examination by a revenue agent
  - By helping to influence tax legislation, or
  - By helping to get a private letter ruling.

- When established procedures are available for review of refund requests, requesting such a refund for

  - Interest or penalty overpayments or
  - Deposits of taxes not properly recorded.

- Requesting a reduction in the assessed value of property under an established taxing authority's review process for hearing such arguments.
- Filing an amended return claiming a refund

  - Based on an issue that is the subject of a test case for another taxpayer or for which a position is being developed by a taxing authority.
  - For an amount that is greater than the threshold for review set by the Joint Committee on Internal Revenue Taxation (last set at $1 million at March 1991) or state taxing authority.

> *NOTE: The key consideration is that the contingent fee is based on an amount **not** determined by the member*

Example of Contingent Fees Not Permitted	The following is an example of a circumstance in which a contingent fee would be not be permitted • Preparing an amended income tax return for a client for a refund of taxes because a deduction was inadvertently omitted in the original return. There is no question as to the propriety of the deduction; rather the claim is filed to correct an omission.
Receipt of Contingent Fees by Member's Spouse	A member's spouse may provide services to a member's attest client for a contingent fee if • The activities of the member's spouse are separate from the member's practice. • The member is not significantly involved in those activities. The member should consider whether a conflict of interest exists (see Chapter 7, Requirements for Integrity and Objectivity (Including Freedom from Conflicts of Interest).
Investment Advisory Services for Attest Client	A member may only provide investment advisory services for an attest client for a fee based on a percentage of the client's investment portfolio if all of the following conditions are met: • The fee is determined as a specified percentage of the client's investment portfolio. • The dollar amount of the portfolio on which the fee is based is determined at the beginning of each period and is adjusted during the period only for additions and withdrawals. • The fee arrangement is not renewed more often than on a quarterly basis. *NOTE: Since the dollar amount is set at the beginning of the period and adjusted only for client additions and withdrawals, but not for increases or decreases based on the portfolio's investment performance, the CPA's fee is not contingent on the portfolio's performance.* When performing such services, the member should consider Rule 101, *Independence*. See the guidance in Chapter 6, Basic Concepts of Rule 101–Independence, and Rule 102–Integrity and Objectivity, and Chapter 14, Performance of Other Services for Clients.

Investment Advisory Services for Nonattest Client

A member or member's firm may provide investment advisory services for a contingent fee to

- The owners, officers, or employees of an attest client.
- A nonattest client employee benefit plan sponsored by an attest client.

The member should, however, consider his or her obligations under

- Interpretation 102-2, *Conflicts of Interest* (Chapter 7) and
- Rule 301, *Confidential Client Information* (Chapter 28).

*NOTE: The SEC and the DOL do **not** agree with the AICPA's view that the following are separate clients from the attest entity:*

- *The owners, officers, or employees of an attest client*
- *A nonattest client employee benefit plan sponsored by an attest client.*

The position of these agencies is that services that would impair independence for the plan would generally have the same effect with respect to the sponsor. See Subsection D of Chapter 14, Performance of Other Services for Clients.

Section B: State Rules

State Rules	CPAs must also consider state laws concerning contingent fees. As of August 17, 2001, forty-five jurisdictions provide for the acceptance of contingent fees and nine jurisdictions prohibit them. Several states are considering different proposals during this year. A chart containing information about contingent fees is updated regularly on the AICPA website at www.aicpa.org/states/uaa/commfees.htm.
	Appendix B contains information on how to contact state boards and state societies.
The Uniform Accountancy Act	The Uniform Accountancy Act, sponsored by NASBA and developed along with the AICPA, permits contingent fees on behalf of nonattest clients. The language is taken from the AICPA's *Code of Professional Conduct.*

Authoritative Sources

1. Rule 302, *Contingent Fees* (302.01).
2. Interpretation 302-1, *Contingent Fees in Tax Matters* (ET 302.02).
3. SEC's Rule 2-01(c)(5), Contingent Fees. *Revision of the Commission's Auditor Independence Requirements*
4. Ethics Ruling No. 17, *Definition of the Receipt of a Contingent Fee or a Commission* (ET 391.033-.04).
5. Ethics Ruling No. 19, *Receipt of Contingent Fees or Commissions by Member's Spouse* (ET 391.037-.038).
6. Ethics Ruling No. 24, *Investment Advisory Services* (ET 391.047-.048).
7. Ethics Ruling No. 25, *Commission and Contingent Fee Arrangements with Nonattest Client* (ET 391.049-.050).

31 RULE 501—ACTS DISCREDITABLE

In This Chapter	*For information on*	*See section*
	Guidance for all members	A
	Guidance for members in public practice	B

Overview of Rule 501

Rule 501 prohibits acts discreditable to the profession. Section A discusses discreditable acts that apply to all members.

Section B discusses discreditable acts that apply to members in public practice.

Section A: Guidance for All Members

Basic Rule	Rule 501 prohibits acts discreditable to the profession.
Employment Discrimination and Harassment	A member who violates any state or federal antidiscrimination law, including laws prohibiting sexual or other forms of harassment, commits a discreditable act. Violation of the law is determined by the courts and is deemed to occur after the member has waived or lost the right to appeal.
False or Misleading Information Resulting from Member's Negligence	The following, when committed through the member's negligence, are discreditable acts: • Making false or misleading entries, or not correcting such entries if the member has the authority to do so. • Signing a materially false or misleading document. • Allowing or directing others to make such entries or sign such documents.
Soliciting or Disclosing CPA Exam Questions and Answers	A member who solicits or knowingly discloses Uniform CPA Exam questions without written authorization of the AICPA commits a discreditable act. *NOTE: This restriction applies to the questions from the Uniform CPA Examination for May 1996 and after. Prior to the May 1996 exam, CPA exam questions and unofficial answers were made available to the public. Beginning in May 1996, the examination became secure. Questions and unofficial answers are no longer published.*
Failing to File a Tax Return or Pay Tax Liability	A member who fails to file tax returns or remit payroll or other taxes collected for others on a timely basis has committed a discreditable act.

Section B: Guidance For Members in Public Practice

Subsection A : Retaining Client Records

Basic Principle

A member who retains client records after the client requests them commits a discreditable act. This is true even if state statutes grant the member a lien on certain records in his or her possession.

NOTE: Some states have rules on retaining client records. Practitioners should consult their state laws and regulations for additional guidance. See Appendix B for information on contacting state boards and state societies.

Definition of Client Records

A client's records are defined as any accounting or other records belonging to the client that were given to the member by, or on behalf of, the client. They do not include a member's workpapers.

NOTE: Many state boards have definitions of "client records" that go beyond the AICPA definition. Under those requirements, since the state board rules are more stringent, those rules should be followed in determining what constitutes " client records" that are required to be provided to a client.

Member's Workpapers Include PBCs

A member's workpapers include, but are not limited to, analyses and schedules prepared by the client (PBCs) at the request of the member. These are the member's property and are not considered client records.

Engagement Terminated Prior to Completion

If the engagement is terminated by either the member or the client prior to completion, a member is required to return only records as defined above.

Example

> A member is preparing a client's tax return. The client terminates the engagement before completion. The member is not required to give the client the tax return. The member is only required to return records provided by the client to the member.

Engagement Completed

If the engagement is complete, the member should return client records.

If asked, the member should also give the client information in the member's workpapers that is not in the client's books and records, and without which the client's financial information is incomplete.

Examples include

- Adjusting, closing, combining or consolidating journal entries.
- Information normally contained in books of original entry and general or subsidiary ledgers.
- Tax or depreciation carryforward information.

The member may require that the client pay all fees before the member provides such information.

Format of Requested Information

The member should provide the information described above in the medium requested, but only if it already exists in that format. For example, the member does not need to convert hardcopy information to an electronic form if it does not exist in that form.

Additional Requests for Information

Once the member has given client records and the additional completing information described above to an appropriate client representative, the member need not provide such information again either to the representative or other individuals associated with the client.

The client representative is the person, such as a general partner or majority shareholder, that has been held out as the client's representative.

Example

> Two individuals associated with a client company are currently on opposing sides in an internal dispute. Both individuals have made separate requests for client records and other information that is required under Rule 501 to be provided. Individual A is a majority shareholder and has been dealing with the member as the company's representative. The member need only provide client records and appropriate information once to Individual A.

Removal of Client Files from an Accounting Firm	If a member who is not an owner of the firm is terminated, the member may not take or keep originals or copies of proprietary information or information from client files without the firm's permission, unless permitted by a contractual agreement.

Subsection B: Failing to Follow Requirements for Government Audits or Requirements of Regulatory Agencies

Standards or Requirements for Government Audits

A member who audits a recipient of government monies or government units must comply with GAAS as well as other relevant guidance for governmental audits. Such guidance includes

- Government audit standards
- Guides
- Procedures
- Statutes
- Rules
- Regulations

A member who accepts such an engagement and fails to comply with relevant guidance commits a discreditable act, unless the member discloses the lack of compliance and reasons for it in his or her report.

Requirements of Governmental Bodies, Commissions, or Other Regulatory Agencies

A member who performs attest or similar services for entities subject to the jurisdiction of governmental bodies, commissions, or other regulatory agencies must comply with applicable GAAS as well as the requirements of those bodies.

Examples of such bodies include

- The Securities and Exchange Commission (SEC).
- The Federal Communications Commission (FCC).
- State insurance commissions.
- Other regulatory agencies that have established such requirements.

A material departure from such requirements is a discreditable act, unless the member discloses that such requirements were not followed and the reasons for not following the requirements in his or her report or in the financial statements.

In addition, a member should follow the requirements of such organizations, as well as GAAP, if the member prepares financial statements or related information, such as management's discussion and analysis, for the purpose of reporting to such bodies.

*NOTE: This guidance applies to members **not** in public practice as well as members in public practice.*

Subsection C: Nonclient Confidentiality

Basic Principle	If a member obtains information from a nonclient source with the understanding that the source and details not be disclosed, the member may not reveal this information without permission.
	NOTE: Confidential client information is discussed in Chapter 29.
Terms of Engagement Should Address Nonclient Confidentiality	In an engagement such as a feasibility study in which it appears that the member will rely on confidential information from nonclient sources, the terms of the engagement should state that the member's outside confidential sources will not be divulged even if they might affect the outcome of the engagement.
Terms of Engagement Are Silent	If the terms of the engagement are silent and the member needs to use outside confidential sources, the member should obtain the client's approval to present recommendations without disclosing confidential information. If client does not agree, the member should withdraw rather than breach confidence or improperly limit the information in his or her final recommendation.

Subsection D: Collection of Notes Issued in Payment

Collection of Notes	If a member's firm has a delinquent client, and the firm made arrangements with a bank to collect notes issued by a client as payment for outstanding fees and notifies the client, this would not violate any part of the *Code of Professional Conduct*.
	NOTE: See also Chapter 13, Unpaid Fees.

Authoritative Sources

1. Rule 501, *Acts Discreditable* (ET 501.01).
2. Interpretation 501-1, *Retention of Client Records* (ET 501.02).
3. Interpretation 501-2, *Discrimination and Harassment in Employment Practices* (ET 501.03).
4. Interpretation 501-3, *Failure to Follow Standards and/or Procedures or Other Requirements in Governmental Audits* (ET 501.04).
5. Interpretation 501-4, *Negligence in the Preparation of Financial Statements or Records* (ET 501.05).
6. Interpretation 501-5, *Failure to Follow Requirements of Governmental Bodies, Commissions, or Other Regulatory Agencies* (Revised) (ET 501.06).
7. Interpretation 501-6, *Solicitation or Disclosure of CPA Examination Questions or Answers* (ET 501.07).
8. Interpretation 501-7, *Failure to File Tax Return or Pay Tax Liability* (ET 501-8).
9. Ethics Ruling No. 2, *Collection of Notes Issued in Payment* (ET 591.003-.004).
10. Ethics Ruling No. 14 of Rule 301, *Use of Confidential Information on Management Consulting Service Engagements* (ET 391.027-.028).
11. Ethics Ruling No. 182, *Termination of Engagement prior to Completion* (ET 591.363-.364).
12. Ethics Ruling No. 189, *Request for Client Records and Other Information* (ET 591.377-.378).
13. Ethics Ruling No.191, *Member Removing Client Files from an Accounting Firm* (ET 591.381-.382).

32 RULE 502—ADVERTISING AND OTHER FORMS OF SOLICITATION

Overview

Rule 502 prohibits false or misleading advertising by members.

Section A contains guidance on acceptable and unacceptable forms of advertising and solicitation by CPAs.

Section B provides additional guidance for CPAs from Treasury Department Circular 230 and the Investment Advisers Act.

Finally, although Rule 502 applies to members in public practice, Section C provides guidance on applying this rule in situations that members not in public practice might encounter.

Section A: AICPA Guidance for Members in Public Practice

Basic Rule	Rule 502 prohibits members in public practice from the following when soliciting clients: • False, misleading, or deceptive advertising. • Coercion. • Overreaching or harassing conduct.
Definition of False, Misleading, or Deceptive Advertising	Examples of prohibited false, misleading or deceptive advertising or solicitation include those that • Create false expectations of favorable outcomes. • Imply that the member can influence a body or official such as a court or regulatory agency. • Represent that services will be performed for a fee when the member knows at the time of representation that the fee is likely to be substantially increased. • Make representations that would deceive or be likely to be misunderstood.
Permitted Forms of Advertising	As a result of a consent agreement between the AICPA and the Federal Trade Commission (FTC), CPAs may now use forms of advertising such as the following *as long as they are not false, misleading, or deceptive*: • In-person solicitation of clients. • Comparative advertising. • Self-laudatory advertising. • Testimonials or endorsements.
Engagements Obtained through Third Parties	Members may obtain clients or customers through the efforts of third parties, as long as the member determines that the promotional efforts of the third parties do not violate the *Code of Professional Conduct*.
Rationale for Engagements Obtained through Third Parties	Members who receive benefits from the actions of third parties must not do through the third parties what they are prohibited from doing themselves.

Use of CPA and Attorney Titles	A member who is both licensed as an attorney and a CPA may simultaneously practice accounting and law. The member may use either a single or separate letterhead, as long as

- The member's use of the CPA designation complies with Rule 502.
- The member conforms with the rules of the applicable Bar Association.

Use of AICPA PFS Designation	A member who holds the AICPA's Personal Financial Specialist (PFS) designation may use it after his or her name. If all partners or shareholders currently hold the designation, "Personal Financial Specialists" may be used on a firm's letterhead and in marketing materials.
Member Interviewed by the Press	When interviewed by a writer or reporter, the member should comply with the *Code of Professional Conduct* and not provide the press with any information for publication that the member himself or herself could not publish.
Serving as Course Instructor	A member who conducts a course should be sure that the promotions for the course do not violate Rule 502. The promotional material may include information on the instructor's background, such as the degrees he or she holds, professional society affiliations, and the name of the firm.
Member's Association with Newsletters and Publications	A newsletter, tax booklet, or similar publication not prepared by the member may be attributed to the member or the member's firm if the member concludes that the information attributed to the member or firm is not false, misleading, or deceptive.

Section B: Other Regulatory Guidance for Members in Public Practice

Treasury Department Circular 230

Treasury Department Circular 230, *Regulations Governing the Practice of Attorneys, Certified Public Accountants, Enrolled Agents, and Enrolled Actuaries and Appraisers Before the Internal Revenue Service,* prohibits CPAs, as well as other professionals, from

- Making false or misleading claims
- Making, directly or indirectly, an uninvited solicitation of employment in matters related to the IRS.

SEC Regulations

The SEC regulates advertising by investment advisers. Rule 206(4)-1 of the Investment Advisers Act, *Advertisements by Investment Advisers*, describes advertising practices that the SEC considers fraudulent, deceptive or manipulative. Advertising, as defined for this purpose, means any written communication addressed to more than one person, or any notice or announcement in a publication or by radio or television, which offers any investment advisory service with regard to securities.

State Regulations

State laws may contain additional requirements on advertising and solicitation. See Appendix B for information on how to contact state boards and state societies.

Section C: Guidance for Members Not in Public Practice

Use of CPA by Controller of Bank	A member who is the controller of a bank may use the CPA title on bank stationery or in paid advertisements that list the bank's officers and directors.
Member Interviewed by the Press	When interviewed by a writer or reporter, the member should comply with the *Code of Professional Conduct* and not provide the press with any information for publication that the member himself could not publish.
Serving as Course Instructor	A member who conducts a course should be sure that the promotions for the course do not violate Rule 502. The promotional material may include information on the instructor's background, such as the degrees he or she holds and professional society affiliations.

Authoritative Sources

1. Rule 502, *Advertising and Other Forms of Solicitation* (ET 502.01).
2. Interpretation 502-2, *False, Misleading or Deceptive Acts in Advertising or Solicitation* (ET 502.03).
3. Interpretation 502-5, *Engagements Obtained through Efforts of Third Parties* (ET 502.06).
4. Rule 206(4)-1of the Investment Advisers Act, *Advertisements by Investment Advisers*
5. Treasury Circular 230, *Regulations Governing the Practice of Attorneys, Certified Public Accountants, Enrolled Agents, and Enrolled Actuaries and Appraisers Before the Internal Revenue Service.*
6. Ethics Ruling No. 33, *Course Instructor* (ET 591.065-.066).
7. Ethics Ruling No. 38, *CPA Title, Controller of Bank* (ET 591.075-.076).
8. Ethics Ruling No. 78, *Letterhead: Lawyer-CPA* (ET 591.155-.156).
9. Ethics Ruling No. 108, *Member Interviewed by the Press* (ET 591.215-.216).
10. Ethics Ruling No. 176, *Member's Association with Newsletters and Publications* (ET 591.351-.352).
11. Ethics Ruling No. 183, *Use of the AICPA Personal Financial Specialist Designation* (ET 591.365-.366).

33 RULE 503—COMMISSIONS AND REFERRAL FEES

In This Chapter   This chapter applies only to CPA firms and members in public
practice. It contains the following sections:

For information on	*See section*
AICPA requirements	A
State requirements	B

Overview   The AICPA once prohibited commissions and referral fees for all
professional services. The AICPA has retained the prohibition for
any professional service when the CPA also provides audit, certain
attestation, or compilation services to the client as described in
Section A.

Some state boards still prohibit commissions and referral fees (see
Section B). Other organizations, such as the SEC, follow the
AICPA rule, except for its application of certain rules to affiliates
of audit clients (see page 228).

Section A: AICPA Requirements

Basic Rule

Rule 503 prohibits a member in public practice from receiving a commission or referral fee from a client when the member or member's firm performs for that client

1. An audit or a review of a financial statement.
2. An examination of prospective financial information.
3. A compilation of a financial statement expected to be used by third parties except when the compilation report discloses a lack of independence.

These services are referred to in this chapter as disqualifying services.

*NOTE: Although the **Code of Professional Conduct** does not define commissions or referral fees, some states define these terms. For example, the New York State Society's Professional Ethics Committee defines a commission as "compensation, except for a referral fee, for recommending or referring any product or service to be supplied by another person." Referral fees are defined as "compensation for recommending or referring any service of a CPA to any person."*

In its guidance on acceptance of fees and commissions, the California Accountancy Act, under Business and Professions Code Section 5061, defines a fee as including, but not being limited to, "a commission, rebate, preference, discount, or other consideration, whether in the form of money or otherwise." Therefore, practitioners should be alert to arrangements for receiving consideration that are not specifically identified as commissions, but that may be encompassed by the ethics rules.

Prohibitions

A member who performs any of the disqualifying services listed in the *Basic Rule* may not receive a commission for recommending or referring

- Any product or service **to a client**.
- Any product or service supplied **by a client**.

NOTE: This prohibition includes both commissions paid to the member by a client and commissions paid by a third-party supplier of products or services. The guidance on commissions and referral fees is similar to that for contingent fees. The reader may also want to consider the guidance in Chapter 30, Rule 302—Contingent Fees.

Period of Applicability

This prohibition applies during

- The period in which the member is engaged to perform any of these disqualifying services, and
- The period covered by any historical financial statements involved in the disqualifying services.

Rationale	The basic purpose of this rule is to ensure the member's objectivity and to avoid a conflict of interest in performing the service.

Basic Rule—Disclosure of Permitted Commissions	A member whose firm does not perform any disqualifying services for a client may receive a commission or referral fee for other types of services, such as personal financial planning, from that client. The member should disclose the commission **to the party to whom the product or service was recommended or referred**.

Documenting Disclosure of Commissions	A number of states require that a CPA issue a separate disclosure document to the party to whom the product or service was recommended (i.e., the client).
NOTE: Even if not required by state law or regulation, the authors believe that this is a good practice.

Example Written Disclosures of Permitted Commissions	One example of a state that requires a written disclosure statement for permitted commissions is California. Some of the California State Board of Accountancy requirements for this statement are

- The fact that the fee or commission is to be paid for professional services and that a fee or commission cannot be accepted solely for the referral of the client to the products or services of a third party.
- A description of the product(s) or service(s) recommended to the client.
- The identity of the third party that will provide the product or service.
- The business relationship of the licensee to the third party.
- A description of any fee or commission that may be received by the licensee.
- The dollar amount or value of the fee or commission payment(s) or the basis on which the payment(s) shall be computed.

When the product or service cannot be specifically identified at the time of the initial disclosure, the licensee must provide this information in a supplemental disclosure within thirty days of the receipt of the fee or commission.

In addition, the disclosure must

- Be on letterhead of the licensee's firm and signed by the member.
- Be signed and dated by the client.
- Contain an acknowledgment by the client that the client has read and understands the information contained in the disclosure.

- Be retained by the member for a period of five years.

The member client should send a copy of the disclosure document to the client.

Disclosure of Permitted Referral Fees

The AICPA rule creates an exception for referral fees that are related to recommending or referring the services of a CPA. Any member who accepts a referral fee for recommending or referring any service of a CPA or who pays a referral fee to obtain a client shall disclose this fact to the client.

NOTE: The member may not perform any disqualifying services for the client and accept a referral fee. Referral fees may be treated differently under state laws from commissions. While some of the guidance in the Code of Professional Conduct mentions both commissions and referral fees, many state laws (e.g., California) expressly prohibit CPAs from accepting a commission or fee solely for referring a client to a third party.

Definition of Receipt of Commission

A commission is considered received when

- The performance of the related services is complete, and
- The fee or the commission is determined.

Example

A member sells a life insurance policy to a client in 20X1. The member's commission payments are determined to be a fixed percentage of future years' renewal premiums. The commission is considered received in the year the policy is sold, (i.e., 20X1), no matter when payments are actually received.

Referral of Products of Others

A member cannot permit others, such as a distributor or agent, to do things that would violate the Code if the member did them. The member is held responsible for the actions of distributors or agents.

Example 1

CPA has Audit Client A. Audit Client A asks CPA to recommend a computer wholesaler for Client A's purchase of new computers. CPA may not receive a commission from the wholesaler for the recommendation.

Example 2

CPA has Audit Client A. Audit Client A asks CPA to recommend a source for Client A's purchase of new computers. CPA refers Client A to distributor B. Client A buys the computer, which distributor B obtains from a wholesaler. CPA may not receive a commission from the wholesaler, even though the referral was actually to the distributor.

Receipt of Commissions by Member's Spouse	A member's spouse refers products or services for a commission to a client for whom the member's firm performs disqualifying services. Rule 503 is not violated if

- The activities of the member's spouse are separate from the member's practice, and
- The member is not significantly involved in those activities.

The member should consider whether a conflict of interest exists (see Chapter 7).

Commission Arrangements with Nonattest Client

A member or member's firm may refer products or services of a nonclient or a nonattest client for a commission to

- The owners, officers or employees of an attest client.
- A nonattest client employee benefit plan sponsored by an attest client.

The member should disclose the commission to the owner, officers, or employees, or to the employee benefit plan.

The member should also consider

- Interpretation 102-2, *Conflicts of Interest* (Chapter 7), and
- Rule 301, *Confidential Client Information* (Chapter 29).

*NOTE: The SEC and the DOL do **not** agree with the AICPA's view that the following are separate clients from the attest entity:*

- *The owners, officers, or employees of an attest client*
- *A nonattest client employee benefit plan sponsored by an attest client*

The position of these entities is that services that would impair independence for the plan would generally have the same effect with respect to the sponsor. See Subsection M of Chapter 14, Performance of Other Services for Clients.

Sales of Products to Clients

A member may purchase a product from a third-party supplier and resell the product to a client, since the profit on the sale does not constitute a commission. The purchase of the product involves the member taking title to the product and having the associated risks of ownership.

Billing for Subcontractor's Services

A member has contracted with a computer hardware maintenance service to provide support for a client's computer operations. The member may bill the client a higher service fee than that charged to the member by the service provider. The increased fee is not a commission.

Section B: State Requirements

State Rules	CPAs must also consider state laws concerning commissions. As of August 17, 2001, forty-five jurisdictions provide for the acceptance of commissions and nine jurisdictions prohibit them. Several states are considering amending their requirements and continuing the trend in recent years to permit such fee arrangements or permit them under limited circumstances. A chart containing information about commissions is updated regularly on the AICPA website at www.aicpa.org/states/uaa/commfees.htm. Appendix B contains information on how to contact state boards and state societies.
The Uniform Accountancy Act	The Uniform Accountancy Act, sponsored by NASBA and developed along with the AICPA, permits commissions with disclosure on behalf of nonattest/noncompilation clients. The language is taken from the AICPA's *Code of Professional Conduct*.

Authoritative Sources

1. Rule 503, *Commissions and Referral Fees*. (ET 503.01).
2. SEC's Rule 2-01(c)(5).
3. Ethics Ruling No. 184, *Definition of the Receipt of a Contingent Fee or a Commission* (ET 591.367-.368).
4. Ethics Ruling No. 185, *Sale of Products to Clients* (ET 591.369-.370).
5. Ethics Ruling No. 186, *Billing for Subcontractor's Services* (ET 591.371-.372)
6. Ethics Ruling No. 187, *Receipt of Contingent Fees or Commissions by Member's Spouse* (ET 591.373-.374)
7. Ethics Ruling No. 188, *Referral of Products of Others* (ET 591. 375-.376).
8. Ethics Ruling No. 192, *Commission and Contingent Fee Arrangements with Nonattest Client* (ET 59.383-.384).
9. California Board of Accountancy Regulations, Section 56, *Commissions—Basic Disclosure Requirement*.

34 RULE 505—FORM OF ORGANIZATION AND NAME

In This Chapter   This chapter applies only to members in public practice. It contains the following sections:

For information on	See section
Permitted forms of organization	A
Misleading firm name	B
Members who own a separate business	C

Overview   Rule 505 applies to both the form and the name of the organization for members in public practice. Section A provides guidance on permitted forms of organization, which must be allowed by law or regulation and also meet the requirements set by the AICPA Council.

Section B provides guidance on determining what is and is not acceptable for a firm name.

Section C provides guidance for a member in public practice who participates in a separate business that performs professional services for which standards are promulgated by bodies designated by Council (e.g., accounting, tax, consulting).

Section A: Permitted Forms of Organization

Basic Rule	Rule 505 states that a member may practice public accounting only in a permitted form of organization. A permitted form of organization must • Be allowed by law or regulation, and • Meet the requirements set by the AICPA Council.
Applicability of Rule 505 to Firms Performing Attest Services	A member in public practice in any firm or organization that does any of the following must comply with the requirements of the AICPA *Council Resolution Concerning Rule 505—Form of Organization and Name* (the Council Resolution). • Performs audits or other engagements under SAS. • Performs reviews under SSARS. • Performs examinations of prospective financial information under SSAE. • Holds out as a firm of CPAs or uses the term "certified public accountant(s)" or the designation CPA in connection with its name.
Applicability of Rule 505 to Firms Performing Compilations	A member who performs compilations under SSARS but practices in a firm or organization that does not meet the definition of a firm or organization as described in, "Applicability of Rule 505 to Firms Performing Attest Services," must comply with the following requirements: • A CPA must have ultimate responsibility for the firm's compilation services and for each business unit performing compilations. (Non-CPA owners could not ultimately be responsible for these services.) • A CPA must individually sign any compilation report. The report may not be signed in the firm's name. For example, John Jones, CPA, an employee of XYZ Wholesale Company, may sign the report, but not under the firm name of XYZ Wholesale Company.
Applicability of Rule 505 to all other Firms	Firms not covered in the two previous sections, "Applicability of Rule 505 to Firms Performing Attest Services" and "Applicability of Rule 505 to Firms Performing Compilations," may take any legally permissible form.

Requirements of the Council Resolution

The requirements of the Council Resolution are

1. CPAs must own a majority of the financial interests and voting rights.

    A nonCPA owner must be actively providing services to the firm's clients as his or her principal occupation. Investors or commercial enterprises not actively providing services to the firm's clients as their principal occupation may not be owners.

2. A CPA must have ultimate responsibility for

    *   All the services provided by the firm, and
    *   Each functional and geographic business unit that performs attest or compilation services, or any other engagements under SAS and SSARS. Non-CPA owners cannot be ultimately responsible for any of these services or engagements.

3. Non-CPAs who become owners after adoption of the Council Resolution must have a baccalaureate degree.

    NOTE: Beginning in 2010, non-CPAs who become owners should also have 150 semester hours of education from an accredited college or university.

4. Non-CPA owners cannot hold themselves out as CPAs, but are be permitted to use the following titles:

    *   Principal
    *   Owner
    *   Officer
    *   Member
    *   Shareholder
    *   Any other title permitted by state law

5. Non-CPA owners must follow the *Code of Professional Conduct*. AICPA members may be held responsible under the *Code* for acts of co-owners.

6. Non-CPA owners must complete the same work-related CPE requirements as AICPA members.

    NOTE: AICPA bylaws require that, effective January 1, 2001, all AICPA members, both in public practice and not in public practice, shall complete 120 hours (or its equivalent) of continuing professional education for each three-year period.

7. Owners shall at all times own their equity and be the beneficial owners of their equity. If the owner stops being actively involved in the firm, his ownership must be transferred to the firm or other qualified owners within a reasonable amount of time.

8. Non-CPA owners cannot be members of the AICPA.

Applicability to Alternative Practice Structures

A traditional CPA firm engaged in auditing and other attestation services might be closely aligned with another organization, public or private, that performs other professional services.

These types of alliances are sometimes called *Alternative Practice Structures* (APS)—a nontraditional structure for the practice of public accounting.

Examples of APSs include American Express Tax and Business Services and Century Business Services.

An APS is in compliance with the financial interests provision (requirement 1) of the Council Resolution if

- CPA owners of the attest firm remain financially responsible under applicable state laws or regulations for the attest work performed.
- The firm is in compliance with the other requirements of AICPA's bylaws, the Council Resolution, and the *Code of Professional Conduct.*

NOTE: A June 2000 change to AICPA Bylaws 2.2 and 2.3 requires that members practicing public accounting in firms not enrolled in an AICPA-approved practice-monitoring program must enroll individually in a peer review program if they perform services, such as compilations, that are subject to peer review. For a model of an APS and for information on APS independence rules, see Chapter 26, Alternative Practice Structures.

Employment by, or Partnership with, Non-CPAs

A member employed in a public accounting firm made up of one or more non-CPA practitioners must comply with the *Code of Professional Conduct.*

If the member becomes a partner in the firm, he or she is responsible for the compliance with the *Code of Professional Conduct* of all persons associated with him or her.

NOTE: The authors believe that if the member becomes a shareholder in the firm, the same guidance would apply.

Example

A member in partnership with a noncertified public accountant would be held accountable if the noncertified partner violated the *Code of Professional Conduct.*

A member who is in a partnership with non-CPAs may sign a report with his or her signature and the designation "Certified Public Accountant" under the firm name. However, it must be clear that the partnership itself was not held out as being composed of CPAs.

Example

Schaller, Nichols, and Guy, Public Accountants
Dan Guy, CPA

Audit with Former Partner

A member's firm, which has been dissolved previously, consisted of one partner certified as a CPA and one noncertified partner. One account has been retained which the two practitioners plan to continue to work on together. Although it is proper for the audit to be carried out jointly by the two partners, the opinion should be presented on plain paper and signed in a manner similar to the following:

> Dan Guy, Certified Public Accountant
> Linda Nichols, Accountant

This form of signature assures the client that both partners participated in the audit, but leaves no doubt as to whether a partnership existed.

State Requirements

Many states now allow CPAs to practice as limited liability companies (LLC), limited liability partnerships (LLP) and general corporations. According to the AICPA's *Digest of State Issues*, as of March 2002

- Fifty-one jurisdictions have passed LLC legislation.
- Fifty-three jurisdictions have passed LLP legislation.
- At least two states have passed bills to allow CPAs to form general corporations.
- Forty-three states have explicitly amended their accountancy statute to provide for these forms of practice.

Most recently, Michigan amended their LLC and PC laws to correspond with changes in the accountancy laws. Several states are seeking to amend their LLC and PC laws to correspond with changes in their accountancy laws.

Also, NASBA's Uniform Accountancy Act (UAA) has sections that allow non-CPAs to have ownership interests in CPA firms if certain conditions are met. A number of states are currently evaluating whether to adopt the UAA.

Section B: Misleading Firm Name

Basic Rule

Rule 505 prohibits members from practicing public accounting under a misleading firm name.

- A successor firm **may** include the names of one or more past owners in the firm name.

Example

A firm is composed of four members who practice under the name of the managing partner. The managing partner is elected to high public office and leaves the partnership. The three remaining members may continue to practice under the managing partner's name followed by the designation "and Company."

- A firm **may not** designate itself as "Members of the American Institute of Certified Public Accountants" unless **all** of its CPA owners are AICPA members

Associations of Accountants Who Are Not Partners

Members who are not partners should not use a joint letterhead showing the names of both members even if they

- Share an office,
- Have the same employees,
- Have a joint bank account, and
- Work together on each other's engagements.

Rule 505 would be violated if any reports were issued under the joint letterhead.

NOTE: The public might assume that a partnership exists when in fact none exists.

Association of Firms That Are Not Partners

Three firms who wished to form an association, but not a partnership, would not be able to use a title such as "Smith, Jones, and Associates." Each firm should use its own name on its letterhead and list the other two firms as correspondents.

Practice of Public Accounting under Name of Association or Group Prohibited

Several CPA firms, who remain separate and distinct, but form an association or group which would have joint advertising, training, professional development, and management assistance, are not allowed to practice public accounting under the name of the association or group.

Practicing under the name of an association or group may confuse the public about the relationship among firms.

Permitted Use of Firm Name Along with Name of Association or Group	However, as long as the firm practiced only in its own firm name it could • Indicate the association or group name elsewhere on the stationery. • List the names of the other firms in the association or group on its stationery.
Firm Name of Merged Partnerships	When two partnerships merge, it is permissible for the newly merged firm to practice under a title that includes the name of a partner who had retired from one of the two firms prior to the merger.
Nonproprietary Partner	A firm may **not** use a designation such as "nonproprietary partner" to describe a high-ranking staff person who was a former partner of merged firms but is not a partner in the merging firm. The use of the term "partner" should be limited to legal partners.
Partner Having Separate CPA Proprietorship	A member may be a partner of a firm of public accountants, none of which are certified as CPAs, and may retain his or her own practice as a CPA. However, clients and others should be advised of this dual position of the member to prevent misunderstanding.
Partnership Roster	A firm may use an established firm name in a different state even if there is some difference in the roster of partners. The firm must otherwise comply with Rule 505, *Form of Organization and Name*.
State Requirements	States may also have regulations concerning the use of the name of the practice. For example, some states prohibit use of a name that implies the existence of a partnership when there is none. See Appendix B for information on contacting state boards and state societies.

Section C: Members Who Own a Separate Business

Applicability of Rules of Conduct to Members Who Own a Separate Business

A member in public accounting who owns an interest in a separate business that performs any of the following services is required to comply with the *Code of Professional Conduct*:

- Accounting
- Tax
- Personal financial planning
- Litigation support services
- Services for which standards are promulgated by bodies designated by Council (e.g., consulting).

NOTE: The following engagements are covered by standards issued by bodies designated by Council:

- *Audits and examinations*
- *Reviews*
- *Compilations*
- *Agreed-upon procedures*
- *Consulting services*
- *Tax*

Example

A member in public practice plans to form a separate business to perform centralized billing services for local doctors. Although the member maintains that this service is similar to one offered by a local bank and therefore not the practice of public accounting, the service is a type performed by public accountants. Therefore, the member could proceed with the business only if he or she complied with the *Code of Professional Conduct*, particularly Rule 502, *Advertising and Other Forms of Solicitation* (Chapter 32) and Rule 505, *Form of Organization and Name*.

Member Controls Business

If a covered member controls the separate business, either individually or collectively with the firm or other covered members of the firm, then all owners and employees of the separate business must comply with all provisions of the *Code of Professional Conduct*. The business is included in the definition of covered member for the purpose of applying the independence rules (see Chapter 9).

Member Does Not Control Business

If the member, individually or collectively with the firm or members of his or her firm, does not control the separate business, the provisions of the *Code of Professional Conduct* apply to the member but not to the entity, its other owners, and employees.

Example

A separate business enters into a contingent fee arrangement with an attest client of the member. If the member controls the separate business, such an arrangement would not be permitted (see Chapter 30, Contingent Fees). If the member does not control the separate business, the separate business would be permitted to enter into the arrangement.

Authoritative Sources

1. Bylaw Section 230R, *Implementing Resolutions under Section 2.3 Requirements for Retention of Membership, Continuing Professional Education for Members.*
2. Rule 505, *Form of Organization and Name* (ET 505.01).
3. Appendix B—Council Resolution Concerning Rule 505, *Form of Organization and Name.*
4. Interpretation 505-2, *Application of Rules of Conduct to Members Who Own a Separate Business* (ET 505.03).
5. Interpretation 505-3, *Application of Rule 505 to Alternative Practice Structures* (ET 505.04).
6. Ethics Ruling No. 3, *Employment by Non-CPA Firm* (ET 591.005-.006).
7. Ethics Ruling No. 134, *Association of Accountants Not Partners* (ET 591.267-.268).
8. Ethics Ruling No. 135, *Association of Firms Not Partners* (ET 591.269-.270).
9. Ethics Ruling No. 136, *Audit with Former Partner* (ET 591.271-.272).
10. Ethics Ruling No. 137, *Nonproprietary Partners* (ET 591.273-.274).
11. Ethics Ruling No. 138, *Partner Having Separate Proprietorship* (ET 591.275-.276).
12. Ethics Ruling No. 140, *Political Election* (ET 591.279-.280).
13. Ethics Ruling No. 141, *Responsibility for Non-CPA Partner* (ET 591.281-.282).
14. Ethics Ruling No. 144, *Title: Partnership Roster* (ET 591.287-.288).
15. Ethics Ruling No.145, *Firm Name of Merged Partnerships* (ET 591.289-.290).
16. Ethics Ruling No.177, *Data Processing: Billing Services* (ET 591.353-.354).
17. Ethics Ruling No.179, *Practice of Public Accounting under Name of Association or Group* (ET 591.357-.358).
18. Ethics Ruling No. 190, *Non-CPA Partner* (ET 591.379-.380).

PART E

OTHER ETHICS GUIDANCE

35 STATEMENTS ON STANDARDS FOR TAX SERVICES AND INTERPRETATIONS (SSTS)

What Are the SSTS?

The Statements on Standards for Tax Services (SSTS) supersede and replace the Statements on Responsibilities in Tax Practice (SRTP). They are enforceable standards of conduct for tax practice under the *Code of Professional Conduct*.

Applicability

The standards apply to all members when

- Recommending tax return positions, and
- Preparing or signing tax returns, including claims for refunds.

Effective Date

The SSTS have been approved by the Tax Executive Committee, were published in the October issue of the *Journal of Accountancy*, and became binding on members as of October 31, 2000.

In This Chapter

	For information on	*See section*
Statement No. 1	*Tax Return Positions*	A
Interpretation No. 1-1	*Realistic Possibility Standard*	B
Statement No. 2	*Answers to Questions on Returns*	C
Statement No. 3	*Certain Procedural Aspects of Preparing Returns*	D
Statement No. 4	*Use of Estimates*	E
Statement No. 5	*Departure from a Position Previously Concluded in an Administrative Proceeding or Court Decision*	F
Statement No. 6	*Knowledge of Error: Return Preparation*	G
Statement No. 7	*Knowledge of Error: Administrative Proceedings*	H
Statement No. 8	*Form and Content of Advice to Taxpayers*	I

*NOTE: The AICPA has issued an Exposure Draft of a proposed Interpretation No. 1-2, **Tax Planning** to Statement on Standards for Tax Services No. 1 **Tax Return Positions**. The Tax Executive Committee* *determined that there was a compelling need for a comprehensive interpretation of a member's responsibilities in connection with tax planning, with the recognition that such guidance would clarify how those standards would apply across the spectrum of tax planning, including those situations involving tax shelters, regardless of how that term is defined. The Interpretation, therefore, includes illustrations that cover a broad range of practice situations. Please check for updates on the John Wiley & Sons, Inc. website at www.wiley.com/ethics.*

Section A: SSTS No. 1, *Tax Return Positions*

Basic Rule— Recommending Tax Positions, Preparing or Signing a Return	SSTS No.1 prohibits members from 1. Recommending a tax position unless the member believes that the position has a realistic possibility of being sustained administratively or judicially if challenged. *NOTE: This is referred to as the realistic possibility standard. See Interpretation No. 1-1.* 2. Knowingly preparing or signing a return that takes a position that the member would not recommend under item 1 above. *NOTE: The taxpayer has the final responsibility for positions taken on the return.* In some cases, a member may conclude that a position does not meet the standard in 1. The taxpayer, however, may still wish to take the position. If the member concludes that the tax position is not frivolous, the member may • Recommend the tax return position as long as the member advises the taxpayer to disclose the position, or • Prepare or sign a return that reflects such a tax position as long as the position is disclosed.
Basic Rule— Advising Taxpayer of Penalties	When recommending tax return positions and preparing or signing a return, a member should, when relevant, advise the taxpayer of • Potential penalties for a tax position, and • The possibility of avoiding penalties through disclosures. *NOTE: Such advice may be given orally. Although a member should advise the taxpayer with respect to disclosure, the taxpayer is responsible for deciding whether and how to disclose.*
Basic Rule— Prohibited Positions	If a position is • Designed to exploit the likelihood of audit or detection, or • Only an arguing position for negotiating with a taxing authority, the member should not recommend such a position, or prepare or sign a return that takes such position.

Basic Rule—The Propriety of Being an Advocate for a Taxpayer	A member should be an advocate for the taxpayer when recommending a tax return position that complies with SSTS No. 1.
Appropriate Disclosure	Appropriate disclosure is determined by • The facts and circumstances of a particular case, and • The authorities regarding disclosure in the applicable taxing jurisdiction.
Definition of a Taxpayer	A taxpayer is defined as a client, a member's employer, or any other recipient of tax services.
Tax Returns Include Information Returns	A tax return is primarily a taxpayer's representation of facts. Under the SSTS, *tax return* includes information return.
Definition of Tax Return Position	A tax return position is • A position taken in a tax return on which the member has specifically provided advice to the taxpayer, or • A position about which a member knows the material facts and, on the basis of those facts, concludes whether the position is appropriate.
Definition of Frivolous Position	A frivolous position is one that is knowingly advanced in bad faith and is patently improper.

Section B: Interpretation No. 1-1, *Realistic Possibility Standard*

Basic Rule

To meet the realistic possibility standard, the member should believe that, based on a reasonable interpretation of the tax law, the position

- Is justified by existing law, or
- Can be supported by a good-faith argument for extending or changing existing law through the courts.

A member should not take into account the likelihood of audit or detection when determining whether this standard has been met.

Relationship to Other IRS Standards

The realistic possibility standard is

- Less stringent than the Internal Revenue Code's substantial authority standard and the "more likely than not" standard that apply to substantial underpayments of tax liability.
- Stricter than the Internal Revenue Code's reasonable basis standard.

Authorities for Determining Realistic Possibility Standard

In determining whether a tax return meets the realistic possibility standard, a member is not limited to authorities considered when determining whether substantial authority exists under the Internal Revenue Code. The member may also rely on

- Well-reasoned treatises.
- Articles in recognized professional tax publications.
- Other commonly used reference tools and sources of tax analyses.

Determining Whether a Realistic Possibility Exists

In determining whether a realistic possibility exists, a member should

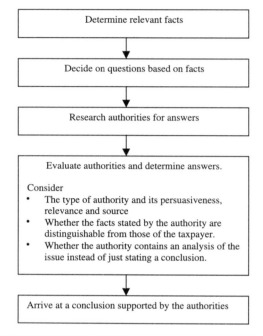

Section C: SSTS No. 2, *Answers to Questions on Returns*

Basic Rule	SSTS No. 2 states that a member, before signing as preparer of a tax return, should make a reasonable effort to get information from the taxpayer needed to answer all questions on the return.

Rationale	A member should try to obtain all answers because • A question and answer may be important in determining the taxable income or loss, or the tax liability. • As preparer, the member must often sign a declaration that the return is true, correct, and complete.

Definition of Questions	The term "questions" includes any request for information. The request need not be stated as a question. Questions are found • On the return, • In the instructions, or • In the regulations.

Omitting an Answer	Reasonable grounds for omitting an answer might include • The information is not easily obtained and the answer does not significantly impact taxable income or loss, or the tax liability shown on the return. • The meaning of the question is uncertain in relation to the particular return. • The answer is very lengthy. In this case, the member should put a statement on the return saying that data will be supplied upon examination. An answer should not be omitted simply because it may not be in the taxpayer's favor. If the taxpayer has a good reason for omitting an answer, the taxpayer does not have to include an explanation of such reason in the return. However, the taxpayer should consider whether the return would be incomplete because of the omission.

Section D: SSTS No. 3, *Certain Procedural Aspects of Preparing Returns*

Basic Rule— Relying on Information from Taxpayer

SSTS No. 3 states that while a member may rely without verification on information provided by the taxpayer or third parties, the member should question such information if it appears incorrect, incomplete or inconsistent.

Example

A taxpayer gives a member an unsupported list of dividends and interest. The member may rely on the list as long as it does not seem to be incorrect, incomplete, or inconsistent.

NOTE: Even though a member is not required to examine underlying documents, a member should encourage the taxpayer to provide appropriate supporting data.

Example

A member should encourage a taxpayer to provide supporting documents to allow the member to thoroughly consider income and deductions from security transactions and from pass-through entities, such as estates, trusts, partnerships, and S corporations.

Basic Rule— Responsibility for Conditions for Deductibility

If a taxpayer must meet certain conditions to support tax treatment of an item, the member should inquire to determine if the condition has been met.

Example

A deduction may require that books and records be maintained, or that supporting documents exist. The member should ask the taxpayer about such records and determine that the condition for the deduction is met.

Basic Rule—Prior Year Returns and Other Relevant Information

A member should

- Consider tax returns from prior years wherever possible.
- Consider relevant information from another taxpayer's return if known to the member and necessary for preparing the original taxpayer's return. The member should comply with any confidentiality rules or laws that would apply to such information.

Section E: SSTS No. 4, *Use of Estimates*

Basic Rule

SSTS No. 4 states that, unless prohibited by law or rule, a member may use a taxpayer's estimates if

- Obtaining exact data is impractical, and
- The member determines that estimates are reasonable based on the facts and circumstances known to the member.

However, SSTS No. 4 also states that estimates should not be presented so as to imply greater accuracy than exists.

Appraisals or Valuations

Appraisals or valuations are not considered estimates under the SSTS.

Specific Disclosure of Estimates

Although it is usually not necessary to disclose that an estimate was used, such disclosure should be made in certain circumstances to avoid misleading taxing authorities as to the degree of accuracy. Such circumstances may exist when the taxpayer

- Has died or is ill at the time the return is due.
- Has not received a Schedule K-1 for a pass-though entity at the time the tax return is due.
- Has pending litigation that might affect the return (e.g., bankruptcy).
- Has lost relevant records because of a fire or computer failure.

Section F: SSTS No. 5, *Departure from a Position Previously Concluded in an Administrative Proceeding or Court Decision*

Basic Rule	SSTS No. 5 allows a member to recommend a position, or sign or prepare a return containing a position, that differs from a position determined in an administrative proceeding or court decision for a taxpayer's prior return. *NOTE: An exception occurs when a taxpayer is bound to a specified treatment for later years, such as by a formal closing agreement.*
Definition of Administrative Proceeding	Administrative proceeding includes an examination by a taxing authority or an appeals conference for a return or claim for refund.
Definition of Court Decision	Court decision refers to a decision by any court having jurisdiction over tax matters.
Examples of When a Different Tax Treatment May Be Recommended in Subsequent Years	Normally, if the tax treatment of an item is determined in an administrative proceeding or court decision for the prior year's return, the member would recommend the same treatment in the current year. However, there may be circumstances in which different tax treatments would be warranted. Examples of such circumstances include • Although taxing authorities tend to act consistently on items covered in prior administrative proceedings, the authorities are not bound to do so. A taxpayer is similarly not bound to the tax treatment of an item consented to in an earlier administrative proceeding. • The prior decision may have been made without supporting documentation that is now available. • A taxpayer may have settled or not appealed the court decision even though the position met the standards in SSTS No. 1, *Tax Return Positions*. • Court decisions, rulings, or authorities that support the taxpayer's position now exist that did not exist during the prior proceeding.

Section G: SSTS No. 6, *Knowledge of Error: Return Preparation*

Basic Rule— Actions on Becoming Aware of an Error	SSTS No. 6 states that if a member becomes aware of an error in a previously filed return or that a return was not filed, the member should
	
	• Promptly inform the taxpayer.
	
	  NOTE: It is the taxpayer's responsibility to decide whether to correct the error.
	
	• Recommend corrective actions.
	
	  NOTE: Such recommendations may be communicated orally.

Basic Rule— Correcting the Error and Notifying Tax Authority	The member may not notify the taxing authority without the taxpayer's permission, except when required by law. *NOTE: The taxpayer, not the member, is responsible for deciding whether to correct the error.* If the taxpayer fails to correct a prior year error, and asks the member to prepare this year's return, the member should consider whether to continue the relationship with the client in the current year. If the member does prepare the current year's return, the member should take steps to avoid repeating the error. *NOTE: A member should consider consulting his or her own legal counsel before deciding upon recommendations to the taxpayer and whether to continue a professional relationship with the taxpayer. When there is a possibility that the taxpayer could be charged with fraud or other criminal misconduct, the taxpayer should be advised to consult his or her legal counsel before taking any action.*
Applicability	SSTS No. 6 applies whether or not the member prepared or signed the return that contains the error.
Definition of Error	An error includes • Any position, omission, or method of accounting that does not meet the standards of SSTS No. 1, *Tax Return Positions,* when the return is filed. • A position in a prior year's return that no longer meets the standards of SSTS No. 1 because of retroactive application of laws, court decisions, or administrative pronouncements. An error does not include an item that does not have a significant effect on the taxpayer's tax liability.

Section H: SSTS No. 7, *Knowledge of Error: Administrative Proceedings*

Basic Rule— Actions on Becoming Aware of an Error	SSTS No. 7 states that if the member is representing a taxpayer in an administrative proceeding and becomes aware of an error in the return, the member should • Notify the taxpayer without delay. • Recommend corrective action. *NOTE: Such recommendation may be communicated orally.*
Basic Rule— Notifying Taxing Authority of Error	Although the member can only notify the taxing authority with the taxpayer's permission, except when required by law, the member should seek such permission from the taxpayer. If the taxpayer refuses, the member should consider withdrawing and discontinuing the relationship with the taxpayer. *NOTE: A member should consider consulting his or her own legal counsel before making recommendations to the taxpayer and deciding whether to continue a professional relationship with the taxpayer. When there is a possibility that the taxpayer could be charged with fraud or other criminal misconduct, the taxpayer should be advised to consult his or her legal counsel before taking any action.*
Applicability	This SSTS applies whether or not the member prepared or signed the return that contains the error. Special considerations may apply when a member has been engaged by legal counsel to assist in matters relating to counsel's client.
Definition of Administrative Proceeding	An administrative proceeding includes an examination by a taxing authority or an appeals conference, but does not include a criminal proceeding.

Section I: SSTS No. 8, *Form and Content of Advice to Taxpayers*

Basic Rule

A member should

- Use his or her good judgment to make sure that tax advice reflects the professional competence of the member and serves the taxpayer's needs.
- Assume that tax advice provided to a taxpayer will the affect the reporting of matters or transactions in the taxpayer's tax returns and should therefore follow SSTS No. 1, *Tax Return Positions*, when giving advice.

A member is not required to

- Follow a standard format or guidelines when providing advice to a taxpayer, either written or orally.
- Communicate with a taxpayer when subsequent developments affect advice previously given unless

  1. The member is assisting a taxpayer in implementing procedures or plans associated with the advice provided.
  2. The member specifically agrees to undertake this obligation.

NOTE: Taxpayers should be made aware that tax advice reflects professional judgment based on an existing situation and that subsequent developments could affect previous advice. A member has no duty to keep informed of the effect of subsequent developments on his or her advice. However, if a member continues to be engaged by a taxpayer and is aware of subsequent events that would have affected advice previously given, the authors recommend that the member notify the client.

Applicability

This SSTS does not cover a member's responsibilities when it is expected that third parties are likely to rely on the advice.

Confidentiality

The member should consider applicable confidentiality rules when providing tax advice.

Form of Advice to the Taxpayer

In deciding on the form of advice to the taxpayer, a member should consider

- How important is the transaction? How large are the amounts involved?
- Is the inquiry specific or general in nature?
- How much time is available to develop advice and submit a recommendation?

- What are the technical complications presented?
- What authorities and precedents exist on this subject?
- How sophisticated is the client in tax matters?
- Should a lawyer be consulted?

Authoritative Sources

---

1. Statements on Standards for Tax Services No. 1, *Tax Return Positions*.
2. Statements on Standards for Tax Services No. 2, *Answers to Questions on Returns*.
3. Statements on Standards for Tax Services No. 3, *Certain Procedural Aspects of Preparing Returns*.
4. Statements on Standards for Tax Services No. 4, *Use of Estimates*.
5. Statements on Standards for Tax Services No. 5, *Departure from a Position Previously Concluded in an Administrative Proceeding or Court Decision*.
6. Statements on Standards for Tax Services No. 6, *Knowledge of Error: Return Preparation*.
7. Statements on Standards for Tax Services No. 7, *Knowledge of Error: Administrative Proceedings*.
8. Statements on Standards for Tax Services No. 8, *Form and Content of Advice to Taxpayers*.
9. Interpretation No. 1-1, *Realistic Possibility Standard*.

36 STATEMENTS ON STANDARDS FOR CONSULTING SERVICES

Introduction

Consulting services differ fundamentally from attest services.

- In an attest service, the practitioner expresses a conclusion about the reliability of another party's assertion.
- In a consulting service, the practitioner develops the findings, conclusions, and recommendations presented. The nature and scope of work is determined by agreement between the practitioner and client, and is frequently performed only for the use and benefit of the client.

To provide guidance on consulting services, the AICPA issued a Statement on Standards for Consulting Services (SSCS).

Applicability

This Statement on Standards for Consulting Services, *Consulting Services: Definitions and Standards*, applies to any AICPA member who holds out as a CPA in public practice while providing consulting services.

NOTE: See Chapter 14 for SECPS restrictions on consulting services for audit clients.

General Standards

Practitioners who perform consulting services must comply with the general standards of the profession described in Rule 201. Rule 201 states that a member shall comply with the following standards and any interpretations issued by bodies designated by Council:

1. **Professional Competence.** A member must only perform services that the member or the member's firm can complete with professional competence.
2. **Due Professional Care.** A member must exercise due professional care when performing professional services.
3. **Planning and Supervision.** A member must adequately plan and supervise the performance of professional services.
4. **Sufficient Relevant Data.** The member must obtain sufficient relevant data to provide a reasonable basis for con-

clusions or recommendations when performing professional services.

NOTE: See Chapter 28 for additional information on Rule 201.

Additional Standards for Consulting Services

Practitioners must also comply with the following additional general standards for consulting services.

1. **Client interest.** A member should serve the client interest by working to accomplish the objectives established in the understanding with the client while maintaining integrity and objectivity.
2. **Understanding with client.** The member should establish an understanding with the client about

   • The responsibilities of the parties.
   • The nature, scope, and limitations of services to be performed.

   This understanding

   • May be written or oral.
   • Should be modified if circumstances significantly change during the engagement.

   NOTE: See Chapter 14, Performance of Other Services for Clients, for additional requirements regarding an understanding with the client when consulting services are performed for an audit/attest client.

3. **Communication with client.** The member should inform the client of

   • Any conflicts of interest under Rule 102 (see Chapter 7),
   • Significant reservations concerning the scope or benefits of the engagement, and
   • Significant engagement findings or events.

Constraints Limit Services to Be Provided

Professional judgment is necessary in applying SSCS. The understanding with the client may establish constraints on the services to be provided. However, even when the agreed-upon scope of services has limitations, the member is **not** required to decline or withdraw from a consulting engagement. The member is required to inform the client of any significant reservations caused by the limitation.

Example

The understanding with the client may limit the practitioner's efforts to gather important relevant data. The member should explain the effect of this limitation to the client.

Consulting Services for Attest Client

The SSCS states that performing consulting services for an attest client does not, in itself, impair independence. However, members and their firms must comply with all applicable independence standards when performing attest services, such as those of the

- AICPA,
- State Boards,
- State societies, and
- Other regulatory agencies, including the SEC.

Definition of Consulting Process

The consulting process refers to the analytical approach applied in performing a consulting service. It typically involves some combination of the following:

- Determining the client's objective.
- Fact-finding.
- Defining problems or opportunities.
- Evaluating alternatives.
- Formulating proposed actions.
- Communicating results.
- Implementing.
- Following up.

Definition of Consulting Services

Consulting services are professional services that use the practitioner's technical skills, education, observations, experiences, and knowledge of the consulting process.

See Exhibit 1 for types of consulting services.

NOTE: In a consulting engagement, the CPA develops the findings, conclusions, and recommendations. In an attest or audit engagement, the CPA expresses a conclusion or opinion about the reliability of a matter (i.e., an assertion) that is the responsibility of another party.

Definition of Consulting Services Practitioner

A consulting services practitioner is

- Any AICPA member holding out as a CPA while performing consulting services for a client, or
- Any other individual performing consulting services for a client for an AICPA member or member's firm holding out as a CPA.

Authoritative Source

---

1. Statement on Standards for Consulting Services, *Consulting Services: Definitions and Standards.*

Exhibit 1—Types of Consulting Services

Service	*Description*	*Examples*
Consultations	The practitioner provides advice in a short time frame, based primarily on existing personal knowledge about • The client, • The circumstances, • The technical matters involved, • Client representations, and • The mutual intent of the parties.	• Reviewing and commenting on a client-prepared business plan • Suggesting computer software for further investigation by the client.
Advisory Services	The practitioner develops findings, conclusions, and recommendation for the client to consider and use in decision making.	• Operational review and improvement study. • Analysis of an accounting system. • Assistance with strategic planning. • Definition of requirements for an information system.
Implementation Services	The practitioner puts an action plan into effect. Client personnel and resources may be combined with the practitioner's to accomplish the implementation objectives. The practitioner is responsible to the client for the conduct and management of engagement activities.	• Providing computer system installation and support. • Executing steps to improve productivity. • Assisting with the merger of organizations.
Transaction Services	The practitioner provides services related to a specific client transaction, usually with a third party.	• Insolvency services. • Valuation services. • Preparation of information for obtaining financing. • Analysis of a potential merger or acquisition. • Litigation services.
Staff and Other Support Services	The practitioner provides appropriate staff and other support to perform client-specified tasks. The staff provided by the member may be directed by the client as needed.	• Data processing facilities management. • Computer programming. • Bankruptcy trusteeship. • Controllership activities.
Product Services	The practitioner provides the client with a product and related professional services to support the product's installation, use, or maintenance.	• Sale and delivery of packaged training programs. • Sale and implementation of computer software. • Sale and installation of systems development methodologies.

37 AN INTERPRETATIVE OUTLINE OF IFAC'S *CODE OF ETHICS FOR PROFESSIONAL ACCOUNTANTS*[1] (Revised January 1998)[2]

INTRODUCTION TO THE CODE

The International Federation of Accountants

The International Federation of Accountants (IFAC) is a nonprofit, nongovernmental, nonpolitical international organization of accounting bodies designed to develop and enhance the worldwide accountancy profession.

The Ethics Committee

The Ethics Committee reports to IFAC's Board. The Committee has responsibility, among other things, to develop the *Code of Ethics for Professional Accountants* (*Code*). The Committee is required to consult with and to advise the Board[3] on all ethics issues and to develop guidance on such issues for the Board's approval. Before the Committee can present an exposure draft amending or creating new guidance to the Board, the Committee must have approval of at least three-fourths of the Committee members.

Applicability of the *Code*

The IFAC *Code* recognizes that the task of developing detailed ethical requirements, implementing those requirements, and enforcing a code of ethics is primarily the responsibility of the member bodies of each country. However, some IFAC member bodies adopt the *Code* as the ethical requirements in their countries. In

---

[1] *Reprinted with permission from the **Guide to International Standards on Auditing and Related Services**, by Dan M. Guy and Douglas R. Carmichael. Published by Practitioners Publishing Company, Fort Worth, Texas.*

[2] *In January 2002, IFAC released and expanded guidance on independence presented in Section 8B. Section 8B applies to assurance engagements when the assurance report is dated on or after December 31, 2004, with earlier application encouraged. The existing rules on independence are presented in Section 8A.*

[3] *The Board consists of the President, the Deputy President, and representatives from eighteen countries, which are elected for two and one-half year terms. The Board supervises the general IFAC work program, the budget, and certain committees and projects.*

situations when a national requirement is in conflict with a provision of the *Code*, the national requirement should be followed.

When a professional accountant performs services in a country other than his or her home country, an important question is which ethical requirements (the IFAC *Code,* the country where the services are applied, or the home country) apply? In this situation, the professional accountant should refer to Section 6 below on "Cross-Border Activities."

Objectives of the
Code

The objectives apply to all professional accountants, whether they are in public practice, industry, commerce, the public sector, or education. However, the objectives are not used to solve specific ethical problems.

To achieve the highest standards of professionalism, professional accountants should adhere to the following objectives:

- *Credibility*
      In the whole of society there is a need for credibility in information and information systems.

- *Professionalism*
      There is a need for individuals who can be clearly identified by clients, employers and other interested parties as professional persons in the accountancy field.

- *Quality of Service*
      There is a need for assurance that all services obtained from a professional accountant are carried out to the highest standards of performance.

- *Confidence*
      Users of the services of professional accountants should be able to feel confident that there exists a framework of professional ethics that governs the provision of those services.

Fundamental
Principles of
Ethics

The fundamental principles apply to all professional accountants, whether they are in public practice, industry, commerce, the public sector, or education. Like the objectives, the fundamental principles are not used to solve specific ethical problems. The fundamental principles are

- *Integrity*
      A professional accountant should be straightforward and honest in performing professional services.[4]

---

[4] *Professional service includes any service performed by a professional accountant that requires accountancy or related skills, including accounting, auditing, tax, consulting, and financial management services.*

- *Objectivity*

   A professional accountant should be fair and should not allow prejudice or bias, conflict of interest or influence of others to override objectivity.

- *Professional Competence and Due Care*

   A professional accountant should perform professional services with due care, competence and diligence, and has a continuing duty to maintain professional knowledge and skill at a level required to ensure that a client or employer receives the advantage of competent professional service based on up-to-date developments in practice, legislation, and techniques

- *Confidentiality*

   A professional accountant should respect the confidentiality of information acquired during the course of performing professional services and should not use or disclose any such information without proper and specific authority or unless there is a legal or professional right or duty to disclose.

- *Professional Behavior*

   A professional accountant should act in a manner consistent with the good reputation of the profession and refrain from any conduct that might bring discredit to the profession.

- *Technical Standards*

   A professional accountant should carry out professional services in accordance with the relevant technical and professional standards. Professional accountants have a duty to carry out with care and skill, the instructions of the client or employer insofar as they are compatible with the requirements of integrity, objectivity and, in the case of professional accountants in public practice, independence. In addition, they should conform with the technical and professional standards promulgated by

   - IFAC (for example, International Standards of Auditing),
   - International Accounting Standards Committee,
   - The member's professional body or other regulatory body, and
   - Relevant legislation.

Organization of the *Code*

The *Code* is divided into three parts.

- Part A applies to all professional accountants unless otherwise specified. Part A contains the following seven sections:

  1. Integrity and Objectivity
  2. Resolution of Ethical Conflicts
  3. Professional Competence
  4. Confidentiality
  5. Tax Practice
  6. Cross-Border Activities
  7. Publicity

- Part B applies only to those accountants in public practice. Part B contains the following seven sections:

  1. Independence
  2. Professional Competence and Responsibilities Regarding the Use of Nonaccountants
  3. Fees and Commission
  4. Activities Incompatible with the Practice of Public Accountancy
  5. Clients' Monies
  6. Relations with Other Professional Accountants in Public Practice
  7. Advertising and Solicitation

- Part C applies to employed professional accountants and may also apply, in appropriate circumstances, to accountants employed in public practice. Part C contains the following four sections:

  1. Conflict of Loyalties
  2. Support for Professional Colleagues
  3. Professional Competence (of Employed Professional Accountants)
  4. Presentation of Information

Important Definitions

Auditor—This term is used and highlighted throughout the following discussion to refer to

  1. All individuals performing services requiring independence.
  2. All partners and proprietors in practice.
  3. All professional employees working on the engagement.
  4. All managerial employees located in an office participating in a significant part of the engagement.

Audit Firm or Practice—These terms refer to a sole practitioner, a partnership or a corporation of professional accountants that offer professional services to the public.

Professional Accountant—A term that includes those persons in public practice (a sole practitioner, partnership, or corporate entity), industry, commerce, the public sector or education.

Professional Accountant in Public Practice—A term that includes each partner or person occupying an equivalent or similar position, and each employee in a practice that provides **audit,** tax, or consulting services to a client. The term also includes professional accountants having managerial responsibilities in public practice.

Part A: Applicable to All Professional Accountants (including auditors, persons in industry, commerce, the public sector, and education)

Section 1

Integrity and Objectivity

All professional accountants/**auditors** must have integrity and objectivity. Integrity includes intellectual honesty, fair dealing, truthfulness, and freedom from conflicts of interest.

All professional accountants/**auditors** should avoid relationships that allow prejudice, bias, or other influences to override objectivity.

Professional accountants/**auditors** should neither accept nor offer gifts or entertainment that might reasonably be believed to have a significant and improper influence on professional judgment. What constitutes an excessive gift or entertainment varies from country to country, but professional accountants/**auditors** should avoid circumstances that would bring their professional reputation into dispute. **Auditors** should also refer to *Acceptance of Goods, Services, and Gifts* under Section 8A.

Section 2

Resolution of Ethical Conflicts

Professional accountants/auditors should be constantly conscious of and be alert to factors that give rise to conflicts of interest. Examples of factors that give rise to conflicts of interest include

- A professional accountant or auditor may be asked to act contrary to technical or professional standards.
- A question of divided loyalty between the professional accountant's **or auditor's** superior and the required professional standards of conduct could occur.

Professional accountants/**auditors** should refer to Section 15 for guidance on how to resolve a conflict of interest matter.

Section 3

Professional Competence[5]	Professional accountants/**auditors** should not portray themselves as having expertise or experience that they do not possess. Maintenance of professional competence requires that professional accountants/**auditors** have a continuing awareness of developments in the accounting profession, including relevant national and international pronouncements on accounting, auditing, and other relevant regulations and statutory requirements. In addition, the **auditor's** firm should adopt a quality control program.

Section 4

Confidentiality	Confidentiality covers (1) disclosure of information and (2) use (including the appearance of use) of information for personal advantage or for the advantage of another. Confidentiality does not apply to disclosure of information that is required to be disclosed by professional standards. Also, statute and common law govern confidentiality; therefore, its application is dependent on national or local law.

Professional accountants/**auditors** must respect the confidentiality of client or employer information. The duty of confidentiality continues even after the client/employer relationship with the accountant/**auditor** has ended.

The accountant/**auditor** should uphold the duty of confidentiality unless

1. The client/employer has given his or her permission to disclose the information.
2. There is a legal duty (for example, to disclose a violation of law to appropriate authorities) or a professional duty (for example, to comply with technical standards and ethical requirements, or to comply with quality review requirements of a national body) to disclose.

Professional accountants/**auditors** are obligated to ensure that assistants under their control, and individuals that they have consulted with, adhere to confidentiality.

---

[5] *IFAC recommends that each member who is active as an accounting professional should participate in a minimum of thirty hours per year, or a minimum of ninety hours for every three-year period, of structured learning.*

After deciding that confidential information should be disclosed but before disclosing such information, the professional accountant/**auditor** should consider

- Whether the information is based on known and substantiated facts.
- The appropriate recipients of the information.
- The legal consequences of disclosing the information.

Finally, the professional accountant/auditor should consider the need to consult with legal counsel and the relevant national professional body.

Section 5

Tax Practice

A professional accountant should follow the following principles in rendering tax services. A professional accountant (an **auditor** may also provide tax advice and prepare the tax return in addition to performing the audit of the client's financial statements)

1. Is entitled to advocate or advance the best position of the client or the employer.[6]
2. Should resolve doubt when there is reasonable support for the position in favor of the client or the employer.
3. Should make sure that the client or the employer is aware of the limitations of the tax advice and tax treatment.
4. Should not indicate to the client or the employer that the tax return preparation or advice given is beyond challenge.
5. Should advise the client or employer that they are responsible for the tax return.
6. Should record material advice given to a client or an employer in a letter or in a memorandum to the files.
7. Should not be associated with any tax return or related communication that

   a. Contains a false or misleading statement.
   b. Contains statements or information that was furnished recklessly or without any knowledge of whether such information is true or false.
   c. Omits or obscures information required to be submitted to tax authorities.

---

[6] *The term "client" applies to the professional accountant in public practice, whereas the term "employer" applies to the employer of the employee professional accountant in industry, commerce, the public sector, or education.*

8. May use estimates in a tax return when such use is generally accepted or it is not practical to obtain exact data. When estimates are used, they should be

    a. Presented as estimates.
    b. Reasonable under the circumstances.

9. Should ordinarily rely on information furnished by the client or the employer if such information appears reasonable. However, where appropriate, encourage supporting data to be provided. In addition, the professional accountant should

    a. Use the client's or the employer's prior years' returns when feasible.
    b. Make inquiries when the information appears to be incorrect or incomplete.
    c. Reference the books and records of the client or the employer.

10. Should promptly advise the client or the employer of any material errors or omissions in a tax return of a prior year or of a failure to file a required tax return. (The professional accountant has this responsibility even if he or she was not associated with the tax return of a prior year. However, the professional accountant is not obligated to inform the revenue authorities and should not do so without client or employer permission.)

11. If the client or the employer does not correct the matter in 10. above, should inform the client or the employer that the professional accountant cannot act for them in connection with the tax return or other related information. Also, consider whether continued association with the client or the employer is consistent with professional standards. (National or local requirements may require the professional accountant to inform the revenue authorities of this decision.)

Section 6

Cross-Border Activities

When a professional accountant/**auditor** (a) performs services outside of his or her home country and (b) the ethical requirements of the two countries differ, the professional accountant/**auditor** should follow the **most demanding** standards considering:

1. IFAC's *Code*.

2. The ethical requirements of the other country.
3. The ethical requirements of the home country, **but only if they are required to be followed for services performed outside the home country**.

NOTE: If a foreign public accounting firm issues an opinion or otherwise performs material services upon which a US (or other) registered public accounting firm relies in issuing all or part of any audit report, that foreign accounting firm is subject to the US Sarbanes-Oxley Act of 2002. Among other matters, this Act established requirements applicable to prohibited nonaudit services, prohibited audit services when certain former accounting firm employees have joined audit clients in certain positions, and prohibited audit services if the lead audit engagement and reviewing partners are not rotated every five years.

Section 7

Publicity

In marketing and promotion, professional accountants/**auditors** should not

1. Use means that bring the professional into disrepute.
2. Make exaggerated claims for the services that they provide, their qualifications, or their experiences.
3. Denigrate the work of other accountants.

Part B: Applicable to Professional Accountants in Public Practice (includes audit, tax, and consulting partners and persons occupying equivalent or similar positions, and each employee providing professional audit, tax, or consulting services)

Section 8A: Current IFAC Independence Rules

**Existing
Independence
Rules**

In January 2002, IFAC released revised guidance on independence, which is presented in the following section (Section 8B). The revised guidance applies to assurance engagements when the assurance report is dated on or after December 31, 2004, with earlier application encouraged. The existing rules on independence are presented below.

NOTE: If a foreign public accounting firm issues an opinion or otherwise performs material services upon which a US (or other) registered public accounting firm relies in issuing all or part of any audit report, that foreign accounting firm is subject to the US Sarbanes-Oxley Act of 2002. Among other matters, this Act established requirements applicable to prohibited nonaudit services, prohibited audit services when certain former accounting firm employees have joined audit clients in certain positions, and prohibited audit services if the lead audit engagement and reviewing partners are not rotated every five years. These prohibitions are noted at appropriate places in this chapter.

Independence

Auditors when undertaking an engagement that involves the expression on an opinion on financial information

1. Should be independent (independence in fact), and
2. Should appear to be independent (independence in appearance).

Financial Involvement with, or in the Affairs of, Clients

If the **auditor** has any of the following involvements, he or she is not independent:

1. A direct financial interest in a client, including its parent, subsidiaries, and affiliates.
2. An indirect material financial interest in a client, for example, by being a trustee of any trust or executor or administrator of any estate if such trust or estate has a financial interest in a client.
3. Loans to or from the client or any officer, director, or principal shareholder of a client.
4. A financial interest in a joint venture with a client or employee(s) of a client.

5. A financial interest in a nonclient that has an investor or investee relationship with the client (as described below).

A. Direct and Indirect Financial Interests

The **auditor** is not independent if he or she has acquired, or is committed to acquire, a direct or indirect material financial interest in a client. A direct financial interest includes an interest held by the spouse or dependent child of the **auditor**. In some countries, the prohibition may extend to other close relatives.

For indirect financial interests of a trustee or estate, the materiality of the financial interest is paramount. That is, the shareholdings, if material to the size of the issued share capital of the client or if material to the total assets of the trust or estate, would impair the **auditor's** independence. The prohibition also covers situations when the **auditor's** spouse or dependent child serves as trustee, executor, or administrator of a trust or an estate.

If a direct or indirect financial interest is involuntarily acquired by inheritance, marriage, or by a merger or acquisition, the **auditor** should dispose of the interest at the earliest practicable date to avoid a loss of independence.

B. Loans to or from Clients

The **auditor** should not make a loan to a client or guarantee a client's debt or accept a loan from a client or a guarantee of the **auditor's** debt. However, (1) loans to or from banks or other similar financial institutions when made under normal lending procedures, terms, and requirements, (2) home mortgages, and (3) deposit accounts with banks and other similar financial institutions are excluded. The prohibition also covers loans and guarantees to or from clients and the **auditor's** spouse or dependent child.

C. Investor[7]—Investee[8] Relationships

Company A (an investor and a client) has a material investment in Company B (an investee and a nonclient). If the **auditor** has any direct or indirect material financial interest in Company B, he or she is not independent with respect to Company A.

Company X (an investor and a nonclient) has a material investment in Company Z (an investee and a client). If the **auditor** has any direct or indirect material financial interest in Company X, he or she is not independent with respect to Company Z.

---

[7] *An "investor" is a parent, general partner, or natural person or corporation that has the ability to significantly influence an investee*

[8] *An "investee" is a subsidiary or an entity subject to the significant influence of an investor.*

D. Client—Nonclient Joint Ventures
    Company G (a client) and Company T (a nonclient) have a joint venture—Company S. If the **auditor** has an immaterial financial interest in Company T, his or her independence would not be impaired with respect to Company G provided that the **auditor** could not significantly influence Company T.

Appointments in Companies

The **auditor** is not independent if, during the period under audit or immediately preceding an assignment, he or she was

1. A member of the board, an officer, or an employee of the client.
2. A partner or an employee of a member of the board, an officer, or an employee of the client.

The *Code* suggests that the period "immediately preceding an assignment" should not be less than two years or as required by legislation.

*Provision of Other Services to **Audit** Clients*

The **auditor's** independence is not impaired by providing advisory services (accounting services, consulting, and tax services) to audit clients, provided there is no involvement in or responsibility assumed for management decisions.

The **auditor** may also prepare accounting records and financial statements (a frequently requested service in small client entities) and maintain his or her independence by observing the following requirements:

1. Do not have any relationship or combination of relationships with the client or any conflict of interest that would impair integrity or independence.
2. The client must accept responsibility for the financial statements.
3. Do not assume the role of employee or of management conducting client operations.
4. Do not eliminate the need to perform audit tests because of the work done preparing accounting records.

Ideally, the staff assistants assigned to the preparation of accounting records should not participate in the audit.

NOTE: If a foreign public accounting firm is subject to the US Sarbanes-Oxley Act of 2002, Section 201, "Services Outside the Scope of Practice of Auditor," makes it unlawful to perform any of the following nonaudit services:

*   *Bookkeeping or other services related to the accounting records or financial statements of the listed audit client.*
*   *Financial information systems design and implementation.*

- *Appraisal or valuation services, fairness opinions, or contribution-in-kind services.*
- *Actuarial services.*
- *Internal audit outsourcing services.*
- *Management functions or human resources.*
- *Broker-dealer, investment advisor, or investment banking services.*
- *Legal services and expert services unrelated to the audit.*

Personal and Family Relationships

If an **auditor,** who is a sole practitioner, partner, or an employee engaged on the assignment, is the spouse or dependent child of the client or a relative living in the client's common household, independence is impaired. In some countries, the range of relationships that impairs independence is wider. In fact, the *Code* indicates that it is up to each IFAC member body to determine what personal and family relationships impair independence.

Fees

If recurring total fees, coming from one client or group of connected clients, are the only or a substantial part of the **audit** firm's gross income, the **auditor** should carefully consider if independence is impaired. Likewise, if fees due from a client remain unpaid for an extended period, especially if prior year fees are not paid before the issuance of the current audit report, the **auditor's** independence may be impaired.

Allowances should be made for new **audit** firm practices and practices that are ceasing operations. Exemptions should also be made for the branch office of an **audit** firm where a given client's fees are a substantial part of the branch's fees. In the latter situation, a partner from another office should review the **audit.**

Contingent Fees

Professional services should not be provided to an **audit,** tax, or consulting client under a contingent fee arrangement in which no fee will be charged unless a specified finding or result is obtained. However, fees are not contingent if a court or other public authority fixes them. In countries where contingent fees are permitted by statute or by an IFAC member body, contingent fee engagements should be limited to those engagements where independence is not required (for example, tax services work would be an acceptable contingent fee arrangement, but a contingent fee **audit** engagement would not be acceptable).

Acceptance of Goods, Services, and Gifts

Professional accountants in public practice/**auditors** and their spouses and dependent children should not accept goods and services except on business terms available to others. Likewise, undue hospitality and gifts that are not commensurate with normal courtesies should not be accepted.

Ownership of Capital and Voting Rights

Ideally, a firm's capital should be owned entirely by professional accountants in public practice/**auditors**. However, others may own a portion of a firm's capital provided that professional accountants in public practice own the majority of capital and voting rights.

Former Partners

A partner in a firm may leave the firm and accept an appointment with an **audit** client. The firm may maintain its independence if the following conditions are met:

1. Payments made to the former partner for his or her interest and for any unfunded vested retirement benefits are fixed as to dates and amounts.
2. The payments in 1. above do not cause substantial doubt about the firm's ability to continue as a going concern.
3. The former partner does not participate or appear to participate in the firm's business or professional activities. (The provision of office space to the former partner constitutes an appearance to participate.)

NOTE: If a foreign public accounting firm is subject to the US Sarbanes-Oxley Act of 2002, Section 206, "Conflicts of Interest," makes it unlawful for that accounting firm to provide audit services to a listed audit client if that client has hired a chief executive officer, controller, chief financial officer, or equivalent person who was employed by the accounting firm and participated in the audit during the last year.

Actual or Threatened Litigation

Litigation involving the professional accountant in public practice/**auditor** and the client may impair the accountant's/**auditor's** independence and objectivity. The commencement or threat of litigation (1) by a client against the accountant/**auditor,** (2) by the accountant/**auditor** against the client alleging fraud or deceit by the client's officers, (3) or by others alleging substandard **audit** performance impairs independence. In these situations, the **auditor's** ability to report fairly and impartially on the client's financial statements and the willingness of the client to disclose information to the **auditor** may be affected. The *Code* recognizes that it not possible to specify precisely the point where it is improper for the **auditor** to report; therefore, the **auditor** should consider the circumstances from an independence-in-appearance perspective.

*Long Association of Senior Personnel with **Audit** Clients*

Long involvement of a senior **auditor** with an **audit** client could be perceived as a threat to objectivity and independence; therefore, the **audit** firm should provide for rotation of senior **auditors** serving the client. When not practical, review procedures or external-consulting arrangements should be established to guard against any reduction in objectivity and independence.

NOTE: If a foreign public accounting firm is subject to the US Sarbanes-Oxley Act of 2002, Section 203, "Audit Partner Rotation," makes it unlawful for that accounting firm to provide audit services if the lead audit and reviewing partners have not been rotated in five years.

Section 8B—Revised IFAC Independence Guidance

In This Section

This section contains the following subsections:

For information on	*See subsection*
Overview and objectives	A
Threats to independence	B
Safeguards	C
Examples	D

Revised Independence Rules

In January 2002, IFAC released revised guidance on independence, which is presented in the following section. The revised guidance applies to assurance engagements when the assurance report is dated on or after December 31, 2004, with earlier application encouraged. The existing rules on independence are presented in Section 8A.

NOTE: If a foreign public accounting firm issues an opinion or otherwise performs material services upon which a US (or other) registered public accounting firm relies in issuing all or part of any audit report, that foreign accounting firm is subject to the US Sarbanes-Oxley Act of 2002. Among other matters, this Act established requirements applicable to prohibited nonaudit services, prohibited audit services when certain former accounting firm employees have joined audit clients in certain positions, and prohibited audit services if the lead audit engagement and reviewing partners are not rotated every five years. These prohibitions are noted at appropriate places in this chapter.

Subsection A: Overview and Objectives

Overview

The IFAC *Code* provides a framework and principles to be used to identify, evaluate, and respond to threats to independence. Professional judgment should be used to evaluate each unique situation and determine those safeguards that should be applied. The new *Code* also presents numerous examples, which are summarized starting at Section D.

Basic Principle	Members of assurance teams, firms, and network firms (when applicable) should be independent of assurance clients.

NOTE: A network firm is an entity under common control, ownership, or management with the firm or any entity that a reasonable and informed third party, having knowledge of all relevant information, would reasonably conclude to be part of the firm nationally or internationally.

Elements of Independence

Independence requires two key elements.

a. **Independence of mind:** Allows an opinion to be offered without being affected by influences that compromise professional judgment. This state of mind allows an individual to act with integrity and exercise objectivity and professional skepticism.

b. **Independence in appearance:** Involves avoiding facts and circumstances that are so significant that a reasonable and informed third party, having knowledge of all relevant information, including safeguards applied, would reasonably conclude that a firm's or a member if the assurance team's integrity, objectivity, or professional skepticism has been compromised.

*NOTE: Although the word "independence" may imply freedom from all economic, financial, and other relationships, such freedom is impossible in a society where every member has relationships with others. Therefore, the **significance** of such relationships is what needs to be evaluated.*

The new *Code* is based on a conceptual approach because it is impossible to define every situation that creates a threat to independence and specify the appropriate responses. Firms and members of assurance teams should also consider whether relationships between individuals outside of the assurance team and the assurance client threaten independence.

Conceptual Framework for Independence Objectives

The conceptual framework assists firms and members of assurance teams in

- Identifying threats to independence.
- Evaluating whether those threats are clearly insignificant.
- When threats are not clearly insignificant, identifying and applying appropriate safeguards to eliminate or reduce the threat to an acceptable level.

When no safeguards are available to reduce the threat to an acceptable level, the only options are to

- Eliminate the threat.
- Refuse to accept or continue the assurance engagement.

Documentation Requirements

When an identified threat to independence is not clearly insignificant, and the firm decides to accept or continue the assurance engagement, the decision should be documented. Such documentation should include

- A description of the identified threats.
- The safeguards used to eliminate or reduce the threats to an acceptable level.

Applicability

The principles below apply to all assurance engagements.

The nature of the threats to independence and the applicability of safeguards will differ based on

- Whether the engagement is an audit engagement or another type of assurance engagement.
- When the assurance engagement is not an audit engagement, the purpose, subject matter, and intended users of the report.

A firm should evaluate the circumstances, nature of the engagement, and threats to independence in deciding

- Whether to accept or continue an engagement.
- The nature of the safeguards to be applied.
- Who should be members of the assurance team.

Independence Requirements for Audit Engagements

Because of the importance of independence in appearance and independence in mind for audit clients, the following are required to be independent of audit clients:

- The members of the assurance team,
- The firm, and
- Network firms.

Independence Requirements for Other Nonaudit Assurance Engagements

Considerations similar to those for audit clients should be made for nonaudit assurance clients. However, a factor that enters the evaluation is whether the assurance report is restricted for use to identified users.

Report Not Restricted	If the report is **not** expressly restricted for use by identified users, the following are required to be independent of the nonaudit assurance client:

- Members of the assurance team, and
- Firms.

Any threats that the firm has reason to believe may be created by network firm interests and relationships should also be evaluated.

Report Restricted	If the report is expressly restricted for use to identified users, safeguards are enhanced because the users are considered knowledgeable and the firm can more easily communicate about safeguards with the users. Therefore

- The members of the assurance team are required to be independent of the client. (Limited consideration of any threats created by network firm interests and relationships may be sufficient.
- In addition, the assurance team members and the firm should not have a material or indirect financial interest in the client.

Related Entities	For listed audit clients, the firm and any network firms must consider the interests and relationships of the client's related entities, which should be identified in advance. For all other assurance clients, when considering and evaluating independence, the assurance team should consider whether the related entity is relevant to the evaluation.

Inadvertent Violations	An inadvertent violation of the IFAC *Code* would generally not compromise independence if

- The firm has established appropriate quality control policies and procedures for independence, and
- Once discovered, a violation is promptly corrected and any necessary safeguards applied.

Significant versus Insignificant Independence Threats	A **clearly insignificant** threat is one that is clearly trivial and inconsequential. In evaluating the significance of threats, both qualitative and quantitative factors should be considered. All other threats are deemed to be significant.

Public Interest Perspective

Certain companies (e.g., listed companies, credit institutions, insurance companies, and pension funds) may have a wide range of stakeholders and therefore be significant from a public interest perspective.

If a member body chooses not to differentiate between listed entity audit engagements and other audit engagements, the listed entity examples should be considered to apply to all audit engagements.

National Perspectives

The conceptual framework for independence requirements for assurance engagements is the international standard in which national standards should be based. **No member body or firm is allowed to apply less stringent standards.**

If, however, a member body or firm is prohibited from complying with certain parts of this section by law or regulation, that body or firm should comply with all other requirements in this section.

A country or culture may use a different definition of relationships (e.g., some national legislators have prescribed lists of individuals who are defined as close family members that differ from those used in the *Code*.) In this case, the firm, network firms, and members of assurance teams should be aware of the differences and follow the more stringent requirements.

Subsection B: Threats to Independence

In This Subsection

This subsection contains the following categories:

For information on	*See category*
Self-interest threat	1
Self-review threat	2
Advocacy threat	3
Familiarity threat	4
Intimidation threat	5

Category 1: Self-Interest Threat

Definition	A self-interest threat occurs when a firm or member of the assurance team could benefit from a financial interest in, or other self-interest conflict with, an assurance client.
Examples	Examples of circumstances that may create this threat include • Direct or material indirect financial interest in an assurance client, including a loan or guarantee to or from an assurance client or its directors or officers; • Undue dependence on total fees from an assurance client; • Economic concern about losing the engagement; • A close business relationship with an assurance client; • Potential for employment with an assurance client; and • Contingent fees relating to assurance engagements.

Category 2: Self-Review Threat

Definition	A self-review threat occurs when (1) a product or judgment from a previous engagement needs to be reevaluated to reach conclusions on the current assurance engagement, or (2) when an assurance team member was formerly a director or officer of the assurance client or was an employee in a position to directly and significantly influence the subject matter of the assurance engagement.
Examples	Examples of circumstances that may create this threat are when an assurance team member • Is, or recently was, a director or officer of the assurance client; • Is, or recently was, an employee of the assurance client in a position to directly and significantly influence the subject matter of the assurance engagement; • Performs services for an assurance client that directly affect the subject matter of the engagement; and • Prepares original data used to generate the financial statements or other records that are the subject matter of the assurance engagement.

Category 3: Advocacy Threat

Definition   An advocacy threat occurs when a firm or assurance team member promotes an assurance client's position or opinion to the point that objectivity may be compromised. This might happen if a firm or assurance team member subordinated their judgment to that of the client.

Examples   Examples of circumstances that may create an advocacy threat include

- Dealing in or promoting the assurance client's shares or other securities, and
- Acting as the assurance client's advocate in litigation or in resolving disputes with third parties.

Category 4: Familiarity Threat

Definition   A familiarity threat occurs when a firm or an assurance team member becomes too sympathetic to the assurance client's interests due to a close relationship with the client or its directors, officers, or employees.

Examples   Examples of some circumstances that may create a familiarity threat include

- An assurance team member has an immediate or close family member who is a director or officer of the assurance client;
- An assurance team member has an immediate or close family member who is an employee of the assurance client and is in a position to directly and significantly influence the subject matter of the assurance engagement;
- A former partner of the firm is a director, officer of the assurance client, or an employee in a position to directly and significantly influence the subject matter of the assurance engagement.
- A senior member of the assurance team has a long association with the assurance client; and

- An assurance team member accepts gifts or hospitality from the assurance client, its directors, officers, or employees, unless the value is clearly insignificant.

Category 5: Intimidation Threat

Definition	An intimidation threat occurs when an assurance team member may not act objectively and exercise professional skepticism due to actual or perceived threats from the directors, officers, or employees of an assurance client.
Examples	Examples of circumstances that may create an intimidation threat include • Threat of replacement over a disagreement about the application of an accounting principle; and • Pressure to lower fees by inappropriately reducing the work performed.

Subsection C: Safeguards

Applying Safeguards	When a threat (1) is identified and (2) is not clearly insignificant, safeguards should be identified and applied to either eliminate the threat or reduce it to an acceptable level. This decision should be documented. Safeguards vary depending on the circumstances. In evaluating safeguards, the conclusions of a reasonable and informed third party with knowledge of all relevant information, including the safeguards applied, should always be considered. The conclusions might be affected by • The significance of the threat. • The nature of the assurance engagement. • The intended users of the assurance report. • The structure of the firm.

Categories of Safeguards	The three broad categories of safeguards are • Safeguards established by the profession, legislation, or regulation. • Safeguards within the assurance client. • Safeguards within the firm's own systems and procedures.
Safeguards Established by the Profession, Legislation, or Regulation	These safeguards include • Educational, training, and experience requirements for entry into the profession; • Continuing education requirements; • Professional standards and monitoring and disciplinary processes; • External review of a firm's quality control system; and • Legislation governing the independence requirements of the firm.
Safeguards within the Assurance Client	These safeguards include • Having persons other than management ratify or approve the appointment of the firm if the initial appointment is done by client management; • Designating competent employees to make managerial decisions at the client; • Establishing policies and procedures that ensure client's commitment to fair financial reporting; • Having internal procedures that ensure objective choices in commissioning nonassurance engagements; and • Having an audit committee or other corporate governance structure that oversees a firm's services
Audit Committees	Audit Committees can play an important governance role when they are independent of client management and can assist the board of directors in determining that a firm is independent when performing the audit. The audit committee of listed entities and the audit firm should have regular communications of matters that might, in the firm's opinion, reasonably to thought to bear on independence. In addition, firms should • Establish policies and procedures to communicate with audit committees or others charged with governance on independence. • For audits of listed entities, communicate orally and in writing, at least annually, all relationships and other matters between the firm, network firms, and the audit client that in the firm's professional judgment may be reasonably thought to bear on independence.

Safeguards within the Firm's Own Systems and Procedures

Safeguards with the firm's own systems and procedures include both firmwide safeguards and engagement-specific safeguards.

Firmwide Safeguards

These safeguards include

- Having firm leadership that emphasizes independence and the public interest;
- Documenting independence policies to identify, evaluate, and apply safeguards to eliminate or reduce independence threats;
- Establishing internal policies and procedures to monitor compliance with the firm's independence policies and procedures;
- Using different partners and teams with separate reporting lines for providing nonassurance services to an assurance client;
- Communicating and providing training on a firm's policies and procedures, and any changes thereto, to all partners and professional staff on a timely basis;
- Providing appropriate training and education of a firm's policies and procedures, and any changes thereto, to all partners and professional staff;
- Designating a member of senior management to oversee the adequate functioning of the safeguarding system;
- Establishing means of advising partners and professional staff of the assurance clients and related entities from which they must be independent;
- Establishing a disciplinary mechanism to promote compliance with policies and procedures; and
- Establishing policies and procedures to

  - Implement and monitor quality control of assurance engagements;
  - Identify interests or relationships between the firm or members of the assurance team and assurance clients;
  - Monitor and, if necessary, manage the reliance on revenue received from a single assurance client;
  - Prohibit individuals who are not members of the assurance team from influencing the outcome of the assurance engagement; and
  - Empower staff to communicate to senior levels within the firm any independence and objectivity issues that concern them. (This includes informing staff of the procedures available to them.)

Engagement-Specific Safeguards

Engagement-specific safeguards include

- Involving an additional professional accountant to review work or advise. This individual could be someone from outside the firm or network firm not otherwise associated with the assurance team;
- Consulting a third party, such as a committee of independent directors, a professional regulatory body, or another professional accountant;
- Rotating senior personnel;
- Discussing independence issues with the audit committee or others charged with governance;
- Disclosing the nature of the services provided and extent of fees charged to those with governance, such as the audit committee;
- Having policies and procedures to ensure that members of the assurance team do not make, or assume responsibility for management decisions for the assurance client.
- Involving another firm to perform or reperform part of the assurance engagement;
- Involving another firm to reperform the nonassurance service to the extent necessary to enable it to take responsibility for that service; and
- Removing an individual from the assurance team, when that individual's financial interests or relationships create an independence threat.

Safeguards Are Not Sufficient or Not Implemented

When the available safeguards are not sufficient to eliminate the threats to independence or to reduce them to an acceptable level, or when a firm chooses not to eliminate the activities or interests creating the threat, the only options are to refuse to perform, or withdraw from, the assurance engagement.

Engagement Period— General

Members of the assurance team and the firm should be independent of the assurance client during the period of the assurance engagement, which starts when the assurance team begins to perform the services and ends when the report is issued, except when the engagement is recurring. If the engagement is expected to recur, the period of engagement ends when either party notifies the other that the professional relationship has terminated or the final report is issued, whichever is later.

Period of Audit Engagement

In an audit engagement, the engagement period includes the period covered by the financial statements reported on by the firm. When an entity becomes an audit client during or after the period covered by the financial statements that the firm will report on, the firm should evaluate the following for any independent threats:

- Financial or business relationships with the audit client during or after the period covered by the financial statements, but before accepting the audit engagement; or
- Services previously provided to the audit client.

Period of Nonaudit Assurance Engagement

In a nonaudit assurance engagement, the firm should consider whether any financial or business relationships or previous services may create threats to independence.

If the firm provided nonassurance services to the audit client during or after the period covered by the financial statements but before the start of the audit services and those services would not be allowed during the period of the audit engagement, the firm should evaluate whether those services create threats to independence. If the threat is not clearly insignificant, the following safeguards should be considered and applied if necessary:

- Discuss the nonassurance services' effect on independence with those charged with governance of the client;
- Obtain the client's acknowledgment of responsibility for the results of the nonassurance services;
- Prevent the personnel who provided the nonassurance services from participating in the audit; and
- Engage another firm to review the results of the nonassurance services or have another firm reperform the nonassurance services to the extent needed to allow it to take responsibility for those services.

Client Becomes a Listed Entity

If a firm provides nonassurance services to a nonlisted audit client, the firm's independence will not be impaired when the client becomes a listed entity as long as

- The nonassurance services previously provided were allowed for nonlisted audit clients;
- The services will stop within a reasonable period of time after the client becomes a listed entity, if they are not allowed for listed audit clients; and
- The firm has established appropriate safeguards to eliminate or acceptably reduce any threats to independence from the previous services.

Subsection D: Examples

In This Subsection   This subsection contains the following categories:

For information on	*See category*
Financial interests	1
Provision of nonassurance services to assurance clients	2
Fees and pricing	3
Loans and guarantees	4
Close business relationships with assurance clients	5
Family and personal relationships	6
Employment with assurance clients	7
Recent service with assurance clients	8
Serving as an officer or director on the board of assurance clients	9
Long association of senior personnel with assurance clients	10
Gifts and hospitality	11
Actual or threatened litigation	12

Overview   This subsection provides numerous examples of potential threats to independence. The examples are not an exhaustive list of circumstances that create threats to independence. Members of assurance teams, firms, and network firms not only should comply with these examples, but should exercise professional judgment and apply the principles in this section to the particular circumstances they face, including circumstances not covered by these examples.

Category 1: Financial Interests

In This Category   This category contains the following subcategories:

For information on	*See category*
General guidance applicable to all assurance clients	1a
Guidance applicable to audit clients	1b
Guidance applicable to nonaudit clients	1c

Subcategory 1a: General Guidance Applicable to All Assurance Clients

Overview

A financial interest in an assurance client may result in a self-interest threat. The key to evaluating the threat is the nature of the financial interest. The following elements of the financial interest should be evaluated:

- The role of the person holding the financial interest.
- The materiality of the financial interest.
- The type (direct or indirect) of financial interest and the degree of control or influence that can be exercised over the intermediary, the financial interest held, or its investment strategy.

*NOTE: **A direct financial interest** is a financial interest that is (1) owned directly by and under the control of an individual or entity (including those managed on a discretionary basis by others) or (2) beneficially owned through a collective investment vehicle, estate, trust, or other intermediary over which the individual or entity has control. **An indirect financial interest** is a financial interest that is beneficially owned through a collective investment vehicle, estate, trust, or other intermediary over which the individual or entity has no control, such as a mutual fund or unit trust.*

Direct Financial Interest or Material Indirect Financial Interest

Scenario

A member of the assurance team or immediate family member has a direct financial interest, or material financial interest, in the assurance client.

Evaluation

The threat created is so significant that only the following safeguards can eliminate or acceptably reduce the threat.

Safeguards

- Dispose of the direct financial interest before joining the assurance team.
- Either dispose of all of the indirect financial interest or reduce holdings to an immaterial amount.
- Remove assurance team member from the engagement.

Financial Interest Received through Inheritance, Gift, or Merger

Scenario

A member of the assurance team, or one of their immediate family members, receives a direct financial interest or material indirect financial interest through an inheritance or a gift, or as a result of a merger.

NOTE: An immediate family member is a spouse (or equivalent) or dependent.

Evaluation

A self-interest threat is created. Evaluate (1) the nature of the relationship between the assurance team member and the close family member, and (2) the materiality of the financial interest. Consider applying the following safeguards as necessary to eliminate or acceptably reduce the threat.

Safeguards

- Dispose of the financial interest at the earliest practical date; or
- Remove the member of the assurance team from the assurance engagement.
- Consider whether additional safeguards are necessary during the period before the financial interest is disposed of or the individual is removed from the assurance team, such as discussing the matter with those charged with governance, or involving an additional professional accountant to review the work done or advise as necessary.

Close Family Member Has Financial Interest

Scenario

A member of the assurance team knows that his or her close family member has a direct or a material indirect financial interest in the assurance client.

NOTE: A close family member is a parent, nondependent child, or sibling.

Evaluation

A self-interest threat may be created. Evaluate the threat and consider

- The nature of the relationship between the member of the assurance team and the close family member.
- The materiality of the financial interest.

Consider and apply safeguards such as the following as necessary.

Safeguards

- Have the close family member dispose of all or a sufficient portion of the financial interest at the earliest practical date;
- Discuss the matter with those charged with governance, such as the audit committee;
- Involve an additional professional accountant who did not take part in the engagement to review the work done by the individual or otherwise advise as necessary; or
- Remove the individual from the assurance engagement.

Direct or Material Indirect Financial Interest Held by Trustee

Scenario

A firm or a member of the assurance team holds a direct financial interest or a material indirect financial interest in the assurance client as a trustee.

Evaluation

A self-interest threat may be created by the possible influence of the trust over the assurance client. Therefore, such an interest should be held only when

- The member of the assurance team, an immediate family member of the member of the assurance team, and the firm are not beneficiaries of the trust;
- The interest held by the trust in the assurance client is not material to the trust;
- The trust is not able to exercise significant influence over the assurance client; and
- The member of the assurance team or the firm does not have significant influence over any investment decisions involving a financial interest in the assurance client.

Financial Interest Held by Individuals Outside the Assurance Team

Scenario

Individuals outside of the assurance team such as the following (and their immediate and close family members) hold a financial interest in a client:

- Partners, and their immediate family members who are not members of the assurance team;
- Partners and managerial employees who provide nonassurance services to the assurance client; and
- Individuals who have a close personal relationship with a member of the assurance team.

Evaluation

A self-interest threat may be created. Evaluate factors such as

- The firm's organizational, operating, and reporting structure; and
- The nature of the relationship between the individual and the member of the assurance team.

If the threat is other than clearly insignificant, consider and apply safeguards such as the following to acceptably reduce the threat.

Safeguards

- Have policies to restrict people from holding such interests when appropriate.

- Discuss the matter with those charged with governance, such as the audit committee; or
- Involve an additional professional accountant who did not take part in the assurance engagement to review the work done or advise as necessary.

Inadvertent Violations

Scenario

An inadvertent violation of this section occurs.

Evaluation

Independence would not be impaired by an inadvertent violation of rules covering a financial interest in an assurance client when

- The firm, and the network firm, have policies and procedures requiring all professionals to promptly report any violations resulting from purchases, inheritance, or other acquisitions of a financial interest in the assurance client.
- The firm, and the network firm, promptly inform the professional to dispose of the financial interest.
- Either the financial interest is disposed of at the earliest practical date after identifying the issue, or the professional is removed from the assurance team.

Consider applying safeguards such as the following when as inadvertent violation has occurred.

Safeguards

- Involve an additional professional accountant who did not participate in the assurance engagement to review the assurance team member's work; or
- Do not allow the individual to participate in any substantive decision-making concerning the assurance engagement.

Subcategory 1b: Guidance Applicable to Audit Clients

Direct Financial Interest in Audit Client

Scenario

A firm, or a network firm, has a direct financial interest in an audit client of the firm.

Evaluation

The self-interest threat created would be so significant that no safeguard could reduce the threat to an acceptable level. The only option is to dispose of the financial interest

Material Indirect Financial Interest in Audit Client	*Scenario* A firm, or a network firm, has a material indirect financial interest in an audit client of the firm. *Evaluation* A self-interest threat is created. The only options are to dispose of all of the indirect interest or reduce holdings to an immaterial amount.
Material Financial Interest with Controlling Interest	*Scenario* A firm, or a network firm, has a material financial interest in an entity that has a controlling interest in an audit client. *Evaluation* The self-interest threat is so significant that no safeguard could reduce the threat to an acceptable level. The only options are to dispose of the financial interest in total or reduce holdings to an immaterial amount.
Firm's Retirement Plan Has Financial Interest in Audit Client	*Scenario* A retirement benefit plan of a firm, or network firm, has a financial interest in an audit client. *Evaluation* A self-interest threat may be created. Evaluate the threat, and if other than clearly insignificant, consider applying safeguards necessary to eliminate or acceptably reduce the threat.
Other Partners in Office in Which Lead Engagement Partner Practices Has Direct or Material Indirect Financial Interest	*Scenario* Another partner in the office in which the lead engagement partner practices in connection with the audit holds a direct or a material indirect financial interest in that audit client. (This would include partners who do not perform assurance engagements and their immediate family members.) *Evaluation* The self-interest threat could be so significant that no safeguard could reduce the threat to an acceptable level. Such partners or their immediate family members should not hold any direct or material indirect financial interests in an audit client. *NOTE: The office in which the lead engagement partner practices in connection with the audit is not necessarily the office to which that partner is assigned. When the lead engagement partner is located in a dif-*

*ferent office from that of the other members of the assurance team, judg-
ment should be applied to decide in which office the partner practices in
connection with that audit.*

**Other Partners
and Managerial
Employees
Provide
Nonassurance
Services to
Audit Client**

Scenario

A partner, other than the audit partner, or a managerial employee
provides nonassurance services to the audit client. The partner or
employee or an immediate family member holds a direct financial
interest or a material indirect financial interest in that client.

Evaluation

If the nonassurance services are not clearly insignificant, the self-
interest threat created would be so significant that no safeguard
could reduce the threat to an acceptable level. Such partners or
their immediate family members should not hold any direct or
material indirect financial interests in an audit client.

**Exception:
Immediate
Family Member
Has Financial
Interest in Audit
Client**

Scenario

An immediate family member of (1) a partner located in the office
in which the lead engagement partner practices in connection with
the audit, or (2) a partner or managerial employee who provides
nonassurance services to the audit client holds a financial interest
in an audit client that is received as a result of their employment
rights, such as pension rights or share options.

Evaluation

Such an interest would not create an unacceptable threat as long as
it is received as a result of their employment rights, and appropriate safeguards, where necessary, are applied to eliminate or acceptably reduce the threat.

**Member or Firm
Has Interest in
Same Entity as
Audit Client**

Scenario

The firm, the network firm, or a member of the assurance team has
an interest in an entity, and an audit client (or director, officer, or
controlling owner of the audit client) also has an investment in that
entity.

Evaluation

A self-interest threat may be created. Independence is not compromised with respect to the audit client if the respective interests
of the firm, the network firm, or member of the assurance team
and the audit client (or director, officer, or controlling owner of
the audit client) are both immaterial and the audit client cannot
exercise significant influence over the entity. If an interest is ma-

terial to either the firm, the network firm, or the audit client, and the audit client can exercise significant influence over the entity, no safeguards are available to reduce the threat to an acceptable level. The firm or the network firm should either dispose of the interest or decline to perform the audit engagement. An assurance team member with a material interest should

- Dispose of the interest.
- Reduce holdings to an immaterial amount.
- Withdraw from the audit.

Subcategory 1c: Guidance Applicable to Nonaudit Clients

Direct Financial Interests in Nonaudit Assurance Client	*Scenario* A firm has a direct financial interest in an assurance client that is not an audit client. *Evaluation* The self-interest threat created would be so significant no safeguard could reduce the threat to an acceptable level. The only appropriate action is to dispose of the financial interest.
Material Indirect Financial Interest in Nonaudit Assurance Client	*Scenario* A firm has a material indirect financial interest in an assurance client that is not an audit client. *Evaluation* A self-interest threat is created. The only appropriate action would be for the firm to either dispose of all of the indirect interest or reduce the holdings to an immaterial amount.
Material Financial Interest in Entity with Controlling Interest in Nonaudit Assurance Client	*Scenario* A firm has a material indirect financial interest in an entity that has a controlling interest in an assurance client that is not an audit client. *Evaluation* The self-interest threat created would be so significant no safeguard could reduce the threat to an acceptable level. The only appropriate action would be for the firm to either dispose of all of the financial interest or reduce the holdings to an immaterial amount.

Restricted Use Report for a Nonaudit Assurance Engagement

When a restricted-use report for an assurance engagement that is not an audit engagement is issued, exceptions to the guidance for all clients and for nonaudit assurance clients is discussed in Subsection A under "Report Restricted."

Category 2: Provision of Nonassurance Services to Assurance Clients

Overview

Although firms often provide nonassurance services to their clients, providing these services may create independence threats to the firm, a network firm, or the members of the assurance team. The perception of threats to independence is particularly important for the provision of such threats. The significance of such threats must be evaluated before the firm accepts an engagement to provide a nonassurance service to an assurance client. In certain cases, the threat may be eliminated or reduced by applying safeguards. However, in other cases, no safeguards are available to reduce the threat to an acceptable level.

NOTE: If a foreign public accounting firm is subject to the US Sarbanes-Oxley Act of 2002, Section 201, "Services Outside the Scope of Practice of Auditor," makes it unlawful to perform any of the following nonaudit services:

- *Bookkeeping or other services related to the accounting records or financial statements of the listed audit client.*
- *Financial information systems design and implementation.*
- *Appraisal or valuation services, fairness opinions, or contribution-in-kind services.*
- *Actuarial services.*
- *Internal audit outsourcing services.*
- *Management functions or human resources.*
- *Broker-dealer, investment advisor, or investment banking services.*
- *Legal services and expert services unrelated to the audit.*

Types of Clients

The following examples discuss providing nonassurance services to an assurance client. Potential threats to independence most frequently occur when providing nonassurance services to an audit client. However, threats to independence may also arise when providing a nonassurance service related to the subject matter of a nonaudit assurance engagement. Factors to consider are the significance of the firm's involvement with the subject matter of the nonaudit assurance engagement, whether any self-review threats are created, and whether any threats to independence could be acceptably reduced by applying safeguards, or whether the nonassurance engagement should be declined. When the nonassurance service is not related to the subject matter of the nonaudit assurance engagement, the threats to independence will generally be clearly insignificant.

Services Provided to a Related Entity, Division, or Discrete Financial Statement Item	Although providing certain nonassurance services to audit clients may create threats to independence so significant that no safeguard could eliminate or acceptably reduce the threat, providing such services to a related entity, division, or discrete financial statement item may be permitted when independence threats have been acceptably reduced by arranging for that related entity, division, or discrete financial statement items to be audited by another firm or by having another firm reperform the nonassurance service to allow it to take responsibility for that service.
General Safeguards	New developments and changes in the business world make it impossible to list all examples of scenarios when providing nonassurance services to an assurance client might create threats to independence, or of the different safeguards that might eliminate these threats or reduce them to an acceptable level. However, the following general safeguards may be particularly relevant in acceptably reducing threats created by providing nonassurance services to assurance clients:

- Establish policies and procedures to prohibit professional staff from making decisions (or assuming responsibility for such decisions) for the assurance client.
- Discuss independence issues related to the nonassurance services with those charged with governance, such as the audit committee.
- Develop policies within the client for oversight responsibility for nonassurance services provided by the firm.
- Involve an additional professional accountant to provide advice on the potential impact of the nonassurance services on independence.
- Involve an additional professional accountant from outside of the firm to provide assurance on a discrete aspect of the assurance engagement.
- Obtain the client's acknowledgment of responsibility for the results of the work performed by the firm.
- Disclose to those charged with governance, such as the audit committee, the nature and extent of fees charged.
- Make sure that personnel providing nonassurance services do not participate in the assurance engagement.

CPA Authorizes, Executes, or Consummates a Transaction	*Scenario* A CPA authorizes, executes, or consummates a transaction, exercises authority on behalf of the assurance client, or has the authority to do so. *Evaluation* This would generally create a self-interest or self-review threat that is so significant that the only options would be to avoid the activity or refuse to perform the assurance engagement.
CPA Determines Which Recommendations of the Firm Should Be Implemented	*Scenario* A CPA determines which recommendations of the firm should be implemented. *Evaluation* This would generally create a self-interest or self-review threat that is so significant that the only options would be to avoid the activity or refuse to perform the assurance engagement.
CPA Reports as Management to Audit Committee	*Scenario* A CPA reports in a management role to those charged with governance. *Evaluation* This would generally create a self-interest or self-review threat that is so significant that the only options would be to avoid the activity or refuse to perform the assurance engagement.
Having Custody of Assurance Client's Assets	*Scenario* A CPA has custody of an assurance client's assets. *Evaluation* This may create self-review or self-interest threats. The significance of the threats should be evaluated. If the threat is other than clearly insignificant, safeguards such as the following should be considered and applied as necessary to eliminate or acceptably reduce the threat. *Safeguards* • Make sure that personnel providing such services do not participate in the assurance engagement.

- Have an additional professional accountant advise on the potential impact of the activities on the independence of the firm and the assurance team.
- Other relevant safeguards set out in national regulations.

Supervising Client Employees in Performing Their Activities

Scenario

A CPA supervises assurance client employees in the performance of their normal recurring activities.

Evaluation

This may create self-review or self-interest threats. The significance of the threats should be evaluated. If the threat is other than clearly insignificant, safeguards such as the following should be considered and applied as necessary to eliminate or acceptably reduce the threat.

Safeguards

- Make sure that personnel providing such services do not participate in the assurance engagement.
- Have an additional professional accountant advise on the potential impact of the activities on the independence of the firm and the assurance team.
- Other relevant safeguards set out in national regulations.

Preparing Source Documents or Original Data

Scenario

A CPA prepares source documents or originates data in electronic or other form that provides evidence for transactions (e.g., purchase orders, payroll time records, and customer orders).

Evaluation

This may create self-review or self-interest threats. The significance of the threats should be evaluated. If the threat is other than clearly insignificant, safeguards such as the following should be considered and applied as necessary to eliminate or acceptably reduce the threat.

Safeguards

- Make sure that personnel providing such services do not participate in the assurance engagement.
- Have an additional professional accountant advise on the potential impact of the activities on the independence of the firm and the assurance team.
- Other relevant safeguards set out in national regulations.

In This Category   This category contains the following subcategories:

For information on	*See category*
Preparing accounting records and financial statements	2a
Valuation services	2b
Provision of taxation services to audit clients	2c
Provision of internal audit services to audit clients	2d
Provision of IT systems services to audit clients	2e
Temporary staff assignments to audit clients	2f
Provision of litigation support services to audit clients	2g
Provision of legal services to audit clients	2h
Recruiting senior management	2i
Corporate finance and similar activities	2j

Subcategory 2a: Preparing Accounting Records and Financial Statements

Preparing Accounting Records or Financial Statements for Audit Clients

Scenario

A firm, or network firm, assists an audit client in preparing accounting records or financial statements. The financial statements are subsequently audited by the firm.

Evaluation

This may create a self-review threat. If the personnel providing such assistance make management decisions, the self-review threat would be so great that it could not be reduced to an acceptable level by any safeguards. Such personnel should not make managerial decisions such as the following:

- Determining or changing journal entries, the classifications for accounts or transaction or other accounting records without obtaining the audit client's approval.
- Authorizing or approving transactions.
- Preparing source documents or originating data (including decisions on valuation assumptions), or changing such documents or data.

Audit Clients That Are Not Listed Entities

Scenario

A firm, or a network firm, provides an audit client that is not a listed entity with routine and mechanical accounting, bookkeeping, or payroll services. Examples of such services include

- Recording transactions for which the audit client has determined or approved the appropriate account classification;
- Posting coded transactions to the audit client's general ledger;
- Preparing financial statements based on information in the trial balance; and
- Posting audit client-approved entries to the trial balance.

Evaluation

The firm, or a network firm, may provide such services to an audit client that is not a listed entity, provided any self-review threat created is reduced to an acceptable level. The threat's significance should be evaluated and, if not clearly insignificant, safeguards such as the following should be considered and applied as necessary to acceptably reduce the threat.

Safeguards

- Ensure that such services are not performed by an assurance team member.
- Establish policies and procedures that prohibit those providing such services from making any managerial decisions for the audit client.
- Require that source data for accounting entries originate with the audit client.
- Require that underlying assumptions originate with and be approved by the audit client.
- Obtain audit client approval for any proposed journal entries or changes affecting the financial statements.

Audit Clients That Are Listed Entities

Scenario

For an audit client that is a listed entity, a firm (1) provides accounting, bookkeeping, or payroll services or (2) prepares financial statements or financial information on which the financial statements reported on by the auditor are based.

Evaluation

Such services may impair, or appear to impair, the independence of the firm or network firm. No safeguard, other than prohibiting the services, could acceptably reduce the threat. Therefore, a firm or a network firm should not, except in emergency situations and when the services fall within the statutory audit mandate, or as discussed in the following, provide such services to listed entities which are audit clients.

Exception: Providing Accounting and Bookkeeping Services to Divisions or Subsidiaries of Listed Entities

Scenario

A firm provides routine or mechanical accounting and bookkeeping services to divisions or subsidiaries of listed audit clients.

Evaluation

Providing such services would not impair independence for the audit client as long as the following conditions are met and the following safeguards are applied.

Conditions

- The services do not involve exercising judgment;
- The divisions or subsidiaries for which the service is provided are collectively immaterial to the audit client, or the services provided are collectively immaterial to the division or subsidiary; and
- The fees to the firm, or network firm, from such services are collectively clearly insignificant.

Safeguards

- The firm, or network firm, does not assume any managerial role or make any managerial decisions.
- The listed audit client accepts responsibility for the results of the work.
- Personnel providing the services do not participate in the audit.

NOTE: If a foreign public accounting firm is subject to the US Sarbanes-Oxley Act of 2002, Section 201, "Services Outside the Scope of Practice of Auditor," makes it unlawful to perform bookkeeping or other services related to the accounting records or financial statements of the listed audit client.

Exception: Providing Accounting and Bookkeeping Services in Emergency Situations

Scenario

A firm provides accounting and bookkeeping services to audit clients in emergency or unusual situations when it is impractical for the audit client to make other arrangements.

Evaluation

Providing accounting and bookkeeping services to audit clients in emergency or other unusual situations would not be an unacceptable threat to independence as long as

- The firm, or network firm, does not assume any managerial role or make any managerial decisions.
- The audit client accepts responsibility for the results of the work.
- Personnel providing the services are not members of the assurance team.

Permitted Services: Providing Technical Assistance and Advice to Client

Scenario

During the audit, client management asks for and receives advice on accounting principles and financial statement disclosure, the appropriateness of controls, and the methods used in determining the stated amounts of assets and liabilities.

Evaluation

Technical assistance and advice promotes the fair presentation of the financial statements and would not generally threaten the firm's independence.

Permitted Services: Assisting Client during the Audit

Scenario

A firm assists an audit client in resolving account reconciliation problems, analyzing and accumulating information for regulatory reporting, assisting in the preparation of consolidated financial statements (including the translation of local statutory accounts to comply with group accounting policies and the transition to a different reporting framework such as International Accounting Standards), drafting disclosure items, proposing adjusting journal entries, and providing assistance and advice in the preparation of local statutory accounts of subsidiary entities.

Evaluation

These services are considered to be a normal part of the audit process and do not, under normal circumstances, threaten independence.

Permitted Services: Preparing Accounting Records When the Subject Matter of the Engagement Is Not Financial Statements

Scenario

A firm is involved in preparing accounting records for an assurance engagement when the subject matter of the assurance engagement is not financial statements. (For example, the firm developed and prepared prospective financial information and subsequently provided assurance on this prospective financial information.)

Evaluation

A self-review threat may be created. The firm should evaluate the self-review threat's significance, and if other than clearly insignificant, safeguards should be considered and applied as necessary to acceptably reduce the threat.

Subcategory 2b: Valuation Services

Definition of Valuation Services	A valuation is composed of • Making assumptions with regard to future developments. • Applying certain methods and techniques. • Combining the above to compute a certain value, or range of values, for an asset, a liability, or a business as a whole. *NOTE: If a foreign public accounting firm is subject to the US Sarbanes-Oxley Act of 2002, Section 201, "Services Outside the Scope of Practice of Auditor," makes it unlawful to perform appraisal or valuation services, fairness opinions, or contribution-in-kind services.*
Performing a Valuation for an Audit Client That Is Incorporated in the Client's Financial Statements	*Scenario* A firm, or network firm, performs a valuation for an audit client that will be incorporated into the client's financial statements. *Evaluation* A self-review threat may be created. If the service involves valuing matters material to the financial statements and also involves a significant degree of subjectivity, the self-review threat created could not be acceptably reduced by applying any safeguard. The only alternatives are either to not provide the services or withdraw from the audit engagement. If the services are not separately, nor in the aggregate, material to the financial statements, or do not involve a significant degree of subjectivity, the self-review threat may be acceptably reduced by applying safeguards such as the following. *Safeguards* • Involve an additional professional accountant not on the assurance team to review the work or advise as necessary. • Confirm the audit client's understanding of the assumptions underlying the valuation and the method to be used. Obtain the client's approval for their use. • Obtain the audit client's acknowledgment of responsibility for the results of the work performed by the firm. • Make sure that the personnel providing such services do not participate in the audit engagement. Consider the following when determining whether the preceding safeguards would be effective: • The extent of the audit client's knowledge, experience, and ability to evaluate the issues concerned.

- The extent of the audit client's involvement in determining and approving significant matters of judgment.
- The degree to which established methods and professional guidelines are applied when performing a particular valuation service.
- For valuations involving standard or established methods, the degree of subjectivity inherent in the item concerned.
- The reliability and extent of the underlying data.
- The degree of dependence on future events which could create significant volatility inherent in the amounts involved.
- The extent and clarity of the financial statement disclosures.

Valuations for Purpose of Filing Tax Returns	*Scenario* A firm, or a network firm, performs a valuation service for an audit client for making a filing or return to a tax authority, computing an amount of tax due by the assurance client, or for tax planning. *Evaluation* These services would not create a significant threat to independence because such valuations are generally subject to external review, such as by a tax authority.
Valuation for Nonaudit Assurance Engagement	*Scenario* A firm performs a valuation that forms part of the subject matter of a nonaudit assurance engagement. *Evaluation* The firm should consider any self-review threats. If the threat is other than clearly insignificant, safeguards should be considered and applied as necessary to eliminate or acceptably reduce the threat.

Subcategory 2c: Provision of Taxation Services to Audit Clients

Provision of Taxation Services to Audit Clients	*Scenario* A firm provides tax services to an audit client. Taxation services are composed of a broad range of services, including compliance, planning, provision of formal taxation opinions, and assistance in the resolution of tax disputes.

Evaluation

Such services generally do not create threats to independence.

NOTE: If a foreign public accounting firm is subject to the US Sarbanes-Oxley Act of 2002, Section 201, "Services Outside the Scope of Practice of Auditor," makes it unlawful for CPA firms to provide other nonaudit services, including tax services, to public company audit clients unless those services are approved in advance by the company's audit committee. In addition, the audit committee approval must be disclosed to investors in periodic reports.

Subcategory 2d: Provision of Internal Audit Services to Audit Clients

General

Internal audit services may involve an extension of the firm's audit service beyond the requirements of generally accepted auditing standards (GAAS), assistance in performing a client's internal audit activities, or outsourcing of the activities. For the purpose of applying the guidance in this section, internal audit services do not include operational internal audit services unrelated to the internal accounting controls, financial systems, or financial statements.

NOTE: If a foreign public accounting firm is subject to the US Sarbanes-Oxley Act of 2002, Section 201, "Services Outside the Scope of Practice of Auditor," prohibits CPA firms from providing internal audit outsourcing to audit clients.

Providing Internal Audit Services to an Audit Client

Scenario

A firm, or a network firm, provides internal audit services to an audit client.

Evaluation

A self-review threat may be created. In evaluating any threats to independence, the nature of the service should be considered.

Performing Procedures under International Standards on Auditing

Scenario

A firm provides services involving an extension of the procedures required to conduct an audit in accordance with International Standards on Auditing.

Evaluation

These services would not impair independence for an audit client as long as the firm's or network firm's personnel do not act (or appear to act) in a capacity equivalent to a member of audit client management.

Providing Assistance with Internal Audit Activities or Outsourcing Activities	*Scenario* A firm, or a network firm, assists in performing a client's internal audit activities or outsources some of the activities. *Evaluation* Any self-review threat created may be acceptably reduced by ensuring that there is a clear separation between the management and control of the internal audit by audit client management and the internal audit activities themselves.
Performing a Significant Portion of the Internal Audit Activities	*Scenario* A firm performs a significant portion of the audit client's internal audit activities. *Evaluation* A self-review threat may be created. The firm, or a network firm, should consider the threats and proceed with caution before taking on such activities. Appropriate safeguards should be put in place. In addition, the firm, or a network firm, should be sure to ensure that the audit client acknowledges its responsibilities for establishing, maintaining, and monitoring the system of internal controls.
Safeguards	Safeguards should be applied in all circumstances to acceptably reduce any threats to independence by ensuring that the audit client

- Is responsible for internal audit activities and acknowledges its responsibility for establishing, maintaining, and monitoring the internal control system.
- Gives responsibility for internal audit activities to a competent employee, preferably within senior management.
- Approves, along with the audit committee or supervisory body, the scope, risk, and frequency of internal audit work.
- Is responsible for evaluating and determining which of the firm's recommendations should be implemented.
- Evaluates the adequacy of the internal audit procedures performed and the findings resulting from the performance of those procedures by, among other things, obtaining and acting on the firm's reports.

In addition, the findings and recommendations resulting from the internal audit activities should be reported appropriately to the audit committee or supervisory body.

The firm should consider whether such nonassurance services should be provided only by personnel not involved in the audit engagement and with different reporting lines within the firm.

Subcategory 2e: Provision of IT Systems Services to Audit Clients

Services Involve Design and Implementation of Financial Information Technology Systems

Scenario

A firm, or a network firm, provides services to an audit client involving the design and implementation of financial information technology systems that are used to generate information that forms part of the client's financial statements.

Evaluation

The self-review threat created is likely to be too significant to allow the provision of such services to an audit client unless appropriate safeguards are applied.

Safeguards

Ensure that the audit client

- Acknowledges its responsibility for establishing and monitoring an internal control system;
- Designates a competent employee, ideally within senior management, to make all management decisions concerning the design and implementation of the hardware or software system;
- Makes all management decisions concerning the design and implementation process;
- Evaluates the adequacy and results of the system's design and implementation; and
- Is responsible for the operation of the system (hardware or software) and the data used or generated by the system.

The firm, or network firm, should also consider whether the nonassurance services should be provided only by personnel not involved in the audit engagements and with different reporting lines within the firm.

NOTE: If a foreign public accounting firm is subject to the US Sarbanes-Oxley Act of 2002, Section 201, "Services Outside the Scope of Practice of Auditor," makes it unlawful to perform financial information systems design and implementation.

Providing Services Related to the Assessment, Design, and Implementation of Internal Accounting Controls and Risk Management Controls

Scenario

A firm, or network firm, provides services related to the assessment, design, and implementations of internal accounting controls and risk management controls.

Evaluation

Such services are not considered to create a threat to independence as long as firm or network firm personnel do not perform management functions.

Subcategory 2f: Temporary Staff Assignments to Audit Clients

Lending Staff to Audit Client

Scenario

A firm, or network firm, lends staff to an audit client.

Evaluation

This may create a self-review threat when the individual can influence the preparation of a client's accounts or financial statements. In practice, such assistance may be given (particularly in emergency situations) but only when it is understood that the firm's or network firm's personnel will not be involved in

- Making management decisions;
- Approving or signing agreements or other similar documents; or
- Exercising discretionary authority to commit the client.

The unique circumstances of the situation should be carefully analyzed to identify whether any threats are created and whether appropriate safeguards should be implemented.

Safeguards

The following safeguards should be applied in all circumstances to acceptably reduce the threat to independence:

- The staff providing the assistance should not have audit responsibility for any function or activity that they performed or supervised during their temporary staff assignment; and
- The audit client should acknowledge its responsibility for directing and supervising the activities of firm, or network firm, personnel.

Subcategory 2g: Provision of Litigation Support Services to Audit Clients

General	Litigation support services may include acting as an expert witness, calculating estimated damages or other amounts that may be receivable or payable as the result of litigation or other legal dispute, and assisting with document management and retrieval in a dispute or litigation.

Litigation Support Services Involve Estimating Amounts or Disclosures in Financial Statements

Scenario

A firm, or network firm, provides litigation support services to an audit client that include the estimation of the possible outcome and affects the amounts or disclosures in the financial statements.

Evaluation

A self-review threat may be created. The significance of any threat created will depend upon

- The materiality of the amounts involved;
- The degree of subjectivity in the matter; and
- The nature of the engagement.

The firm, or network firm, should evaluate the significance of any threat created and, if the threat is other than clearly insignificant, consider and apply safeguards such as the following that are necessary to eliminate or acceptably reduce the threat.

Safeguards

- Establish policies and procedures to prohibit personnel assisting the audit client from making managerial decisions on behalf of the client;
- Use professionals who are not members of the assurance team to perform the service; or
- Involve others, such as independent experts.

Litigation Support Services Involve Managerial Decisions on Client's Behalf

Scenario

A firm, or network firm, provides litigation support services that involve making managerial decisions on behalf of the audit client.

Evaluation

If the role undertaken by the firm, or network firm, involved making managerial decisions on behalf of the audit client, the threats created could not be acceptably reduced by applying any safeguard. The firm, or network firm, should not perform this type of service for an audit client.

Subcategory 2h: Provision of Legal Services to Audit Clients

General	Legal services are any services for which the person providing the services must either be admitted to practice before the courts of the jurisdiction in which such services are to be provided, or have the required legal training to practice law. Such services encompass a wide and diversified range of areas including both corporate and commercial services to clients, such as contract support, litigation, mergers and acquisition advice, and support and the provision of assistance to clients' internal legal departments.

Legal Services Provided to Audit Client	*Scenario* A firm, or a network firm, provides legal services to an audit client. *Evaluation* Such services may create both self-review and advocacy threats. The threats need to be evaluated, depending on • The nature of the service to be provided; • Whether the service provider is separate from the assurance team, and; • The materiality of any matter in relation to the entities' financial statements. The safeguards described under "Provision of Nonassurance Services to Assurance Clients" under the heading "General Safeguards" may reduce any threats to independence to an acceptable level. When the threat to independence cannot be reduced to an acceptable level, the only available actions are to refuse to provide such services or withdraw from the audit engagement. If the firm provides legal services to an audit client that involve matters that would not be expected to have a material effect on the financial statements, the services would not create an unacceptable threat to independence.

Legal Services to Support Audit Client in the Execution of a Transaction	*Scenario* A firm provides legal services to support an audit client in executing a transaction (e.g., contract support, legal advice, legal due diligence, and restructuring). *Evaluation* Such services may create self-review threats. However, safe-

guards may be available to reduce these threats to an acceptable level. Such services would not generally impair independence, provided that

- Members of the assurance team are not involved in providing the service; and
- In relation to the advice provided, the audit client makes the ultimate decision or, in relation to the transactions, the service involves the execution of what has been decided by the audit client.

Firm Serves as Advocate for Client in Dispute or Litigation: Amounts Involved Are Material

Scenario

A firm serves in an advocacy role for an audit client in litigation or resolving a dispute. The amounts involved are material in relation to the financial statements of the audit client.

Evaluation

These services would create advocacy and self-review threats so significant no safeguard could reduce the threat to an acceptable level. Therefore, the firm should not perform this type of service for an audit client.

Firm Serves as Advocate for Client in Dispute or Litigation: Amounts Involved Are Not Material

Scenario

A firm acts in an advocacy role for an audit client in litigation or resolving a dispute. The amounts involved are **not** material to the financial statements of the audit client.

Evaluation

The firm should evaluate the significance of any advocacy and self-review threats created and, if the threat is other than clearly insignificant, consider and apply safeguards necessary to eliminate the threat or acceptably reduce it.

Safeguards

- Establish policies and procedures to prohibit individuals assisting the audit client from making managerial decisions on behalf of the client; or
- Use professionals who are not members of the assurance team to perform the service.

Firm Partner or Employee Appointed as Audit Client's General Counsel

Scenario

A partner or an employee of the firm, or network firm, is appointed as General Counsel for an audit client.

Evaluation

Such an appointment would create self-review and advocacy threats that are so significant no safeguards could reduce the threats to an acceptable level. The position of General Counsel is generally a senior management position with broad responsibility for the legal affairs of a company. Members of a firm, or network firm, should not accept such an appointment for an audit client.

Subcategory 2i: Recruiting Senior Management

Recruiting Senior Management for an Assurance Client

Scenario

A firm, or a network firm, recruits senior management for an assurance client, such as those in a position to affect the subject of the assurance engagement.

Evaluation

Such a situation may create current or future self-interest, familiarity, and intimidation threats. The significance of the threat will depend upon

- The role of the person to be recruited; and
- The nature of the assistance sought.

Acceptable Services

The firm could generally provide the following services;

- The firm reviews the professional qualifications of a number of applicants and provides advice on their suitability for the post.
- The firm produces a short list of candidates for interview, as long as it has been drawn up using criteria specified by the assurance client.

Unacceptable Services

The firm should not make management decisions, such as whom to hire. Such decisions should be left to the client.

Subcategory 2j: Corporate Finance and Similar Activities

Providing Corporate Finance Services to an Assurance Client	*Scenario* A firm, or a network firm, provides corporate finance services, advice, or assistance to an assurance client. *Evaluation* Such services may create advocacy and self-review threats. For certain types of services, the threats are so significant that no safeguards could be applied to reduce the threat to an acceptable level.
Promoting, Dealing in, or Underwriting an Assurance Client's Shares	*Scenario* A firm promotes, deals in, or underwrites an assurance client's shares. *Evaluation* Such services are not compatible with providing assurance services. In the case of an audit client, the independence threats created would be so significant no safeguards could be applied to reduce the threats to an acceptable level.
Committing Client to Transaction or Consummating Transaction for Client	*Scenario* A firm commits the assurance client to the terms of a transaction or consummates a transaction on behalf of the client. *Evaluation* This would create a threat so significant that no safeguard could reduce the threat to an acceptable level.
Assisting a Client in Developing Corporate Strategies	*Scenario* A firm assists a client in developing corporate strategies. *Evaluation* These services may create advocacy or self-review threats; however, safeguards such as the following may be available to reduce these threats to an acceptable level: *Safeguards* • Establish policies and procedures to prohibit individuals assisting the assurance client from making managerial decisions for the client;

- Use professionals who are not members of the assurance team to provide the services; and
- Ensure that the firm does not commit the assurance client to the terms of any transaction or consummate a transaction for the client.

Assisting in Identifying, or Introducing a Client to, Possible Sources of Capital That Meet the Client Specifications or Criteria

Scenario

A firm assists in identifying, or introducing a client to, possible sources of capital that meet the client specifications or criteria.

Evaluation

These services may create advocacy or self-review threats; however, safeguards such as the following may be available to reduce these threats to an acceptable level:

Safeguards

- Establish policies and procedures to prohibit individuals assisting the assurance client from making managerial decisions for the client;
- Use professionals who are not members of the assurance team to provide the services; and
- Ensure that the firm does not commit the assurance client to the terms of any transaction or consummate a transaction for the client.

Providing Structuring Advice and Assisting a Client in Analyzing the Accounting Effects of Proposed Transactions

Scenario

A firm, or a network firm, provides structuring advice and assists a client in analyzing the accounting effects or proposed transactions.

Evaluation

These services may create advocacy or self-review threats; however, safeguards such as the following may be available to reduce these threats to an acceptable level:

Safeguards

- Establish policies and procedures to prohibit individuals assisting the assurance client from making managerial decisions for the client;
- Use professionals who are not members of the assurance team to provide the services; and
- Ensure that the firm does not commit the assurance client to the terms of any transaction or consummate a transaction for the client.

Category 3: Fees and Pricing

Fees Are Large Portion of Firm's Total Fees

Scenario

The total fees generated by an assurance client represent a large proportion of a firm's total fees.

Evaluation

Due to the size of the fees, the dependence on that client or client group, along with concern about the possibility of losing the client, may create a self-interest threat. The threat's significance depends on factors such as

- The structure of the firm; and
- Whether the firm is well established or newly created.

Evaluate the threat's significance and if threat is other than clearly insignificant, consider and apply safeguards such as the following as necessary to acceptably reduce the threat.

Safeguards

- Discuss the extent and nature of fees charged with those charged with governance such as the audit committee;
- Take steps to reduce the dependence on the client;
- Have external quality control reviews performed; and
- Consult a third party, such as a professional regulatory body or another professional accountant.

Fees Represent Large Portion of One Partner's Revenue

Scenario

The fees generated by the assurance client represent a large proportion of the revenue of an individual partner.

Evaluation

A self-interest threat may be created. The threat's significance should be evaluated and, if the threat is other than clearly insignificant, the following safeguards should be considered and applied to acceptably reduce the threat.

Safeguards

- Implement policies and procedures to monitor and implement quality control of assurance engagements; and
- Involve an additional professional accountant who was not a member of the assurance team to review the work done or advise as necessary.

Fees Due from Client Are Unpaid for Significant Period of Time	*Scenario* Fees due from an assurance client for professional services remain unpaid for a long time. *Evaluation* A self-interest threat may be created, especially if a significant part is not paid before issuing the assurance report for the following year. Payment of such fees should generally be required before the report is issued. The following safeguards may be applied. *Safeguards* • Discuss the level of outstanding fees with those charged with governance, such as the audit committee. • Involve an additional professional accountant who did not participate in the assurance engagement to provide advice or review the work performed. • Consider whether the overdue fees might be equivalent to a loan to the client and whether, because of the significance of the overdue fees, it is appropriate for the firm to continue its relationship with the client.
Fee Charged Is Lower than Comparable Fees	*Scenario* A firm obtains an assurance engagement at a significantly lower fee level than that charged by the predecessor firm, or quoted by other firms. *Evaluation* A self-interest threat is created. To reduce the threat to an acceptable level, the firm must demonstrate that • Appropriate time and qualified staff are assigned to the task. • All applicable assurance standards, guidelines, and quality control procedures are being complied with.
Contingent Fees	Contingent fees are fees calculated on a predetermined basis relating to the outcome or result of a transaction or the result of the work performed. *NOTE: Fees are not regarded as being contingent if a court or other public authority has established them.*

Contingent Fee Charged for Assurance Engagement

Scenario

A firm charges a contingent fee for an assurance engagement.

Evaluation

This creates self-interest and advocacy threats that cannot be reduced to an acceptable level by applying any safeguard. A firm should not have a fee arrangement for an assurance engagement when the amount of the fee is contingent on the result of the assurance work or on items that are the subject matter of the assurance engagement.

Contingent Fee Charged for a Nonassurance Service for Assurance Client

Scenario

A firm charges a contingent fee for a nonassurance service provided to an assurance client.

Evaluation

This may also create self-interest and advocacy threats. If the amount of the fee for a nonassurance engagement was agreed to, or contemplated during the engagement and was contingent on that engagement's result, the threats could not be reduced to an acceptable level by the application of any safeguard and such arrangements may not be accepted.

For other types of contingent fee arrangements, the significance of the threats created will depend on factors such as

- The range of possible fee amounts;
- The degree of variability;
- The basis on which the fee is to be determined;
- Whether the outcome or result of the transaction is to be reviewed by an independent third party; and
- The effect of the event or transaction on the assurance engagement.

Evaluate the significance of the threats, and if the threats are other than clearly insignificant, safeguards such as the following should be considered and applied as necessary to acceptably reduce the threats.

Safeguards

- Disclose to the audit committee, or others charged with governance, the extent of nature and extent of fees charged;
- Have the final fee reviewed or determined by an unrelated third party; or
- Have quality control policies and procedures in place.

Category 4: Loans and Guarantees

Loan from Client Bank to Firm

Scenario

A bank or similar institution is an assurance client of a firm. The bank makes a loan or a guarantee of a loan to the firm.

Evaluation

The loan or guarantee would not create a threat to independence as long as

- The loan is made under normal lending procedures, terms, and requirements; and
- The loan is immaterial to both the firm and the assurance client.

If the loan is material to the assurance client or the firm, it may be possible, by applying safeguards such as the following, to reduce the self-interest threat to an acceptable level.

Safeguard

- Involve an additional professional accountant from outside the firm, or network firm, to review the work performed.

Loan from Client Bank to Immediate Family Member

Scenario

An assurance client bank (or similar institution) makes a loan to an assurance team member or member of his/her immediate family. Such loans could include a home mortgage, bank overdraft, car loan, or credit card balance.

Evaluation

The loan would not create an independence threat if the loan is made under normal lending procedures, terms, and requirements.

Deposits Made by Firm to Client Bank

Scenario

A firm or member of the assurance team makes a deposit with, or holds a brokerage account with, a client bank.

Evaluation

Deposits or accounts would not create a threat to independence if the deposit or account is held under normal commercial terms.

Loan Made by Firm to Client That Is Not a Bank	*Scenario* The firm (or member of assurance team) makes a loan to an assurance client that is not a bank (or similar institution) or guarantees the client's borrowing. *Evaluation* Unless the loan or guarantee is immaterial to both the firm (or member of the assurance team) and the client, the self-interest threat is so significant that no safeguard could reduce the threat to an acceptable level.
Loan Made to Firm by Client That Is Not a Bank	*Scenario* The firm (or member of assurance team) accepts a loan from (or guarantee by) a nonbank assurance client. *Evaluation* Unless the loan or guarantee is immaterial to both the firm (or member of the assurance team) and the client, the self-interest threat is so significant that no safeguard could reduce the threat to an acceptable level.
Loans Involving Audit Clients	If any of the preceding examples involve an audit engagement, the guidance should be applied to the firm, all network firms, and the audit client.

Category 5: Close Business Relationships with Assurance Clients

Close Business Relationships with Assurance Clients	*Scenario* A close business relationship exists between a firm (or a member of the assurance team) and the assurance client or its management, or between the firm, a network firm, and an audit client. Examples include • Having a material financial interest in a joint venture with the assurance client or a controlling owner, director, officer, or other individual who performs senior managerial functions for that client; • Plans to combine services or products of the firm with services or products of the assurance client and to market the package with reference to both parties; and • Arrangements under which the firm distributes or markets

the assurance client's products or services, or the assurance client distributes or markets the products or services of the firm.

Evaluation

Such relationships involve a commercial or common financial interest and may create self-interest and intimidation threats. For an assurance client, no safeguards could reduce the threat to an acceptable level (unless the financial relationship is immaterial and the relationship is clearly insignificant to the firm, the network firm, and the audit client). The only possible actions are to

- End the business relationship;
- Reduce the relationship's significance and reduce the financial interest to an immaterial level; or
- Refuse to perform the assurance engagement.

If the business relationship exists between the client and a member of the assurance team (not the firm or network firm), the only appropriate safeguard would be to remove the individual from the assurance team.

Business Relationships Involving Interest Held by Firm When Audit Client Also Holds Interest

Scenario

A business relationship involves an interest held by the firm, a network firm, or a member of the assurance team or their immediate family in a closely held entity when the audit client or a director or officer of the audit client, or any group thereof, also has an interest in that entity.

Evaluation

These relationships do not create threats to independence provided

- The relationship is clearly insignificant to the firm, the network firm, and the audit client;
- The interest held is immaterial to the investor, or group of investors; and
- The interest does not give the investor, or group of investors, the ability to control the closely held entity.

Buying Goods or Services from Assurance Client

Scenario

The firm (or network firm) or a member of the assurance team buys goods or services from an assurance client.

Evaluation

This would not generally create a threat to independence providing the transaction is in the normal course of business and on an arm's-length basis. However, depending upon the nature and magnitude of the transactions, a self-interest threat may be created. If the threat created is other than clearly insignificant, safeguards such as the following should be considered and applied as necessary to reduce the threat to an acceptable level.

Safeguards

- Eliminate or reduce the magnitude of the transaction;
- Remove the individual from the assurance team; or
- Discuss the issue with the audit committee or others charged with governance.

Category 6: Family and Personal Relationships

Family or Personal Relationships between Individuals at Firm and Client

Scenario

Family and personal relationships exist between a member of the assurance team and a director, officer, or certain employees of the assurance client.

Evaluation

Such relationships may create self-interest, familiarity, or intimidation threats. Each unique relationship would need to be carefully evaluated, and safeguards applied as necessary. The significance of the threat depends on

- The individual's responsibilities on the assurance engagement;
- The closeness of the relationship; and
- The role of the family member or individual within the client.

Immediate Family Members

Scenario

An immediate family member of a member of the assurance team is a director, an officer, or an employee of the assurance client in a position to exert direct and significant influence over the subject matter of the assurance engagement, or was in such a position during any period covered by the engagement. For example, the spouse of a member of the audit team is an employee of the client who can exert direct and significant influence on the preparation of the audit client's accounting records or financial statements.

Evaluation

Since this is such a close relationship, the threats to independence can be reduced to an acceptable level only by removing the individual from the assurance team or withdrawing from the assurance engagement.

Close Family Members

Scenario

A close family member of a member of the assurance team is a director, an officer, or an employee of the assurance client in a position to exert direct and significant influence over the subject matter of the assurance engagement.

Evaluation

Threats to independence may be created. The significance of the threats will depend on

- The position the close family member holds with the client; and
- The role of the professional on the assurance team.

Evaluate the significance of the threat, and if other than clearly insignificant, consider and apply safeguards such as the following as necessary to reduce the threat to an acceptable level.

Safeguards

- Remove the individual from the assurance team;
- Where possible, structure the responsibilities of the assurance team so that the professional does not deal with matters that are within the responsibility of the close family member; and
- Establish policies and procedures to empower staff members to communicate to senior members of the firm any independence and objectivity issues that concern them.

Close Relationships other than Immediate or Close Family Members

Scenario

A person, other than an immediate or close family member of a member of the assurance team, has a close relationship with the member of the assurance team and is a director, an officer, or an employee of the assurance client in a position to exert direct and significant influence over the subject matter of the assurance engagement.

Evaluation

Self-interest, familiarity, or intimidation threats may be created. Therefore, members of the assurance team are responsible for identifying any such persons and for consulting in accordance with firm procedures. When evaluating the significance of any threat created and the safeguards appropriate to eliminate or acceptably reduce the threat, consider matters such as the closeness of the relationship and the individual's role within the assurance client.

Close Relationship between Partner or Employee Not Assigned to Assurance Engagement and Member of Client

Scenario

A personal or family relationship exists between a partner or employee of the firm who is not a member of the assurance team and a director, an officer, or an employee of the assurance client in a position to exert direct and significant influence over the subject matter of the assurance engagement.

Evaluation

Self-interest, familiarity, or intimidation threats may be created. Partners and employees of the firm are responsible for identifying any such relationships and for consulting in accordance with firm procedures. When evaluating the significance of any threat created and the safeguards appropriate to eliminate or acceptably reduce the threat, consider the closeness of the relationship, the interaction of the firm professional with the assurance team, the position held within the firm, and the role of the individual within the assurance client.

Inadvertent Violations

Scenario

A firm inadvertently violates this section as it relates to family and personal relationships.

Evaluation

The independence of the firm or member of the assurance team would not be impaired when

- The firm has established policies and procedures requiring all professionals to promptly report any breaches resulting from changes in the employment status of their immediate or close family members or other personal relationships that create threats to independence;
- The firm either restructures the responsibilities of the assurance team so that the professional does not deal with matters that are within the responsibility of the person with whom he or she is related or has a personal relationship, or if this is not possible, the firm promptly removes the professional from the assurance engagement; and
- Additional care is given to reviewing the work of the professional.

Safeguards

When an inadvertent violation occurs, consider and apply the following safeguards:

- Involve an additional professional accountant who did not participate in the assurance engagement to review the assurance team member's work; or
- Exclude the individual from any substantive decision-making concerning the assurance engagement.

Category 7: Employment with Assurance Clients

Assurance Team Member Is Subsequently Employed by Client

Scenario

A director, an officer, or an employee of the assurance client in a position to exert direct and significant influence over the subject matter of the assurance engagement was a member of the assurance team or partner of the firm.

NOTE: If a foreign public accounting firm is subject to the US Sarbanes-Oxley Act of 2002, Section 206, "Conflicts of Interest," makes it unlawful for that accounting firm to provide audit services to a listed audit client if that client has hired a chief executive officer, controller, chief financial officer, or equivalent person who was employed by the accounting firm and participated in the audit during the last year.

Evaluation

The employment by the client may create self-interest, familiarity, or intimidation threats to the firm or assurance team member's independence, especially when significant connections remain between the individual and his or her former firm. The significance of the threats depends upon

- The individual's new position at the assurance client;
- The involvement the individual will have with the assurance team;
- The period of time that has passed since the individual was a member of the assurance team or firm; and
- The individual's former position within the assurance team or firm.

Evaluate the threat's significance and, if the threat is other than clearly insignificant, consider and apply safeguards such as the following to reduce the threat to an acceptable level.

Safeguards

- Consider modifying the plan for the assurance engagement.
- Assign an assurance team to the subsequent assurance engagement that has sufficient experience in relation to the individual who has joined the assurance client.
- Involve an additional professional accountant who was not a member of the assurance team to review the work done or advise.
- Have a quality control review of the assurance engagement.

The following safeguards are necessary in all cases to reduce the threat to an acceptable level:

- The individual is not entitled to any benefits or payments from the firm unless such payments are made under fixed predetermined arrangements. In addition, any amount owed to the individual should not be significant enough to threaten the firm's independence.
- The individual does not continue to participate or appear to participate in the firm's business or professional activities.

Current Assurance Team Member May Be Subsequently Employed by Client

Scenario

An assurance team member participates in the engagement while having reason to believe that he or she may join the assurance client some time in the future.

Evaluation

A self-interest threat is created. This threat can be reduced to an acceptable level by applying all of the following safeguards.

Safeguards

- Establish policies and procedures requiring that the individual notify the firm when entering serious employment negotiations with the assurance client.
- Remove the individual from the assurance engagement.
- Consider performing an independent review of any significant judgments made by that individual while on the engagement.

Category 8: Recent Service with Assurance Clients

Former Employee of Client Joins Assurance Team

Scenario

A former officer, director, or employee of the assurance client serves as member of the assurance team.

Evaluation

This situation may create self-interest, self-review, and familiarity threats, particularly when the assurance team member has to report on subject matter he or she had prepared, or elements of the financial statements he or she had valued, while with the assurance client. Further evaluation depends on the period involved.

- *Employment occurred during the period covered by the assurance report.* If a member of the assurance team had served as an officer or director of the assurance client, or had been an employee in a position to exert direct and significant influence over the subject matter of the assurance engagement during the period covered by the assurance report, the threat created would be so significant no safeguard could reduce the threat to an acceptable level. Such individuals should not be assigned to the assurance team.
- *Employment occurred prior to the period covered by the assurance report.* If an assurance team member had served as an officer or director of the assurance client, or had been an employee in a position to exert direct and significant influence over the subject matter of the assurance engagement, self-interest, self-review, and familiarity threats may be created. (For example, an individual may have performed work or made a decision in the prior period while employed by the client that will be evaluated as part of the current assurance engagement.) The significance of the threats will depend upon

  - The individual's position with the assurance client.
  - The period of time that has passed since the individual left the assurance client.
  - The individual's role in the assurance team.

Evaluate the significance of the threat, and if other than clearly insignificant, consider and apply safeguards such as the following to reduce the threat to an acceptable level.

Safeguards

- Involve an additional professional accountant to review the work done by the individual as part of the assurance team or as necessary; or
- Discuss the issue with those charged with governance, such as the audit committee.

Category 9: Serving as an Officer or Director on the Board of Assurance Clients

---

Serving as an Officer of Director on the Board of Assurance Clients	*Scenario* A partner or employee of the firm serves as an officer or as a director on the board of an assurance client. *Evaluation* The self-review and self-interest threats created would be so significant no safeguard could reduce the threats to an acceptable level. If an individual accepts such a position, the firm would have to either refuse to perform or withdraw from the engagement.
Member of Network Firm Serves as an Officer or Director on Board of Audit Client	*Scenario* A partner or employee of a network firm serves as an officer or as a director on the board of an **audit** client. *Evaluation* The threats created would be so significant no safeguard could reduce the threats to an acceptable level. If an individual accepts such a position, the firm would have to either refuse to perform or withdraw from the engagement.
Position of Company Secretary	*Scenario* A partner or employee of the firm or a network firm serves as Company Secretary for an audit client. *Evaluation* Duties of the Company Secretary may range from administrative duties such as personnel management and the maintaining of company records and registers, to overseeing compliance with regulations or providing advice on corporate governance issues. While

the position may have differing responsibilities in different jurisdictions, this position generally implies close association with the
entity. If a partner or employee of a firm or network firm serves
as Company Secretary for an audit client, the self-review and advocacy threats created would generally be so significant that no
safeguard could reduce the threat to an acceptable level.

*NOTE: When the practice is specifically permitted under local law,
professional rules, or practice, the duties and functions should be limited
to routine and formal administrative matters such as preparing minutes
and maintaining statutory returns. Routine administrative services supporting the company secretarial function or advising on company secretarial administration matters is generally not perceived to impair independence, as long as client management makes all relevant decisions.*

Category 10: Long Association of Senior Personnel with Assurance Clients

**General
  Provisions**

Scenario

Over a long period of time, the same senior personnel have remained on an assurance engagement.

Evaluation

A familiarity threat may be created. The significance of the threat
will depend upon

- The amount of time that the individual has been a member
  of the assurance team.
- The individual's role on the assurance team.
- The firm's structure.
- The nature of the assurance engagement.

Evaluate the significance of the threat, and if other than clearly
insignificant, consider applying safeguards such as the following.

Safeguards

- Rotate the senior personnel off the assurance team;
- Involve an additional professional accountant not on the assurance team to review the work done by the senior personnel or provide advice; or
- Have independent internal quality reviews performed.

Audit Clients That Are Listed Entities

Scenario

The same lead engagement partner has remained for a prolonged period on the audit of a client that is a listed entity.

Evaluation

A familiarity threat may be created. Apply safeguards such as the following.

Safeguards

- Rotate the lead engagement partner after a predefined period, normally no more than seven years.
- Allow a further period of time, normally two years, to elapse before allowing that partner to resume lead engagement partner role.

NOTE: If a foreign public accounting firm is subject to the US Sarbanes-Oxley Act of 2002, Section 203, "Audit Partner Rotation," makes it unlawful for that accounting firm to provide audit services if the lead audit and reviewing partners have not been rotated in five years.

Audit Client Becomes a Listed Entity

Scenario

An audit client becomes a listed entity and the lead engagement partner has remained on the audit for a prolonged period.

Evaluation

Consider the length of time the lead engagement partner has served the client in that capacity and determine when the partner should be rotated. However, the partner may continue to serve as the lead engagement partner for two additional years before rotating off the engagement.

In certain circumstances such as the following, there is some flexibility in the timing of rotation:

- When the lead engagement partner's continuity is especially important to the audit client, for example, when there will be major changes to the audit client's structure that would coincide with the lead engagement partner's rotation.
- When rotation is not possible or does not constitute an appropriate safeguard, due to the size of the firm.

In all such circumstances when the lead engagement partner is not rotated after a predefined period, apply equivalent safeguards to reduce any threats to an acceptable level.

Firm Size Limits Rotation of Audit Partners	*Scenario* A firm has only a few audit partners with the necessary knowledge and experience to serve as lead engagement partner on a listed entity audit client. *Evaluation* Rotation of the lead partner may not be an appropriate safeguard. The firm should apply other safeguards, such as the following, to reduce the threat to an acceptable level. *Safeguards* • Involve an additional professional accountant who was not otherwise associated with the assurance team to review the work done or advise as necessary. This individual could be someone from outside the firm or someone within the firm who was not associated with the assurance team.

Category 11: Gifts and Hospitality

Accepting Gifts and Hospitality	*Scenario* A firm or a member of the assurance team accepts gifts or hospitality from an assurance client. *Evaluation* This may create self-interest and familiarity threats, unless the value is clearly insignificant. The threats to independence cannot be reduced to an acceptable level by applying any safeguard. A firm or a member of the assurance team should not accept gifts or hospitality.

Category 12: Actual or Threatened Litigation

Actual or Threatened Litigation	*Scenario* Litigation between the firm or a member of the assurance team and the client takes place (or appears likely).

Evaluation

A self-interest or intimidation threat may be created. The firm and the client's management may be placed in adversarial positions by litigation, affecting management's willingness to make complete disclosures and be completely candid. The significance of the self-interest threat will depend upon

- The materiality of the litigation;
- The nature of the assurance engagement; and
- Whether the litigation relates to a prior assurance engagement.

Evaluate the significance of the threat and apply the following safeguards, if necessary, to reduce the threats to an acceptable level. If such safeguards do not reduce the threat to an appropriate level, withdraw from, or refuse to accept, the assurance engagement.

Safeguards

- Disclose to the audit committee, or others charged with governance, the extent and nature of the litigation;
- If the litigation involves a member of the assurance team, remove that individual from the assurance team; or
- Involve an additional professional accountant in the firm who was not an assurance team member to review the work done or provide advice.

Section 9

Professional Competence and Responsibilities Regarding the Use of Nonaccountants

Professional accountants in public practice/**auditors** should refrain from agreeing to perform services for which they are not competent unless competent advice and assistance are obtained. Assistance may be obtained from experts such as other accountants, lawyers, actuaries, engineers, geologists, and valuation specialists. When using these other experts, the professional accountant must take steps to see that such experts are aware of the fundamental ethical principles (see page 260). In supervising these experts, the professional accountant may

1. Ask the experts to read the appropriate ethical codes.
2. Require written confirmation of the experts' understanding of the ethical requirements.
3. Provide consultation when potential conflicts arise.

If the professional accountant is not satisfied that the ethical requirements will be followed, the engagement should not be accepted or, if in process, terminated.

Section 10

Fees and Commissions

Professional Fees

The fees that professional accountants in public practice/**auditors** charge should reflect the value of the services performed. In determining the fees to be charged, the professional accountant in public practice/**auditor** should consider the

1. Skill and knowledge required for the service.
2. Level of training and experience needed.
3. Time spent or to be spent.
4. Degree of responsibility required.

A professional accountant in public practice/**auditor** should not quote a fee for current or future services when it is likely at the time of making the quote that such fee will be substantially increased.

The professional accountant in public practice/**auditor** in quoting a fee should be satisfied that the fee provides for

1. Performing quality work.
2. Using due care to comply with all professional standards and quality control procedures.

The professional accountant in public practice/**auditor** should also be satisfied that the client is not misled about the scope of services that will be provided and the basis for charging future fees.

The professional accountant is public practice/**auditor** should make sure that the client understands the basis on which fees are calculated and the billing arrangements. This understanding should be obtained before the commencement of the engagement. Preferably, the understanding should be in writing.

Commissions

In countries where commissions are permitted either by statute or member body, and the professional accountant in public practice accepts such a commission, this fact should be disclosed to the client.

Subject to the above, a professional accountant in public practice/**auditor** should not pay a commission to obtain a client or accept a commission for referral of a client, including payment and receipt of fees between professional accountants when no services are performed.

In addition, a professional accountant in public practice/**auditor** should not accept a commission for the referral of products or services of others.

Arrangements for the purchase of an accounting practice, or portions thereof, are not considered to be commissions.

Section 11

Activities Incompatible with the Practice of Public Accountancy

A professional accountant in public practice/**auditor** should not concurrently engage in any business, occupation, or activity that impairs integrity, objectivity, independence, or the reputation of the profession.

Also, the simultaneous engagement in another business, occupation, or activity that does not allow the delivery of professional services in accordance with the fundamental ethical principles is inconsistent with the practice of public accountancy.

Section 12

Clients' Monies[9]

In some countries national law does not permit a professional accountant in public practice/**auditor** to hold clients' monies. Where it is permitted, the professional accountant in public practice/**auditor** should not hold clients' monies if he or she believes that such monies were obtained from, or are to be used in, illegal activities.

When holding clients' monies, the professional accountant in public practice/**auditor** should

1. Keep such monies in one (a general clients' monies account) or more bank accounts, separately from personal or firm monies.
2. Deposit such monies without delay to the appropriate bank account.
3. Place such monies in an interest-bearing account with the concurrence of the client within a reasonable time if it is

---

[9] *Clients' monies are defined as any monies, including document of title to money or documents that can be converted to money such as bills of exchange, promissory notes, or bearer bonds, received by a professional accountant in public practice/auditor to be held or paid out according to client instructions.*

likely that monies will remain in the account for a significant period of time.

4. Draw from the client bank account only on the instructions of the client.

5. Use such monies only for the purpose for which they are intended.

6. Pay firm fees due from a client from the bank account only after notifying the client of the amount and the client agrees to the withdrawal.

7. Credit all interest earned on clients' monies to client accounts.

8. At all times, be ready to account for clients' monies to the client.

9. Provide a statement of account to the client at least once a year.

10. Safeguard documents that can be converted to money against unauthorized use.

Section 13

Relations with Other Professional Accountants in Public Practice

Accepting New Assignments

There are three ways a receiving accountant/**auditor**[10] may be involved in accepting new assignments in this section

1. The client's business expansion results in branches or subsidiary companies at locations where an existing accountant/**auditor**[11] does not practice and the existing accountant/**auditor** in consultation with the client or the client requests a receiving accountant/**auditor** to perform work at such locations.

2. The client needs special services or skills that the existing **accountant/auditor** does not have and the existing accountant/**auditor** in consultation with the client or the client requests a receiving accountant/**auditor** to perform such specialized services.

3. The client request a receiving accountant's/**auditor's** opinion (a second opinion) on the application of an ac

---

[10] *A receiving accountant/**auditor** is a professional accountant in public practice/**auditor** to whom the client's existing accountant/**auditor** or the client has referred **audit**, accounting, tax, consulting, or similar appointments.*

[11] *An existing accountant/**auditor** is a professional accountant in public practice/**auditor** who currently holds an **audit**, accounting, tax, consulting, or similar appointment with a client.*

counting principle or an **audit** or reporting matter relative to specific circumstances or transactions.

In each of the three situations above, there is an assumption that the existing accountant/auditor will continue to provide existing professional services to the client. In these three situations, the receiving accountant/auditor should

1. When asked to provide services or advice, make inquiries as to whether the potential client has an existing accountant/auditor.
2. Limit the services provided to the specific referral from the existing accountant/auditor or the client unless otherwise requested by the client.
3. Support the existing accountant's/auditor's current relationship with the client.
4. Do not express any criticism of the professional services of the existing accountant/**auditor**.
5. Regard a request from the client for services that are clearly distinct from the services being provided by the existing accountant/**auditor** or that are clearly distinct from the initial referral request for services as a separate request to provide services or advice.
6. Before accepting an assignment in 5. above, advise the client of the obligation to immediately communicate, preferably in writing, with the existing accountant/**auditor** to advise the existing accountant/**auditor** of the client's request and to ask for all relevant information, if any, needed to perform the assignment.
7. If the client insists that the communication in 6. above not be made, decide whether the client's reasons are valid (a mere disinclination by the client for the communication is not a satisfactory reason). For situations involving second opinions, there is a requirement for communication with the existing accountant/**auditor** in order for the receiving **accountant/auditor** to obtain a full understanding of the facts and circumstances. In addition, the receiving accountant/**auditor,** with the client's permission, is required to provide a copy of the final report to the existing accountant/**auditor**. If the client does not agree to these communications, the assignment should not be accepted.
8. Comply with the instructions received from the existing accountant/**auditor** or the client unless they conflict with relevant legal or other requirements.
9. Keep the existing accountant/**auditor** informed of the general nature of the services being performed.

In the three new assignment situations above, the existing accountant/**auditor** should maintain contact with the receiving accountant/**auditor** and cooperate with and assist them.

Superseding Another Professional Accountant/Auditor in Public Practice

Before accepting an appointment involving recurring professional services (**audit,** accounting, tax, consulting, or other), the proposed accountant/**auditor** should

1. Ascertain if the prospective client has advised the existing accountant/**auditor** of the proposed change.
2. Ascertain if the prospective client has given the existing accountant/**auditor** permission, preferably in writing, to discuss the client's affairs fully and freely.
3. Request permission from the prospective client to communicate with the existing accountant/**auditor**. If not permitted to communicate with the existing accountant/**auditor,** in absence of exceptional circumstances or obtaining the necessary facts by other means, decline the appointment.
4. Ask the existing accountant/**auditor,** preferably in writing, to

   a. Provide information about matters that are important in deciding whether to accept the appointment. (Unpaid fees do not preclude acceptance of the appointment.
   b. Provide all the necessary details needed to make a decision about acceptance.

5. If a response from the existing accountant/**auditor** is not received and there is no knowledge of exceptional circumstances about the engagement, communicate with the existing accountant/**auditor** by other means.
6. If information is not received from 5. above, send a letter to the existing accountant/**auditor,** stating an assumption that there is no professional reason why the appointment should not be accepted and that there is an intention to accept the appointment.

In situations where competitive bids are used, the accountant/**auditor** submitting a bid or tender should state in the submission that if the appointment results in the replacement of an existing **accountant/auditor,** acceptance of the appointment is contingent on performing the six steps above.

In responding to the proposed accountant/**auditor,** the existing accountant/**auditor** should

1. Ensure that the client has given permission to respond fully and freely to the proposed accountant/**auditor**.
2. Reply, preferably in writing, identifying reasons, if any, why the proposed accountant/**auditor** should not accept the appointment. If permission in 1 above is denied, communicate that to the proposed accountant/**auditor**.
3. Disclose all information needed by the proposed **accountant/auditor** relevant to his or her decision to accept or not accept the appointment.
4. Promptly transfer to the new accountant/**auditor** all books and papers of the client unless there is a legal right to withhold such information.

Section 14

Advertising[12] and Solicitation[13]

Member bodies determine whether advertising and solicitation are permitted. When advertising and solicitation are permitted by a member body, it should be

1. Presented in an objective manner.
2. Decent, honest, and truthful.
3. In good taste.

It should not

1. Create false, deceptive or unjustified expectations.
2. Imply the ability to influence any court, tribunal, regulatory agency, or similar body.
3. Consist of self-laudatory statements that are not fact-based.
4. Make comparisons with other professional accountants in public practice/**auditors**.
5. Contain testimonials or endorsements.
6. Contain representations that or likely to cause a reasonable person to misunderstand or be deceived.
7. Make unjustified claims to be an expert or specialist.

A professional accountant in public practice/**auditor** in a country where advertising is permitted should not advertise in newspapers or magazines published or distributed in a country where advertising is prohibited. Likewise, a professional accountant in public practice/**auditor** in a country where advertising is prohibited

[12] *Advertising is defined as the communication of information to the public about the services or skills provided by professional accountants in public practice/**auditors** with the objective of obtaining professional business.*
[13] *Solicitation is defined as an approach to a potential client for the purpose of obtaining professional business.*

should not advertise in newspapers or magazines published in a country where advertising is permitted.

Publicity by Professional Accountants in Public Practice/Auditors in a Country Where Advertising Is Not Permitted

In a country where advertising is not permitted, publicity is acceptable provided that it

1. Is not false, misleading, or deceptive.
2. Is in good taste.
3. Is professionally dignified.
4. Avoids frequent repetition of, and undue prominence being given to, the name of the accountant/**auditor**.

The following topics discuss acceptable and unacceptable publicity in those countries where advertising is not permitted.

Appointments and Awards—These items should receive publicity, but the accountant/**auditor** should not make use of such opportunities for personal professional advantage.

Newspaper and Magazine Announcements—Such announcements may be used to inform the public of a new practice, partnership personnel changes, and address changes provided that they are limited to bare facts and that consideration is given to the area of distribution of the medium.

Seeking Employment or Professional Business—An accountant/**auditor** may use any medium to seek employment or a partnership. However, an accountant /**auditor**

1. May not publicize for subcontract work in a manner that seeks to procure professional business.
2. May publicize for subcontract work in the professional press but should omit his or her name, address, and telephone number.
3. May write a letter or make a direct approach to another accountant/**auditor** when seeking employment or business.

Directories (Non-Firm)—A professional accountant in public practice/**auditor** may be listed in a directory if the directory or the entry therein is not considered an advertisement. Entries should be limited to name, address, telephone number, professional description and other information needed to enable a user to contact the person or organization.

Brochures and Firm Directories—An accountant/**auditor** may issue these items to clients or others that request them provided that the brochure or firm directory

1. Is a factually and objectively worded account of services provided.

2. Contains only names of partners, office addresses, and names and addresses of associated firms and correspondents.

Books, Articles, Interviews, Lectures, Radio and Television Appearances—Accountants /**auditors** when engaged in any of these activities on professional subjects may state their name, professional qualifications, and the name of their firm. However, they should not identify the services that their firm provides.

Training Courses, Seminars, etc.—Accountants/**auditors** may invite clients, staff, or other professional accountants to their training courses or seminars. However, other persons should not be invited unless their request to attend is unsolicited.

Booklets and Documents Containing Technical Information—These items bearing the name of the accountant/**auditor** may be issued to staff, clients, other professional accountants, and others that request the information.

Stationery and Nameplates—These items should comply with the requirements of national law and requirements of the member body. They should not, however, list services provided or the firm's specialization.

Staff Recruitment—Staff vacancies may be communicated to the public through any medium where such items normally appear. The announcement may present details as to services provided to clients but it should not contain promotional elements. Moreover, the announcement should not contain any suggestion that the firm's services are superior to other firms as a consequence of size, associations, or other reasons. More latitude is available in a section of the medium devoted to vacancies than elsewhere in that medium.

Publicity on Behalf of Clients—Accountants/**auditors** may publicize staff vacancies on behalf of clients provided the announcement is for the client.

Inclusion of the Accountant's/Auditor's Name in a Document Issued by a Client—When clients publish documents that contain the accountant's/**auditor's** name, the accountant/**auditor** should advise the client that his or her permission must be obtained before the document is published. This requirement protects the public from being misled. The same consideration applies when the accountant/**auditor** holds an office in a private capacity in an organization (for example, a charitable organization). That is, the accountant/**auditor** should ensure that the public is not misled to believe that his or her association is that of an independent **auditor**.

Part C: Applicable to Employed Professional Accountants[14] (applies, when applicable, to auditors)

Section 15

Conflict of Loyalties to Employers and the Profession	An employed professional accountant, **including an auditor,** cannot be required to

1. Break the law.
2. Breach the rules and standards of the profession.
3. Put their name on, or be associated with, a statement that materially misrepresents facts.

Furthermore, an employed professional accountant cannot lie to or mislead **auditors,** including misleading by keeping silent.

Differences in views between an employed professional accountant and the employer entity about accounting or ethical matters should be resolved within the entity according to the entity's policy. If following such policy does not resolve the matter, the employed professional accountant should discuss the matter with his or her immediate supervisor (unless the supervisor is involved in the matter), and if still not resolved, with higher levels of management or nonexecutive directors. If the matter cannot be resolved, the employed professional accountant may have no other course of action but to consider resigning. The employed professional accountant should communicate his or her reasons for resigning in an information memorandum to the entity but not to others unless legally or professionally required to do so.

Section 16

Support for Professional Colleagues	An employed professional accountant, **including an auditor,** having authority over others should deal with differences of opinion in a professional manner.

---

[14] *A professional accountant employed in industry, commerce, the public sector, or education.*

Section 17

**Professional
  Competence (of
  Employed
  Professional
  Accountants)**

An employed professional accountant should not mislead the employer as to his or her expertise or experience when undertaking significant tasks for which the employed professional accountant has not had sufficient training or experience. In addition, the employed professional accountant should seek appropriate expert advice and assistance.

Section 18

**Presentation of
  Information**

An employed professional accountant/**auditor** should present financial information fully, honestly, and professionally so that users can understand in its context.

An employed professional accountant should maintain financial and nonfinancial information in a manner that describes clearly the true nature of transactions, assets or liabilities. A professional accountant should also record entries in a timely and proper manner.

38 WHERE TO GO FOR MORE INFORMATION

Introduction

A CPA may have additional questions about how to apply ethics guidance that are not addressed in this book. He or she will then need to do additional research or know where to go to ask questions.

Guidance within a CPA's Firm

A CPA firm may have

- Ethics/independence policies tailored for the firm. Such policies may be more restrictive than AICPA, SEC, ISB, state society or state board requirements.
- An individual responsible for ethics matters in an office, region or line of service.
- Materials on ethics in the firm's library (electronic or paper-based).
- An independence system or database. This system or database usually contains information on the firm's clients (e.g., a restricted client list) so that members of the firm can monitor their compliance with independence requirements.

A CPA should always check his or her firm's policy first on how to deal with ethics questions. If additional research is needed, the following are sources of information.

AICPA

The AICPA's *Code of Professional Conduct* is reproduced at www.aicpa.org/about/code/index.htm.

For questions, call the AICPA's Professional Ethics Team at 1-888-777-7077 (or e-mail to ethics@aicpa.org).

Inquiries can also be submitted in writing to

Professional Ethics Team
American Institute of Certified Public Accountants
Harborside Financial Center
201 Plaza Three
Jersey City, NJ 07311

SECPS	For the AICPA's SEC Practice Section (SECPS) Independence Quality Controls, go to www.aicpa.org/members/div/secps/inmerefinal.htm.
	For questions, call the AICPA's SECPS staff at 1-888-777-7077.
	For the SECPS's restrictions on consulting services, see item h. of the SECPS's *Requirements of Members* at www.aicpa.org/members/div/secps/require.htm (see Chapter 14 for additional information on these restrictions).
Independence Standards Board	Although the ISB was dissolved on July 31, 2001, the ISB materials are reproduced at www.cpaindependence.org.
SEC	Guidance on independence can be found in Rule 2-01 of Regulation S-X. Contact publishers such as CCH at www.cch.com or RIA at www.riahome.com.
	The SEC's no-action letters can be found in publications such as
	SEC No-Action Letters, published by CCH, Incorporated. For more information, go to www.cch.com.
	Analysis of Key SEC No-Action Letters by Robert J. Haft, 1999-2000 edition, West Group, St. Paul, MN.
	The SEC's November 2000 rules revision can be found at www.sec.gov/rules/final/33-7919.htm. General information on auditor independence can be found at www.sec.gov/hot/auditor.htm.
	Since the adoption of the Commission's Revised Rules on Auditor Independence in November 2002, the SEC staff has received questions regarding the implementation and interpretation of the rules. The SEC encourages these questions and related correspondence regarding auditor independence. Questions should be directed to the Assistant Chief Accountant (currently Sam Burke or Esmeralda Rodriguez) in the Office of the Chief Accountant, Mail Stop 1103, 450 Fifth Street, N.W., Washington, DC 20549; telephone 202-942-4400. Questions regarding disclosure in proxy statements should be directed to the Office of Chief Counsel in the Division of Corporation Finance at 202-942-2900. The staff's responses to certain questions received to date can be found at www.sec.gov/info/accountants/audindep/audinfaq.htm.
Department of Labor	DOL Regulation 2509.75-9, *Interpretive Bulletin Relating to Guidelines on Independence of Accountant Retained by Employee Benefit Plan*, is at www.dol.gov/dol/allcfr/Title_29/Part_2509/29CFR2509.75-9.htm.

Questions should be addressed to the Office of Chief Accountant Help Desk at 202-219-8770 or 212-219-6666.

GAO

The GAO's new Yellow Book independence requirements are at www.gao.gov/govaud/agagas3.pdf.

Answers to frequently asked questions on these requirements can be found at www.gao.gov/govaud/d02870g.pdf.

For questions on the independence requirements of the Yellow Book, contact Marsha Buchanan, Asst. Director Financial Management and Assurance at 202-512-9321 or e-mail to buchananm@gao.gov.

FDIC

Information about the Federal Deposit Insurance Corporation's (FDIC) rules and regulations can be found at www.fdic.gov/regulations/laws/rules/2000-8500.html.

Answers to frequently asked questions on these requirements can be found at www.gao.gov/govaud/d02870g.pdf.

HUD

Information on HUD's independence requirements can be found in the HUD handbooks at www.hud.gov/offices/adm/handbks_forms/handbooks2.cfm#hnmlr.

APPENDIX A

GLOSSARY

Accounting role or financial reporting oversight role—Defined by the SEC to mean a role in which a person is in a position to or does

(i) Exercise more than minimal influence over the contents of the accounting records or anyone who prepares them; or

(ii) Exercise influence over the contents of the financial statements or anyone who prepares them, such as when the person is a member of the board of directors or similar management or governing body, chief executive officer, president, chief financial officer, chief operating officer, general counsel, chief accounting officer, controller, director of internal audit, director of financial reporting, treasurer, vice president of marketing, or any equivalent position.

Affiliates—Construed broadly, affiliates include persons associated with the client in a decision-making capacity such as officers, directors, and substantial stockholders, as well as entities that directly or indirectly control, are controlled by, or are under common control with the client. An example might be either a subsidiary or a parent company.

Alternative dispute resolution—Techniques used to resolve disputes without litigation.

Alternative Practice Structures (APS)—A nontraditional structure for the practice of public accounting in which a traditional CPA firm engaged in auditing and other attestation services might be closely aligned with another organization, public or private, that performs other professional services (e.g., tax and consulting).

American Institute of Certified Public Accountants (AICPA)—The national professional organization for all certified public accountants (CPAs).

Attest engagement—An attest engagement is an engagement that requires independence as defined in AICPA Professional Standards.

Attest engagement team—The attest engagement team consists of individuals participating in the attest engagement, including those who perform concurring and second partner reviews. The attest engagement team includes all employees and contractors retained by the firm who participate in the attest engagement, irrespective of their functional classification (for example, audit, tax, or management consulting services). The attest engagement team excludes specialists as discussed in SAS No. 73, *Using the Work of a Specialist* [AU section 336], and individuals who perform only routine clerical functions, such as word processing and photocopying.

Chain of Command—Defined by the SEC as all persons who

(i) Supervise or have direct management responsibility for the audit, including at all successively senior levels through the accounting firm's chief executive;
(ii) Evaluate the performance or recommend the compensation of the audit engagement partner; or
(iii) Provide quality control or other oversight of the audit.

Client—A client is any person or entity, other than the member's employer, that engages a member or a member's firm to perform professional services or a person or entity with respect to which professional services are performed. For purposes of this paragraph, the term "employer" does not include

    a. Entities engaged in the practice of public accounting; or
    b. Federal, state, and local governments or component units thereof provided the member performing professional services with respect to those entities

        i. Is directly elected by voters of the government or component unit thereof with respect to which professional services are performed; or
        ii. Is an individual who is (1) appointed by a legislative body and (2) subject to removal by a legislative body; or
        iii. Is appointed by someone other than the legislative body, so long as the appointment is confirmed by the legislative body and removal is subject to oversight or approval by the legislative body.

Client's records—Any accounting or other records belonging to the client that were given to the member by, or on behalf of, the client.

Close relative—A close relative is a parent, sibling, or nondependent child.

Code of Professional Conduct (the Code)—The Code was adopted by the membership of the AICPA to provide guidance and rules to all members on various ethics requirements. The Code consists of (1) Principles, (2) Rules, (3) Interpretations, and (4) Ethics Rulings.

Conflict of interest—A conflict of interest may occur if a member performs a professional service for a client or employer, and the member or his or her firm has a relationship with another person, entity, product, or service that could, in the member's professional judgment, be viewed by the client, employer, or other appropriate parties as impairing the member's objectivity.

Consulting process—The analytical approach applied in performing a consulting service. The process typically involved some combination of the following:

- Determining the client's objective
- Fact-finding
- Defining problems or opportunities
- Evaluating alternatives
- Formulating proposed actions
- Communicating results
- Implementing
- Following up

Consulting services—Professional services that use the practitioner's technical skills, education, observations, experiences, and knowledge of the consulting process.

Consulting services practitioner—Any AICPA member holding out as a CPA while performing consulting services for a client, or any other individual performing consulting services for a client for an AICPA member or member's firm holding out as a CPA.

Consumer—Defined in the seventh edition of Black's Law Dictionary as "a person who buys goods or services for personal, family, or household use with no intention of resale."

Contingent fee—A fee for performing any service in which the amount of the fee (or whether a fee will be paid) depends on the results of the service.

Covered member—A covered member is defined by the AICPA as

    a. An individual on the attest engagement team;

    b. An individual in a position to influence the attest engagement;

    c. A partner or manager who provides nonattest services to the attest client beginning once he or she provides ten hours of nonattest services to the client within any fiscal year and ending on the later of the date (1) the firm signs the report on the financial statements for the fiscal year during which those services were provided or (ii) he or she no longer expects to provide ten or more hours of nonattest services to the attest client on a recurring basis;

    d. A partner in the office in which the lead attest engagement partner primarily practices in connection with the attest engagement;

    e. The firm, including the firm's employee benefit plans; or

    f. An entity whose operating, financial, or accounting policies can be controlled (as defined by generally accepted accounting principles [GAAP] for consolidation purposes) by any of the individuals or entities described in (a) through (e) or by two or more such individuals or entities if they act together.

Covered person—A covered person is defined by the SEC as the following partners, principals, shareholder, and employees of an accounting firm;

    1. The "audit engagement team";

    2. The "chain of command";

    3. Any other partner, principal, shareholder, or managerial employee of the accounting firm who has provided ten or more hours of nonaudit services to the audit client for the period beginning on the date such services are provided and ending on the date the accounting firm signs the report on the financial statements for the fiscal year during which those services are provided, or who expects to provide ten or more hours of nonaudit services to the audit client on a recurring basis; and

    4. Any other partner, principal, or shareholder from an "office" of the accounting firm in which the lead audit engagement partner primarily practices in connection with the audit.

Council—The Council of the American Institute of Certified Public Accountants.

Direct financial interest—A direct financial interest is created when a member invests in a client entity.

Disqualifying services—Term used to refer to the following services, which when performed for a client prohibit the member from accepting a contingent fee or commission:

a. An audit or a review of a financial statement.
b. An examination of prospective financial information.
c. A compilation of a financial statement expected to be used by third parties except when the compilation report discloses a lack of independence.

See Chapter 30 on contingent fees and Chapter 33 on commissions.

Ethics Rulings—Part of the *Code of Professional Conduct*. Rulings summarize the application of rules and interpretations to a particular set of factual circumstances.

Financial Statements—A presentation of financial data, including accompanying notes, if any, intended to communicate an entity's economic resources and/or obligations at a point in time or the changes therein for a period of time, in accordance with generally accepted accounting principles or a comprehensive basis of accounting other than generally accepted accounting principles.

Incidental financial data to support recommendations to a client or in documents for which the reporting is governed by Statements on Standards for Attestation Engagements and tax returns supporting schedules do not, for this purpose, constitute financial statements. The statement, affidavit, or signature of preparers required on tax returns neither constitutes an opinion of financial statements nor requires a disclaimer of such opinion.

Firm—A form of organization permitted by state law or regulation whose characteristics conform to resolutions of Council that is engaged in the practice of public accounting. Except for the purpose of applying Rule 101, *Independence*, the firm includes the individual owners thereof.

Former practitioner—A proprietor, partner, shareholder or equivalent of a firm, who leaves by resignation, termination, retirement, or sale of all or part of the practice.

Holding out as a CPA—Includes any action initiated by a member, whether or not in public practice, that informs others of his or her status as a CPA. This would include, for example, any oral or written representation to another regarding CPA status, use of the CPA designation on business cards or letterhead, the display of a certificate evidencing a member's CPA designation, or listing as a CPA in local telephone directories.

Immediate family—Immediate family is a spouse, spousal equivalent, or dependent (whether or not related).

Indemnification agreement—A contract between two parties whereby one party agrees to compensate or reimburse a second party for certain losses or expenses incurred.

Independence in fact—To be *independent in fact* (mental independence), the CPA must have integrity and objectivity. If there is evidence that independence is actually lacking, the auditor is not independent in fact.

Independence in appearance—If there are circumstances that a reasonable person might believe are likely to impair independence, the CPA is not independent in appearance. To be **recognized** as independent, the auditor must be free from any obligation to or interest in the client, its management, or its owners.

Independence Standards Board (ISB)—A standard-setting body designated by the AICPA and SEC to establish independence requirements for auditors of public companies. The ISB was dissolved on July 31, 2001.

Indirect financial interest—An indirect financial interested is created when a member invests in a nonclient entity that has a financial interest in a client.

Individual in a position to influence the attest engagement—An individual in a position to influence the attest engagement is one who

a.   Evaluates the performance or recommends the compensation of the attest engagement partner;
b.   Directly supervises or manages the attest engagement partner, including all successively senior levels above that individual through the firm's chief executive;
c.   Consults with the attest engagement team regarding technical or industry-related issues specific to the attest engagement; or
d.   Participates in or oversees, at all successively senior levels, quality control activities, including internal monitoring, with respect to the specific attest engagement.

Institute—The American Institute of Certified Public Accountants.

Integrity—An element of character fundamental to professional recognition. It is the quality from which public trust derives and the benchmark against which a member must ultimately test all decisions.

Internal audit outsourcing—Internal audit outsourcing involves performing audit procedures that are generally of the type considered to be extensions of audit scope applied in the audit of financial statements. Examples of such procedures might include confirming receivables, analyzing fluctuations in account balances, and testing and evaluating the effectiveness of controls.

Interpretations of rules of conduct—Part of the Code of Professional Conduct. Interpretations are pronouncements issued by the AICPA's Division of Professional Ethics to provide guidelines concerning the scope and application of the rules of conduct.

Investment club—A group of individuals who pool their money, select investments, and invest the pooled funds in the selected investment.

ISB—see Independence Standards Board.

JEEP—see Joint Ethics Enforcement Program.

Joint closely held investment—A joint closely held investment is an investment in an entity or property by the member and the client (or the client's officers or directors, or any owner who has the ability to exercise significant influence over the client) that enables them to control (as defined by GAAP for consolidation purposes) the entity or property.

Joint Ethics Enforcement Program (JEEP)—The AICPA and most state societies cooperate in the Joint Ethics Enforcement Program (JEEP) in bringing enforcement actions against their members.

Joint Trial Board—The Joint Trial Board hears cases referred by the ethics committee and recommends appropriate disciplinary, remedial, or corrective action.

Key position—A key position is a position in which an individual

   a. Has primary responsibility for significant accounting functions that support material components of the financial statements;
   b. Has primary responsibility for the preparation of the financial statements; or
   c. Has the ability to exercise influence over the contents of the financial statements, including when the individual is a member of the board of directors or similar governing body, chief executive officer, president, chief financial officer, chief operating officer, general counsel, chief accounting officer, controller, director of internal audit, director of financial reporting, treasurer, or any equivalent position.

For purposes of attest engagements not involving a client's financial statements, a key position is one in which an individual is primarily responsible for, or able to influence, the subject matter of the attest engagement, as described above.

Loan—A loan is a financial transaction, the characteristics of which generally include, but are not limited to, an agreement that provides for repayment terms and a rate of interest. A loan includes, but is not limited to, a guarantee of a loan, a letter of credit, a line of credit, or a loan commitment.

Manager—A manager is a professional employee of the firm who has either of the following responsibilities:

   a. Continuing responsibility for the overall planning and supervision of engagements for specified clients.
   b. Authority to determine that an engagement is complete subject to final partner approval if required.

Member—A member, associate member, or international associate of the American Institute of Certified Public Accountants.

Multidisciplinary practices (MDP)—Arrangements in which CPAs share fees with attorneys or other professionals.

National Association of State Boards of Accountancy (NASBA)—A voluntary organization composed of the state boards of accountancy. It promotes communication, coordination, and uniformity among state boards.

Objectivity—The principle of objectivity imposes the obligation to be impartial, intellectually honest, and free of conflicts of interest. Objectivity is a state of mind, a quality that lends value to a member's services.

Office—An office is a reasonably distinct subgroup within a firm, whether constituted by formal organization or informal practice, where personnel who make up the subgroup generally serve the same group of clients or work on the same categories of matters. Substance should govern the office classification. For example, the expected regular personnel interactions and assigned reporting channels of an individual may well be more important than an individual's physical location.

Office participating in a significant portion of the engagement—Offices include the office having primary client responsibility (i.e., the engagement office) for a multi-office engagement and depends on the significance of work performed relative to the overall engagement effort. (Guidance on assessing this significance is provided in Chapter 9.)

Partner—A partner is a proprietor, shareholder, equity or nonequity partner, or any individual who assumes the risks and benefits of firm ownership or who is otherwise held out by the firm to be the equivalent of any of the aforementioned.

PEEC—see Professional Ethics Executive Committee.

Period of the professional engagement—The period of the professional engagement begins when a member either signs an initial engagement letter or other agreement to perform attest services or begins to perform an attest engagement for a client, whichever is earlier. The period lasts for the entire duration of the professional relationship (which could cover many periods) and ends with the formal or informal notification, either by the member or the client, of the termination of the professional relationship or by the issuance of a report, whichever is later. Accordingly, the period does not end with the issuance of a report and recommence with the beginning of the following year's attest engagements.

Practice of public accounting—The practice of public accounting consists of the performance for a client, by a member or a member's firm, while holding out as CPA(s), the professional services of accounting, tax, personal financial planning, litigation support services, and those professional services for which standards are promulgated by bodies designated by Council, such as Statements of Financial Accounting Standards, Statements on Auditing Standards, Statements on Standards for Accounting and Review Services, Statements on Standards for Consulting Services, Statements of Governmental Accounting Standards, and Statements on Standards for Attestation Standards.

However, a member or a member's firm, while holding out as CPA(s), is not considered to be in the practice of public accounting if the member or the member's firm does not perform, for any client, any of the professional services described in the preceding paragraph.

Principles—Positive statements of responsibility in the *Code of Professional Conduct* that provide the framework for the rules, which govern performance.

Professional Ethics Executive Committee (PEEC)—The AICPA's senior technical committee that promulgates professional ethics requirements. The objectives of the PEEC are to develop standards of ethics, promote understanding and voluntary compliance with such standards, establish and present changes of violations of the standards and the AICPA's bylaws to the Joint Trial Board for disciplinary action in cooperation with the State Societies under the Joint Ethics Enforcement Program (JEEP), improve the profession's enforcement procedures, coordinate the subcommittees of the Professional Ethics Division, and promote the efficiency and effectiveness of JEEP Program.

Professional services—Includes **all services** performed by a member while **holding out** as a CPA.

Rules—Broad but specific descriptions of conduct that would violate the responsibilities stated in the principles in the *Code of Professional Conduct.*

Securities and Exchange Commission (SEC)—A federal government regulatory agency with responsibility for administering the federal securities laws.

Significant influence—According to Accounting Principles Board Opinion No. 18, *The Equity Method of Accounting for Investments in Common Stock,* and its interpretations, significant influence exists when the investor owns from 20-50% of the investee's voting shares, although circumstances exist where such influence is present with under 20% ownership, or conversely is absent with holdings of 20% or greater.

State boards of accountancy—State government regulatory organizations. Each state government issues a license to practice within the particular state under that state's accountancy statute.

State societies of CPAs—Voluntary organizations of CPAs within each individual state.

Statements on Standards for Tax Services (SSTS)—SSTS superseded and replaced the AICPA's Statements on Responsibilities in Tax Practice (SRTP). They are enforceable standards of conduct for tax practice under the *Code of Professional Conduct*.

Unpaid fees—Fees for (1) audit and (2) other professional services that relate to certain prior periods that are delinquent as of the date the current year's audit engagement begins, if the client is an SEC registrant, or the date the audit report is issued for non-SEC clients (i.e., AICPA rule).

Yellow Book—*Governmental Auditing Standards* issued by the General Accounting Office.

APPENDIX B

HOW TO CONTACT THE STATE BOARDS AND STATE SOCIETIES

State	State Board	State Society
Alabama	Alabama State Board of Public Accountancy P.O. Box 300375 Montgomery, AL 36130-0375 Phone: 334-242-5700 Fax: 334-242-2711 www.asbpa.state.al.us/	Alabama Society of CPAs 1103 South Perry Street Montgomery, AL 36104 Phone: 334-834-7650 or 800-227-1711 www.accpa.org

Alaska	Alaska State Board of Public Accountancy
	Dept. of Community and Economic Development
	Division of Occupational Licensing,
	  Box 110806
	Juneau, AK 99811
	Phone: 907-465-3811
	Fax: 907-465-2974
	www.dced.state.ak.us/occ/pcpa.htm
		Alaska Society of CPAs
		341 W. Tudor Road, #105
		Anchorage, Alaska 99503
		Phone: 907-562-4334 or
		  800-478-4334
		Fax: 907-562-4025
		www.akcpa.org

Arizona	Arizona State Board of Accountancy
	100 N 15th Ave., Suite 165
	Phoenix, AZ 85007
	Phone: 602-364-0900
	Fax: 602-364-0903
	www.accountancy.state.az.us
		Arizona Society of Certified Public
		  Accountants
		2120 North Central Avenue, Suite 100
		Phoenix, AZ 85004
		Phone: 602-252-4144 or
		  888-237-0700 (in Arizona)
		Fax: 602-252-1511
		www.ascpa.com

Arkansas	Arkansas State Board of Accountancy
	101 East Capitol, Suite 430
	Little Rock, AR 72201
	Phone: 501-682-1520
	Fax: 501-682-5538
	www.state.ar.us/asbpa
		Arkansas Society of Certified Public
		  Accountants
		11300 Executive Center Drive
		Little Rock, AR 72211-4352
		Phone: 501-664-8739 or
		  800-482-8739 (in Arkansas)
		Fax: 501-664-8320
		www.arcpa.org

California	California Board of Accountancy 2000 Evergreen Street, Suite 250 Sacramento, CA 95815-3832 Phone: 916-263-3680 Fax: 916-263-3675 www.dca.ca.gov/cba	California Society of CPAs 1235 Radio Road Redwood City, CA 94065-1217 Phone: 800-9CALCPA www.calcpa.org

Colorado	Colorado State Board of Accountancy 1560 Broadway Suite 1340 Denver, CO 80202 Phone: 303-894-7800 Fax: 303-894-7802 www.dora.state.co.us/accountants	Colorado Society of CPAs 7979 East Tufts Avenue, Suite 500 Denver, CO. 80237-2845 Phone: 303-773-2877 or 800-523-9082 (in Colorado) www.cocpa.org
Connecticut	Connecticut State Board of Accountancy Secretary of the State 30 Trinity Street, P.O. Box 150470 Hartford, CT 06106 Phone: 860-509-6179 Fax: 860-509-6247 www.sots.state.ct.us/SBOA/SBOAindex.html	Connecticut Society of Certified Public Accountants 845 Brook Street, Building 2 Rocky Hill, CT 06067-3405 Phone: 860-258-4800 Fax: 860-258-4859 www.cs-cpa.org
District of Columbia	District of Columbia Board of Accountancy 941 North Capitol Street, N.E. Room 7200 Washington, DC 20002 Phone: 202-442-4461 Fax: 202-442-4528 www.dcra.org/acct/newboa.shtm	Greater Washington Society of CPAs 1023 15th Street, N.W., 8th Floor Washington, DC 20005-2602 Phone: 202-789-1844 Fax: 202-789-1847 www.gwscpa.org
Delaware	Delaware State Board of Accountancy Cannon Building, Suite 203 861 Silver Lake Blvd. Dover, DE 19904 Phone: 302-744-4505 Fax: 302-739-2711 www.professionallicensing.state.de.us/boards/ accountancy/index.shtml	Delaware Society of CPAs 3512 Silverside Road 8 The Commons Wilmington, Delaware 19810 Phone: 302-478-7442 Fax: 302-478-7412 www.dscpa.org
Florida	Florida Board of Accountancy 240 NW 76 Drive, Suite A Gainesville, FL 32607 Phone: 850-487-1395 Fax: 352-333-2508 www.state.fl.us/dbpr/cpa/index.shtml	Florida Institute of Certified Public Accountants P.O. Box 5437 Tallahassee FL 32314-5437 Phone: 850-224-2727 Fax: 850-222-8190 www.ficpa.org
Georgia	Georgia State Board of Accountancy 237 Coliseum Drive Macon, GA 31217-3858 Phone: 478-207-1400 Fax: 478-207-1410 www.sos.state.ga.us/plb/accountancy	Georgia Society of CPAs 3340 Peachtree Road N.E., Suite 2700 Atlanta, GA 30326-1026 Phone: 404-231-8676 or 800-330-8889 Fax: 404-237-1291 www.gscpa.org
Guam	Guam Board of Accountancy Suite 508, GCIC Building 414 W. Soledad Ave. Hagatna, GU 96910 Phone: 671-477-1050 Fax: 671-477-1045 www.guam.net/gov/gba	Guam Society of CPAs 361 South Marine Drive Tamuning, GU 96911 Phone: 671-646-3884 Fax: 671-649-4265

Hawaii	Hawaii Board of Public Accountancy Department of Commerce & Consumer Affairs P.O. Box 3469 Honolulu, HI 96801-3469 Phone: 808-586-2694 Fax: 808-586-2689 No website	Hawaii Society of CPAs P.O. Box 1754 Honolulu, HI 96806 Phone: 808-537-9475 Fax: 808-537-3520 www.hscpa.org
Idaho	Idaho State Board of Accountancy P.O. Box 83720 Boise, ID 83720-0002 Phone: 208-334-2490 Fax: 208-334-2615 Email: isba@boa.state.id.us www.state.id.us/boa	The Idaho Society of Certified Public Accountants 250 Bobwhite Ct., Suite 240 Boise, ID, 83706 Phone: 208-344-6261 Fax: 208-344-8984 www.idcpa.org

Illinois	Illinois Board of Examiners
	505 E. Green, Room 216
	Champaign, IL 61820-5723
	Phone: 217-333-1565
	Fax: 217-333-3126
	www.illinois-cpa-exam.com/cpa.htm
	
	Illinois Public Accountants Registration
	  Committee
	Public Accountancy Section
	320 W. Washington Street, 3rd Floor
	Springfield, IL 62786
	Phone: 217-785-0800
	Fax: 217-782-7645
	www.dpr.state.il.us
		Illinois Society of CPAs
		Chicago Office
		222 South Riverside Plaza,
		  Suite 1600
		Chicago, Illinois 60606
		Phone: 312- 993-0407
		Fax: 312-993-9954
		www.icpas.org

Indiana	Indiana Board of Accountancy Indiana Prof. Licensing Agc., Indiana Gov. Ctr. S. 302 West Washington St., Room E034 Indianapolis, IN 46204-2700 Phone: 317-232-2980 Fax: 317-232-2312 www.state.in.us/pla/bandc/accountancy	Indiana Society of CPAs 8250 Woodfield Crossing Blvd., #100 Indianapolis, IN 46240-2054 Phone: 317-726-5000 Fax: 317-726-5005 www.incpas.org
Iowa	Iowa Accountancy Examining Board 1920 S.E. Hulsizer Avenue Ankeny, IA 50021-3941 Phone: 515-281-4126 Fax: 515-281-7411 www.state.ia.us/iacc	Iowa Society of CPAs 950 Office Park Road, Suite 300 West Des Moines, IA 50265-2548, Phone: 515-223-8161 or 800-659-6375 (in Iowa) Fax: 515-223-7347 www.iacpa.org
Kansas	Kansas Board of Accountancy Landon State Office Building 900 S.W. Jackson, Suite 556 Topeka, KS 66612-1239 Phone: 785-296-2162 Fax: 785-291-3501 www.ksboa.org	Kansas Society of Certified Public Accountants 400 SW Wanamaker Rd., Suite 200 Topeka, KS 66604-0291 Phone: 785-272-4366 FAX: 785-272-4468 www.kscpa.org

Kentucky	Kentucky State Board of Accountancy 332 West Broadway, Suite 310 Louisville, KY 40202-2115 Phone: 502-595-3037 Fax: 502-595-4500 www.state.ky.us/agencies/boa	Kentucky Society of Certified Public Accountants 1735 Alliant Avenue Louisville, Kentucky 40299-6326 Phone: 502-266-5272 or 800-292-1754 (in Kentucky) Fax: 502-261-9512 www.kycpa.org
Louisiana	State Board of CPAs of Louisiana 601 Poydras Street, Suite 1770 New Orleans, LA 70130 Phone: 504-566-1244 Fax: 504-566-1252 www.cpaboard.state.la.us	Society of Louisiana Certified Public Accountants 2400 Veterans Blvd., Suite 500 Kenner, LA 70062-4739 Phone: 504-464-1040 or 800-288-5272 Fax: 504-469-7930 www.lcpa.org
Maine	Maine Board of Accountancy Department of Prof. & Fin. Regulation Division of Lic. & Reg., 35 State House Station Augusta, ME 04333 Phone: 207-624-8627 Fax: 207-624-8637 www.state.me.us/pfr/olr/categories/cat11.htm	Maine Society of Certified Public Accountants 153 U.S. Route 1, Suite 8 Scarborough, ME 04074-9053 Phone: 207-883-6090 or 800-660-2721 Fax: 207-883-6211 www.mecpa.org
Maryland	Maryland State Board of Public Accountancy 500 N. Calvert Street, Room 308 Baltimore, MD 21202-3651 Phone: 410-230-6322 Fax: 410-333-6314 www.dllr.state.md.us/license/occprof/account.html	Maryland Association of Certified Public Accountants 1300 York Road, Building C Lutherville, MD 21093 Phone: 410-296-6250 Fax: 410-296-8713 www.macpa.org
Massachusetts	Massachusetts Board of Public Accountancy 239 Causeway Street Suite 500 Boston, MA 02114 Phone: 617-727-1806 Fax: 617-727-0139 www.state.ma.us/reg/boards/pa/default.html	Massachusetts Society of Certified Public Accountants 105 Chauncy Street 10th floor Boston, MA 02111 Phone: 617-556-4000 or 800-392-6145 Fax: 617-556-4126 www.mscpaonline.org
Michigan	Michigan Board of Accountancy Dept. of Consumer & Industry Services P.O. Box 30018 Lansing, MI 48909-7518 Phone: 517-241-9223 Fax: 517-241-9280 www.cis.state.mi.us/bcs/occ/accttoc.htm	Michigan Association of Certified Public Accountants P.O. Box 5068 Troy, MI 48007-5068 Phone: 248-267-3700 Fax: 248-267-3737 www.michcpa.org
Minnesota	Minnesota State Board of Accountancy 85 East 7th Place, Suite 125 St. Paul, MN 55101 Phone: 651-296-7938 Fax: 651-282-2644 www.boa.state.mn.us	Minnesota Society of Certified Public Accountants 1650 West 82nd Street, Suite 600 Bloomington, MN 55431 Phone: 952-831-2707 Fax: 952-831-7875 www.mncpa.org

Mississippi	Mississippi State Board of Public Accountancy 653 North State Street Jackson, MS 39202-3304 Phone: 601-354-7320 Fax: 601-354-7290 Email: email@msbpa.state.ms.us www.msbpa.state.ms.us	Mississippi Society of CPAs Highland Village, Suite 246 Jackson, MS 39211 Phone: 601-366-3473 or 800-772-1099 Fax: 601-981-6079 www.ms-cpa.org

Missouri	Missouri State Board of Accountancy
	P.O. Box 613
	Jefferson City, MO 65102
	Phone: 573-751-0012
	Fax: 573-751-0890
	www.ded.state.mo.us/regulatorylicensing/
	  professionalregistration/account
		Missouri Society of CPAs
		275 N. Lindbergh Blvd., Suite 10
		St. Louis, MO 63141
		Phone: 314-997-7966 or
		  800-264-7966
		Fax: 314-997-2592
		www.mocpa.org

Montana	Montana State Board of Public Accountants
	301 S Park
	P.O. Box 200513
	Helena, MT 59620-0513
	Phone: 406-841-2388
	Fax: 406-841-2309
	www.discoveringmontana.com/dli/bsd/license/bsd
	  -boards/pac-board/board-page.htm
		Montana Society of Certified Public
		  Accountants
		33 South Last Chance Gulch, Suite 2B
		Helena, MT 59601
		Phone: 406-442-7301 or
		  800-272-0307
		Fax: 406-443-7278
		www.mscpa.org

Nebraska	Nebraska State Board of Public Accountancy P.O. Box 94725 Lincoln, NE 68509-4725 Phone: 402-471-3595 Fax: 402-471-4484 www.nol.org/home/BPA	Nebraska Society of CPAs 635 South 14th Street, Suite 330 Lincoln, Nebraska 68508 Phone: 402-476-8482 or 800-642-6178 (in Nebraska) Fax: 402-476-8731 www.nescpa.com
Nevada	Nevada State Board of Accountancy 200 South Virginia Street Suite 670 Reno, NV 89501-2408 Phone: 775-786-0231 Fax: 775-786-0234 www.nvaccountancy.com	Nevada Society of CPAs 5250 Neil Rd., Suite 205 Reno, NV 89502-6567 Phone: 775-826-6800 or 800-554-8254 Fax: 775-826-7942 www.nevadacpa.org
New Hampshire	New Hampshire Board of Accountancy 6 Chenell Drive, Suite 220 Concord, NH 03301 Phone: 603-271-3286 Fax: 603-271-8702 www.state.nh.us/accountancy	New Hampshire Society of CPAs 1750 Elm Street, Suite 403 Manchester, NH 03104 Phone: 603-622-1999 Fax: 603-626-0204 www.nhscpa.org
New Jersey	New Jersey State Board of Accountancy 124 Halsey Street, 6th Floor P.O. Box 45000 Newark, NJ 07101 Phone: 973-504-6380 Fax: 973-648-2855 www.state.nj.us/lps/ca/nonmed.htm	New Jersey Society of CPAs 425 Eagle Rock Avenue Roseland, NJ 07068-1723 Phone: 973-226-4494 Fax: 973-226-7425 www.njscpa.org

New Mexico	New Mexico Public Accountancy Board 1650 University N.E. Suite 400-A Albuquerque, NM 87102 Phone: 505-841-9108 Fax: 505-841-9101 www.rld.state.nm.us/b&c/accountancy/index.htm	The New Mexico Society of Certified Public Accountants 1650 University NE, Suite 450 Albuquerque, NM 87102-1733 Phone: 505-246-1699 or 800-926-2522 Fax: 505-246-1686 www.nmcpa.org
New York	New York State Board for Public Accountancy State Education Department Cultural Education Center, Room 3013 Albany, NY 12230 Phone: 518-474-3836 Fax: 518-473-6282 www.op.nysed.gov/cpa.htm	New York State Society of Certified Public Accountants 530 Fifth Avenue New York, NY 10036 Phone: 800-633-6320 Fax: 212-719-3364 www.nysscpa.org
North Carolina	North Carolina State Board of CPA Examiners 1101 Oberlin Road, Suite 104 P.O. Box 12827 Raleigh, NC 27605-2827 Phone: 919-733-1422 Fax: 919-733-4209 www.cpaboard.state.nc.us	North Carolina Association of Certified Public Accountants 3100 Gateway Centre Blvd. Morrisville, NC 27560-9241 Phone: 919-469-1040 Fax: 919-469-3959 www.ncacpa.org
North Dakota	North Dakota State Board of Accountancy 2701 S. Columbia Road Grand Forks, ND 58201-6029 Phone: 701-775-7100 Fax: 701-775-7430 Email: ndsba@pioneer.state.nd.us www.state.nd.us/ndsba	North Dakota CPA Society 2701 S. Columbia Rd. Grand Forks ND 58201 Phone: 701-775-7100 Fax: 701-775-7430 www.ndscpa.org
Ohio	Accountancy Board of Ohio 77 South High Street, 18th Floor Columbus, OH 43215-6128 Phone: 614-466-4135 Fax: 614-466-2628 www.state.oh.us/acc	The Ohio Society of CPAs 535 Metro Place South Dublin, OH 43017-7810 Phone: 614-764-2727 or 800-686-2727 Fax: 614-764-5880 www.mysocietyonline.com
Oklahoma	Oklahoma Accountancy Board 4545 Lincoln Blvd., Suite 165 Oklahoma City, OK 73105-3413 Phone: 405-521-2397 Fax: 405-521-3118 www.state.ok.us/~oab	Oklahoma Society of CPAs 1900 NW Expy. Suite 910 Oklahoma City, OK 73118-1898 Phone: 405-841-3800 or 800-522-8261 (in Oklahoma) Fax: 405-841-3801 www.oscpa.com
Oregon	Oregon State Board of Accountancy 3218 Pringle Road, S.E. #110 Salem, OR 97302-6307 Phone: 503-378-4181 Fax: 503-378-3575 www.boa.state.or.us/boa.html	The Oregon Society of Certified Public Accountants PO Box 4555 Beaverton, Oregon 97076-4555 Phone: 503-641-7200 Fax: 503-626-2942 www.orcpa.org

Pennsylvania
Pennsylvania State Board of Accountancy
P.O. Box 2649
Harrisburg, PA 17105-2649
Phone: 717-783-1404
Fax: 717-705-5540
www.dos.state.pa.us/bpoa/cwp/view.asp?a=1104
&q=432428

Pennsylvania Institute of CPAs
1650 Arch Street, 17th Floor
Philadelphia, PA 19103
Phone: 215-496-9272 or
888-CPA-2001 (in Pennsylvania)
Fax: 215-496-9212
www.picpa.org

Puerto Rico
Puerto Rico Board of Accountancy
P.O. Box 3271
Old San Juan Station
San Juan, PR 00904-3271
Phone: 809-722-2122
Fax: 809-721-8399

Colegio de Contadores Publicos
Autorizados de Puerto Rico
Edif. Capital Center
Avenue Arterial Hostos #3
Buxon 1401, Hato Rey, PR 00918
Phone 787-754-1950
Fax: 787-753-0212
www.prscpa.org

Rhode Island
Rhode Island Board of Accountancy
233 Richmond Street, Suite 236
Providence, RI 02903-4236
Phone: 401-222-3185
Fax: 401-222-6654
www.dbr.state.ri.us/account.html

Rhode Island Society of CPAs
45 Royal Little Drive
Providence, RI 02904
Phone: 401-331-5720
Fax: 401-454-5780
www.riscpa.org

South Carolina
South Carolina Board of Accountancy
P.O. Box 11329
Columbia, SC 29211
Phone: 803-896-4770
Fax: 803-896-4554
www.llr.state.sc.us/POL/accountancy/INDEX.ASP

South Carolina Association of CPAs
570 Chris Drive
West Columbia, SC 29169
Phone: 803-791-4181 or
888-557-4814 (in South Carolina)
Fax: 803-791-4196
www.scacpa.org

South Dakota
South Dakota Board of Accountancy
301 East 14th Street, Suite 200
Sioux Falls, SD 57104-5022
Phone: 605-367-5770
Fax: 605-367-5773
www.state.sd.us/dcr/accountancy

South Dakota CPA Society
P.O. Box 1798
Sioux Falls, SD 57101-1798
Phone: 605-334-3848
Fax: 605-334-8595
www.sdcpa.org

Tennessee
Tennessee State Board of Accountancy
500 James Robertson Parkway
2nd Floor
Nashville, TN 37243-1141
Phone: 615-741-2550
Fax: 615-532-8800
www.state.tn.us/commerce/tnsba

Tennessee Society of CPAs
201 Powell Place
Brentwood, TN 37027
Phone: 615-377-3825 or
800-762-0272
Fax: 615-377-3904
www.tscpa.com

Texas
Texas State Board of Public Accountancy
333 Guadalupe
Tower III, Suite 900
Austin, TX 78701-3900
Phone: 512-305-7800
Fax: 512-305-7854
www.tsbpa.state.tx.us

Texas Society of Certified Public
Accountants
14860 Montfort Drive, Suite 150
Dallas, TX 75254-6705
Phone: 800-428-0272
Fax: 972-687-8500
www.tscpa.org

Utah
Utah Board of Accountancy
160 East 300 South
Salt Lake City, UT 84114
Phone: 801-530-6628
Fax: 801-530-6511
www.dopl.utah.gov/licensing/accountancy.html

Utah Association of CPAs
220 East Morris Avenue, Suite 320
Salt Lake City, UT 84115
Phone: 801-466-8022
Fax: 801-485-6206
www.uacpa.org

Vermont	Vermont Board of Public Accountancy Office of Professional Regulation 26 Terrace Street, Drawer 09 Montpelier, VT 05609-1106 Phone: 802-828-2837 Fax: 802-828-2465 www.vtprofessionals.org/opr1/accountants	Vermont Society of CPAs 100 State Street, Suite 500 Montpelier, VT 05602 Phone: 802-229-4939 Fax: 802-223-0360 www.vtcpa.org
Virginia	Virginia Board of Accountancy 3600 West Broad Street, Suite 696 Richmond, VA 23230 Phone: 804-367-8505 Fax: 804-367-2475 www.boa.state.va.us	Virginia Society of CPAs 4309 Cox Road Glen Allen, VA 23060 Phone: 800-733-8272 Fax: 804-273-1741 www.vscpa.com
Virgin Islands	Virgin Islands Board of Public Accountancy P.O. Box 3016 No. 1A Gallows Bay Market Place Christiansted, St. Croix, VI 00822 Phone: 809-773-4305 Fax: 809-773-9850 www.usvi.org/dlca/licensing/cpa.html	Virgin Islands Society of CPAs P.O. Box 3016 Christiansted, St. Croix, VI 00822-3016 Phone: 809-733-4305 Fax: 809-773-9850 www.viscpa.org
Washington	Washington State Board of Accountancy P.O. Box 9131 Olympia, WA 98507-9131 Phone: 360-753-2586 Fax: 360-664-9190 www.cpaboard.wa.gov	Washington Society of CPAs 902 140th Ave NE Bellevue, WA 98005-3480 Phone: 425-644-4800 Fax: 425-562-8853 www.wscpa.org
West Virginia	West Virginia Board of Accountancy 122 Capitol Street, Suite 100 Charleston, WV 25301 Phone: 304-558-3557 Fax: 304-558-1325 www.state.wv.us/wvboa	West Virginia Society of CPAs 900 Lee St., Suite 1201 Charleston, West Virginia 25301 Phone: 304-342-5461 Fax: 304-344-4636 www.wvscpa.org
Wisconsin	Wisconsin Accounting Examining Board 1400 East Washington Avenue P.O. Box 8935 Madison, WI 53708-8935 Phone: 608-266-5511 Fax: 608-267-3816 www.drl.state.wi.us/Regulation/applicant-information/dod139.html	Wisconsin Institute of CPAs 235 N. Executive Drive, Suite 200 Brookfield, WI 53005 Phone: 262-785-0445 or 800-772-6939 Fax: 262-785-0838 www.wicpa.org
Wyoming	Wyoming Board of Certified Public Accountants 2020 Carey Avenue, Suite 100 Cheyenne, WY 82001 Phone: 307-777-7551 Fax: 307-777-3796 www.cpaboard.state.wy.us	Wyoming Society of CPAs 1603 Capitol Avenue, Suite 413 Cheyenne, WY 82001 Phone: 307-634-7039 Fax: 307-634-5110 www.wyocpa.org

ETHICS FOR CPAS:
MEETING EXPECTATIONS IN CHALLENGING TIMES

SELF-STUDY
CPE PROGRAM

WILEY

JOHN WILEY & SONS, INC.

About This Course

We are pleased that you have selected our course. A course description that is based on *Ethics for CPAs: Meeting Expectations in Challenging Times* follows:

Prerequisites:	**None**
Recommended CPE credits:	**8 hours**
Knowledge level:	**Basic**
Area of study:	**Accounting and Auditing Ethics***

The credit hours recommended are in accordance with the AICPA Standards for CPE Programs. Since CPE requirements are set by each state, you need to check with your State Board of Accountancy concerning required CPE hours and fields of study.

If you decide to take this course, follow the directions on the following page. Each course unit costs $59.00. Methods of payment are shown on the answer forms.

Each CPE exam is graded no later than two weeks after receipt. The passing score is at least 70%. John Wiley & Sons, Inc. will issue a certificate of completion to successful participants to recognize their achievement.

Photocopy one copy of the answer sheet for each additional participant who wishes to take the CPE course. Each participant should complete the answer form and return it with the $59 fee for each self-study course.

The enclosed self-study CPE program will expire on January 31, 2004. Completed exams must be postmarked by that date.

---

* *This program may qualify in some states for ethics continuing professional education requirements. Please check with your state board.*

Directions for the CPE Course

The course includes reading assignments and objectives, discussion questions and answers, and a publisher-graded examination. To earn eight hours of CPE credit, follow these steps:

1. Read the learning objectives.
2. Study chapters 1 to 37 in *Ethics for CPAs: Meeting Expectations in Challenging Times.*
3. Answer the discussion questions and refer to the answers to assess your understanding of the respective chapter.
4. Study material in any weak areas again.
5. Upon completion, take the publisher-graded examination. Record your answers by writing true, false, or a letter (a-d) on the line for that question on the answer form.
6. Upon completion of the examination, cut out the answer sheet, put it in a stamped envelope, and mail to the address below:

> Ethics for CPAs: Meeting Expectations in Challenging Times
> CPE Program Director
> John Wiley & Sons, Inc.
> 7222 Commerce Center Drive
> Suite 240
> Colorado Springs, CO 80919

CONTINUING PROFESSIONAL EDUCATION: SELF-STUDY

OBJECTIVES

Studying Chapters 1 through 37 should enable you to

- Apply the ethics guidance of

  - The AICPA Code of Professional Conduct
  - SEC
  - DOL (audits of employee benefit plans)
  - GAO (audits of state and local governmental units)
  - Other organizations

- Apply this guidance in firms of all sizes having public company, private entity, governmental entity, and employee benefit plan clients.

- Describe the Joint Ethics Enforcement Program (JEEP) and the conduct of an investigation and trial board hearing.

- Describe the steps a member should take if involved in a disciplinary action under JEEP.

- Explain the importance of independence, integrity, and objectivity to public confidence in audit, examination (SSAE terminology), review, and agreed-upon procedures engagements.

- Describe the rationale underlying independence rules and their interpretations and their general economic and social framework.

- Distinguish between the independence requirements of the various organizations.

- Summarize the key elements of a firm's quality assurance policies and procedures relevant to independence.

- Distinguish between the general standards of professional competence, due professional care, planning and supervision, and sufficient relevant data.

- Explain the member's duty to comply with the standards promulgated by bodies designated by Council.

- Describe the representations by members in public practice when departures from generally accepted accounting principles exist.

- Describe a member's responsibility to keep client information confidential.

- Determine when a member is or is not permitted to receive commissions, referral fees, and contingent fees.

- Explain what constitutes a discreditable act.

- Distinguish between prohibited and permitted forms of advertising and solicitation.

- Explain the requirements for permitted forms of organization and firm names.

- Explain the requirements of the Statements on Standards for Tax Services and the Statement on Standards for Consulting Services.

- Describe the requirements of IFAC's *Code of Ethics for Professional Accountants*.

DISCUSSION QUESTIONS

1. If an auditor is technically proficient and applies extensive auditing procedures, but lacks independence, the financial statements are
   a. Unaudited.
   b. Semireliable.
   c. Reliable.
   d. None of the above.

2. Rule 102 on integrity and objectivity applies to all CPAs
   a. In public practice who provide professional services.
   b. Who provide professional services, no matter where employed.
   c. In public practice who provide auditing and attestation services.
   d. Who provide professional services imbued with the public interest.

3. A member or member's firm that is not independent can issue
   a. An audit report.
   b. An examination report under the SSAE.
   c. A review report.
   d. A compilation report for a private company.

4. Company A, an audit client, owns 50% of a joint venture. Company Z, a nonclient, owns the remaining 50% of the joint venture. CPA auditor has a material financial interest in Company Z. CPA is independent with respect to
   a. The joint venture.
   b. Company A.
   c. Company Z.
   d. None of the above.

5. An audit client has unpaid fees outstanding as of the date that fieldwork begins for the current audit. The client has paid those past due fees by the time the audit report is issued.
   a. Independence is impaired under the AICPA and SEC rules.
   b. Independence is not impaired under the AICPA rule and **may** not be impaired under the SEC rules.
   c. Independence is impaired under the AICPA rules, but not under the SEC rules.
   d. Independence is not impaired under either AICPA or SEC rules.

6. Loans to and from clients that are not financial institutions
   a. Will impair independence without regard to materiality.
   b. If material, will cause an impairment of independence.
   c. Will not impair independence if the loan is "permitted."
   d. Will not impair independence if the loan is "grandfathered."

7. A member serves as treasurer of a campaign organization that is supporting a candidate for mayor. The member is not independent with respect to
   a. The candidate's political party.
   b. The municipality of which the candidate may become mayor.
   c. The campaign organization.
   d. All of the above.

8. An audit manager is performing an audit engagement. Which of the following employment relationships may impair independence under AICPA rules?
   a. Employment in a key position of the auditor's spouse by the client.
   b. Employment in a key position of the auditor's dependent relative by the client.
   c. Employment in a key position of the auditor's parent by the client.
   d. All of the above.

9. According to the AICPA rules, a CPA firm will not be independent if an audit partner's husband owns more than ___% of the equity securities in an audit client.
   a. 5.
   b. 10.
   c. 15.
   d. 25.

10. Acceptance of a gift from a client will not impair independence if
   a. The recipient discloses the gift to the CPA firm.
   b. The gift is lavish, but not excessive considering the audit fee.
   c. The gift is a wedding present.
   d. The item received is a token gift.

11. A lawsuit is brought against a CPA firm by an audit client. Independence would be considered to be impaired in all of the following circumstances except
   a. The present management alleges audit scope was inadequate.
   b. The present management alleges an audit adjustment violated GAAP.
   c. The present management alleges a state tax return prepared by the CPA firm incorrectly computed the tax liability for a minor amount.
   d. The present management alleges failure to communicate a reportable condition in internal control.

12. If the client agrees to indemnify the member for knowing misrepresentations, the member
   a. Is not independent under AICPA or SEC rules.
   b. Is not independent under AICPA rules, but is independent under SEC rules.
   c. Is not independent under SEC rules, but may be independent under AICPA rules.
   d. Is independent under both AICPA and SEC rules.

13. Which of the following situations would impair independence for a city government client?
   a. The auditor is elected to the city council.
   b. The auditor serves on a citizen's advisory committee to study a possible new structure in the form of government.
   c. The auditor owned city bonds but sold the bonds upon being engaged as the auditor.
   d. The auditor's spouse is running for mayor at the next election.

14. A CPA firm is in an alliance with a public company in an alternative practice structure. The partners of the firm are also employees of a professional services subsidiary of the public company. The chief executive of the professional services subsidiary has a direct financial interest in an audit client of the CPA firm. The partners report directly to the chief executive in their capacity as employees. Which of the following best describes the effect on independence of the CPA firm?
   a. Independence is not impaired because the chief executive is not an owner or employee of the CPA firm.
   b. Independence is impaired because the chief executive is subject to the same requirements as a member and any direct financial interest impairs independence.
   c. The chief executive is not a member, but independence would nevertheless be impaired if the financial interest is material to the chief executive's net worth.
   d. None of the above.

15. A firm's responsibilities for the adherence of its personnel to professional requirements on independence can be fully satisfied by
    a. Adoption of adequate quality control policies and procedures related to independence.
    b. Adherence by its personnel to professional requirements on independence.
    c. Both a. and b. together.
    d. Either a. or b. individually.

16. Which of the following bodies is not designated to issue standards by AICPA Council?
    a. Consulting Services Executive Committee.
    b. Panel on Audit Effectiveness.
    c. Tax Executive Committee.
    d. Auditing Standards Board.

17. Which of the following is **true**?
    a. A member should never disclose the name of a client without the client's specific consent.
    b. A member may use a records retention agency to store client's records.
    c. A member may not accept an engagement to perform services that involve examining confidential information about competitors.
    d. A member may not be compelled by a subpoena to disclose confidential client information.

18. According to AICPA rules, a member in public practice may accept a contingent fee from a client
    a. Only when the contingent fee is disclosed.
    b. Only if the member does not perform an audit or review for the client.
    c. Only if the member does not perform an audit, review, or certain other attest or compilation services for the client.
    d. A member in public practice may never accept a contingent fee.

19. After an engagement is complete, a member is obligated to provide which of the following upon request of the client?
    a. Analyses and schedules prepared by the client at the request of the member.
    b. Member's workpapers.
    c. Consolidating journal entries found in the member's workpapers that are not in the client's books and records.
    d. All of the above.

20. Which is a prohibited form of advertising, even if it is not false, misleading, or deceptive?
    a. In-person solicitation of clients.
    b. Comparison of services provided to those of another firm.
    c. Celebrity endorsements.
    d. None of the above.

21. Which of the following is **not** one of the requirements of the Council Resolution concerning Rule 505—*Form of Organization and Name*?
    a. CPAs must own a majority of the financial interests and voting rights.
    b. A CPA must have ultimate responsibility for all compilation services.
    c. A non-CPA owner is not eligible for membership in the AICPA.
    d. A non-CPA owner cannot use the title of "Principal."

True or False Questions

22. The names of members subject to JEEP investigations are always published in The CPA Letter.

23. A divorced spouse would be included in the AICPA's definition of immediate family member. **C**

24. A lack of independence concerning a direct or indirect financial interest can be remedied by placing securities in a blind trust. **F**

25. Under the AICPA rules, a covered member would include all partners in the CPA firm regardless of which office they practice in. **F**

26. The SEC includes the entity's general counsel in its list of individuals having the ability to exercise significant influence, but the AICPA does not. **F**

27. Under the GAO's independence rules, an auditor would be permitted to prepare draft notes to the financial statements using information determined and approved by management. **T**

28. If a member is a stockholder, partner, director, officer, or employee for an entity other than his or her CPA firm and the member submits financial statements for distribution to third parties, the member must communicate in writing his or her relationship with the other entity, and should not imply that the member is independent. **F**

29. The FTC now requires that accountants doing tax returns for individual nonbusiness clients provide notice of their privacy policies and practices to clients. **T**

30. If a member maintains financial records for an employee benefit plan, Department of Labor regulations state that the member is not independent. **T**

ANSWERS TO DISCUSSION QUESTIONS

1. **The answer is a.** If an auditor is not independent, any procedures that the auditor might perform, no matter how extensive, would not be in accordance with GAAS. The auditor is precluded from expressing an opinion on the financial statements and the financial statements would be, for all practical purposes, unaudited. Answers b. and c. would not be correct because no reliability can be assumed if the financial statements are unaudited. Answer d. is incorrect because the statements would be considered unaudited.

2. **The answer is b.** Rule 102 applies to all CPAs who provide professional services, no matter where employed. This includes CPAs in industry, government, and education who provide tax, consulting, and a variety of other services. Answer a. is incorrect because Rule 102 applies to everyone who provides professional services, not just those in public practice. Answer c. is incorrect because Rule 102 applies to all professionals, not just those in public practice, and applies to all professional services, not just audit and attestation services. Finally, answer d. is incorrect because Rule 102 applies to all professional services, not just those imbued with the public interest.

3. **The answer is d.** Independence is not required for compilation engagements. The auditor should disclose the lack of independence in the compilation report but not the reason for the lack of independence. All of the other engagements—audits (answer a.), reviews (answer c.), and examination reports under the SSAE (answer b.)—require independence.

4. **The answer is d.** CPA auditor has a material financial interest in the nonclient investee, Company Z. The member could be influenced by the nonclient investor, thereby impairing the member's independence with respect to Company Z. Independence is also impaired with respect to the nonclient and the joint venture. Therefore, the CPA would not be independent with respect to the joint venture (answer a.), Company A (answer b.), or Company Z (answer c.).

5. **The answer is b.** Under the AICPA rules, independence is impaired if the fees are delinquent for more than one year prior to the current audit report date. Therefore, since the fees were

paid by the report date, independence is not impaired under the AICPA rule. Therefore, answers a. and c. are incorrect. Under SEC rules, fees that are material in relation to the current audit fee should be paid before the current audit begins, to avoid impairing independence. Such fees were **not** paid at the time that current audit work began in this example. However, since there are two exceptions to the SEC rule that (1) allow for a commitment to pay the fees prior to the audit report being issued or (2) allow for an agreement to make periodic payments, the correct answer is that independence may not be impaired under SEC rules. Because of these exceptions, answer d. is incorrect.

6. **The answer is a.** Loans to and from clients that are not financial institutions will impair independence without regard to materiality. Therefore, answer b. is incorrect. Answers c. and d. are not correct because exceptions for grandfathered loans and permitted loans apply only to loans from financial institutions.

7. **The answer is c.** A member who serves as treasurer of a campaign organization that supports a candidate for mayor would not be independent with respect to the campaign organization. Answers a. and b. are incorrect because independence with respect to the political party or the municipality are not impaired. Because independence is only impaired with respect to the campaign organization, answer d. is also incorrect.

8. **The answer is d.** All of the relationships listed—spouse, dependent relative, or dependent child—are ascribed to the member. Thus, if the member's spouse, dependent relative, or dependent child is employed by the client in a key position, the CPA firm is not independent. Answers a., b., and c. are therefore all incorrect because employment in a key position by any of the individuals listed would impair independence.

9. **The answer is a.** According to the AICPA, if (1) any partner or professional employee, (2) any immediate family member, spouse, spousal equivalent, or dependent of anyone in (1), or (3) any group of persons in (1) or (2) above owns more than 5% of the equity securities of an audit client, the CPA firm is not independent. The SEC rule is more stringent than the AICPA rule above in that any close family member (parent, nondependent child, or sibling) is included in the ownership/control group, if any such group has filed a Schedule 13D or 13G with the SEC indicating beneficial ownership of more that 5% or control of an audit client. In addition, if a close family member of a partner controls an audit client, the CPA firm is not independent. Since answers a., b., and d. are all more than 5%, all three answers would be incorrect.

10. **The answer is d.** A member should not accept more than a token gift from a client. Answer a. is not correct because an individual cannot mitigate the appearance of a lack of independence by disclosing the gift to the CPA firm. Answer b. is not correct because the gift cannot be accepted if it is lavish, no matter what its relationship to the audit fee. Answer c. is not correct because a wedding present is a gift that might give the appearance of impairing independence. However, the prohibition against accepting gifts has to be interpreted sensibly and handled diplomatically.

11. **The answer is c.** Litigation impairs independence when present management of a client brings litigation alleging deficiencies in the member's audit work. Therefore, independence would be impaired for the situations described in answers a., b., and d. Independence would **not** be impaired if litigation relates to an engagement that does not require independence, such as tax work, and the alleged damages are not material to the member's firm or the client company.

12. **The answer is c.** The AICPA permits a member to include an indemnification clause in an engagement letter without impairing independence if the indemnification is restricted to knowing misrepresentations made by the client's management. However, the member who inserted such a clause in an engagement letter would not be independent under SEC rules be-

cause the SEC considers indemnification to be against public policy. Since the SEC prohibits indemnification, answers b. and d. are incorrect. Answer a. is not correct because although the member is not independent under SEC rules, the member may be independent under AICPA rules.

13. **The answer is a.** If a member serves as an elected city legislator, such as on city council, independence is impaired with respect to the city even though the city manager is elected, rather than appointed, by the legislature. Answers b. and d. are both examples of situations that would not impair independence. Answer c. is also not correct because the city bonds were sold before independence was required. If, however, a member owned even an immaterial amount of the bonds at the beginning of the work on the engagement, independence would be impaired.

14. **The answer is b.** The chief executive of the professional services subsidiary is a direct superior and is subject to the same independence requirements as a member with respect to New Firm's audit and attest services clients. A direct financial interest would impair independence for a member. Therefore answer a. is not correct. Answer c. is incorrect because a direct superior is subject to the same independence requirements as a member. Direct financial interests impair independence without regard to materiality. Finally, because answer b. is the correct answer, answer d. is not correct.

15. **The answer is c.** A firm's responsibilities for the adherence of its personnel to professional requirements on independence is fully satisfied only by both adopting adequate quality control policies and procedures related to independence and by the adherence of all professional personnel to all applicable professional requirements on independence. Answers a., b., and d. are not correct because both adoption of the policies and procedures and adherence are needed.

16. **The answer is b.** The Panel on Audit Effectiveness is not an AICPA body, but instead is a separate entity established in 1998 by the Public Oversight Board in response to a request by the Securities and Exchange Commission. The Panel conducted a comprehensive review and evaluation of the way independent audits of financial statements of publicly traded companies are performed and assessed the effects of recent trends in auditing on the quality of audits and on the public interest. Answers a., c., and d. are all bodies designated to issue standards by AICPA Council as described in Chapter 28.

17. **The answer is b.** A member may use a records retention agency. Answer a. is false because a member may disclose the name of a client as long as doing so does not reveal confidential information. Answer c. is incorrect because a member may accept such an engagement as long as the member does not violate confidentiality. Answer d. is false because Rule 301 does **not** relieve a member of an obligation to comply with a legally enforceable subpoena or summons.

18. **The answer is c.** A member in public practice may only receive a contingent fee if the member does not perform an audit, review, or certain other attest or compilation services for the client. Answer a. is not correct because disclosure would not prevent impairment of independence when the member performs audits, reviews, or other attest services. Answer b. is not correct because certain other attest or compilation services may also impair independence and prevent acceptance of a contingent fee. Answer d. is not correct because a public practice member may accept a contingent fee if the member does not perform services listed in answer c.

19. **The answer is c.** These entries should be provided to allow the client to complete the client's financial records. Answers a. and b. are not correct because they represent the member's workpapers, which do not need to be provided to the client. Answer d. is not correct because

only consolidating journal entries need to be provided, not the analyses, schedules, or work-papers.

20. **The answer is d.** All of the above are permitted forms of advertising, as long as they are not false, misleading, or deceptive. Therefore, answer d is correct and answers a., b., and c. are incorrect because other answers would also be correct since they are all permitted forms of advertising.

21. **The answer is d.** All of the answers (answers a, b, and c) are requirements except for d. A non-CPA owner may use the title of Principal.

22. **This answer is false.** The results of the investigation and the name of the member will not be published in *The CPA Letter*, unless the matter is presented to a hearing panel and the panel finds the member guilty.

23. **The answer is false.** As long as the covered member/person and the former spouse are legally divorced, the former spouse would not be included in the immediate family.

24. **The answer is false.** This would not be an acceptable remedy. Independence would be impaired.

25. **The answer is false.** The definition of covered member would apply to the partners who are on the attest engagement team, provide a minimum number of nonattest services to the client, or are in the office in which the lead attest engagement partner primarily practices.

26. **The answer is false.** Both the SEC and the AICPA include an entity's general counsel in their respective lists of individuals having the ability to exercise significant influence.

27. **The answer is true.** This **would** be considered one of the permitted services under the GAO's independence rules as long as it met the two overarching principles. However, other services, such as maintaining or preparing the audited entity's basic accounting records, would be prohibited.

28. **The answer is false.** The member is required to make the communication, but the *Code of Professional Conduct* does not require that the communication be in writing. However, the authors strongly recommend that such communication be in writing.

29. **The answer is true.** Accountants who provide tax planning, financial planning, or tax preparation services to individual nonbusiness clients should be aware of these new rules that went into effect on July 1, 2001.

30. **The answer is true.** Although the DOL has not specifically clarified the meaning of "maintenance of financial records," the basic principle is that independence would be impaired. Some DOL officials maintain that posting a general ledger from client-prepared underlying records and preparing participant account balances for a defined benefit plan impairs independence.

PUBLISHER-GRADED EXAMINATION

Multiple-
Choice

1. The organization created by the Sarbanes-Oxley Act of 2002 that has the responsibility for establishing and enforcing ethics standards is
    a. The Professional Ethics Executive Committee.
    b. The Public Accounting Oversight Board.
    c. The Independence Standards Board.
    d. The Joint Ethics Enforcement Program.

Multiple-
Choice

2. The Sarbanes-Oxley Act prohibits an auditor from all of the following **except:**
    a. Designing a client's financial information systems.
    b. Performing actuarial services.
    c. Making investment decision on behalf of client management.
    d. Providing guidance in determining whether specific derivatives meet the criteria as hedges.

Multiple-
Choice

3. Which of the following prohibit providing internal audit services to an audit client?
    a. The Sarbanes-Oxley Act and the AICPA's *Code of Professional Conduct.*
    b. The AICPA's *Code of Professional Conduct* and the GAO's new independence requirements.
    c. The Sarbanes-Oxley Act and the GAO's new independence requirements.
    d. The Sarbanes-Oxley Act, the AICPA's *Code of Professional Conduct,* and the GAO's new independence requirements.

Multiple-
Choice

4. Which of the following bookkeeping services is prohibited by the GAO?
    a. Posting coded transactions to the entity's financial records.
    b. Preparing a trial balance based on management's chart of accounts.
    c. Preparing draft notes to the financial statements based on information determined and approved by management.
    d. Maintaining depreciation schedules for which management has determined the method of depreciation, rate of depreciation, and salvage value of the assets.

Multiple-
Choice

5. Which of the following is one of the GAO's overarching principles for performing nonaudit services for audit clients?
    a. Auditors should not provide nonaudit services that involve performing management functions.
    b. Auditors should not provide nonaudit services for which the fee is greater than 10% of the audit fee.
    c. Auditors may provide nonaudit services in relation to a specific audit engagement as long as such services do not exceed forty hours.
    d. Auditors may provide nonaudit services as long as safeguards requiring certain documentation are implemented.

Multiple-
Choice

6. A partner leaves his firm and becomes the CFO of one of the firm's public clients. Under the Sarbanes-Oxley Act, independence would be impaired if the partner participated in the audit of the client company
    a. During the one-year period preceding the date of the company's financial statements.
    b. During the one-year period preceding the start of the current audit.
    c. During the two-year period preceding the date of the company's financial statements.
    d. During the two-year period preceding the start of the current audit.

7. Which of the following is included in the list of individuals having the ability to exercise significant influence under the SEC rules, but not under the AICPA rules?
   a. Director of Internal Audit.
   b. Treasurer.
   c. Vice-President of Marketing.
   d. General Counsel.

8. Which of the following is true of the Independence Standards Board?
   a. It is charged with establishing the independence requirements that apply to auditors of private companies.
   b. It is charges with establishing independence requirements that apply to auditors of government agencies.
   c. It can remove a CPA's license to practice for violation of independence requirements.
   d. It was dissolved on July 31, 2001.

9. Which of the following is a possible consequence of impaired independence?
   a. Lawsuits against the firm by clients and other third parties.
   b. Sanctions against the firm by the SEC.
   c. Loss of investor confidence in audit results.
   d. All of the above.

10. Which of the following loans from a client would impair independence?
    a. A line of credit from a nonfinancial institution client for an amount that was immaterial to the member's net worth.
    b. A loan made from a financial institution client prior to its becoming an audit client.
    c. A credit card balance of $4,500.
    d. All of the above.

11. A client owes its auditor fees for professional services provided from January 15 to January 30, 20X1. The auditor expects to begin work in the current year's engagement on February 1, 20X2, and issue the report on March 1, 20X2. Under the AICPA rules, the client must pay the fees by which date to avoid impairing independence?
    a. January 15 20X1.
    b. January 30, 20X1.
    c. February 1, 20X2.
    d. March 1, 20X2.

12. Under the SEC rules, which of the following relatives of an audit manager would impair independence if they owned 5% of equity securities in a client?
    a. Mother.
    b. Brother.
    c. Stepson.
    d. All of the above.

13. Which of the following would **not** be included in the definition of member?
    a. A brother.
    b. A spouse.
    c. An unrelated dependent.
    d. All of the above would be included in the definition of member.

Multiple-
Choice

14. Which of the following would impair independence for a member who provides consulting or advisory services to a private company audit client on corporate finance matters?
    a. Assisting in identifying or introducing the client to possible sources of capital that meet the client's specifications or criteria.
    b. Maintaining custody of client securities.
    c. Assisting in drafting an offering document or memorandum.
    d. Being named as a financial advisor in a client's private placement memoranda.

Multiple-
Choice

15. Independence is required for all of the following **except:**
    a. A comfort letter.
    b. A review report.
    c. A compilation report.
    d. An examination of a financial forecast.

Multiple-
Choice

16. Which of the following statements is true?
    a. Independence is required under Statement of Auditing Standards (SAS), but not Statements on Standards for Attestation Engagements (SSAE) or Statements on Standards for Accounting and Review Services (SSARS).
    b. Independence is required under SAS and SSAE, but not SSARS.
    c. Independence is required under SAS and SSARS but not SSAE.
    d. Independence is required under SAS, SSAE, and SSARS.

Multiple-
Choice

17. Which of the following organizations cooperate in the Joint Ethics Enforcement Program (JEEP) in bringing enforcement actions against their members?
    a. AICPA and SEC.
    b. AICPA and state societies.
    c. AICPA, SEC, and IFAC.
    d. AICPA, SEC, the GAO, and state societies.

Multiple-
Choice

18. An audit manager has XYZ Manufacturing as an audit client. The manager receives a substantial discount on products from XYZ. This discount is not available to members of the general public. What is the effect on independence?
    a. Independence is impaired.
    b. Independence is not impaired if the discount is disclosed to the firm.
    c. Independence is not impaired if the discount is disclosed to the firm and to the client.
    d. Independence is not impaired.

Multiple-
Choice

19. Which of the following exceptions to indemnification agreements is allowed by the AICPA?
    a. A client indemnifies a member for damages from lawsuits and claims relating to client acts.
    b. A client indemnifies a member for knowing misrepresentations made by client's management.
    c. A member indemnifies the client for damages from lawsuits and claims relating to client acts.
    d. All of the above are permitted under the AICPA rules, but not SEC rules.

<table>
<tr><td>Multiple-
Choice</td><td>20. When defining a covered member under the SEC rules, the attest engagement team would consist of all of the following except:
   a. A second-partner reviewer on the engagement.
   b. A contractor who completed audit procedures.
   c. A staff accountant.
   d. All of the above would be included in the definition of the attest engagement team.</td></tr>
</table>

Multiple-Choice

20. When defining a covered member under the SEC rules, the attest engagement team would consist of all of the following except:
    a. A second-partner reviewer on the engagement.
    b. A contractor who completed audit procedures.
    c. A staff accountant.
    d. All of the above would be included in the definition of the attest engagement team.

Multiple-Choice

21. The AICPA's definition of covered member includes a partner or manager who provides nonattest services to the attest client beginning once he or she provides _____ hours of nonattest services to the client within any fiscal year.
    a. 5.
    b. 10.
    c. 20.
    d. 40.

Multiple-Choice

22. Ownership of which of the following would be considered a prohibited direct financial interest?
    a. Bonds issued by the client.
    b. Shares of a client's preferred stock.
    c. Investment in a client's common stock through an investment club.
    d. All of the above.

Multiple-Choice

23. Which of the following is not an example of a conflict of interest that impairs independence?
    a. A member has been approached to provide services in connection with the purchase of real estate from a client of the member's firm.
    b. A member refers a client to ABC Service Bureau, in which a partner in the member's firm holds a material interest.
    c. A member has been asked to perform litigation services for the plaintiff in connection with a lawsuit filed against a client of the member's firm.
    d. All of the above are conflicts of interest.

Multiple-Choice

24. An audit manager invests in a client mutual fund that holds stock in one of the audit manager's clients. Which of the following is true concerning independence with respect to the client mutual fund?
    a. Independence is impaired only if the value of the stock is material to the member.
    b. Independence is impaired only if the value of the stock is material to the member's firm.
    c. Independence is impaired only if the value of the stock is material to the client.
    d. Independence is impaired without regard to materiality.

Multiple-Choice

25. All of the following may impair independence **except:**
    a. A member performs management functions for a client.
    b. A member serves as a voting trustee of the client.
    c. A member serves on an advisory board.
    d. A member serves as a director of the client.

Multiple-
Choice

26. A CPA firm makes payments to a former practitioner who has accepted employment with a private company client after retirement from the firm. In order for the firm to be independent with respect to the client, all of the following provisions are required under AICPA rules **except:**
   a. The payments must be made subject to a written agreement.
   b. The payments must not be material to the CPA firm.
   c. The payments cannot be related to current firm revenues.
   d. The payments must be calculated based on an underlying formula that remains fixed during the payout period.

Multiple-
Choice

27. Auditors of public companies must follow the independence requirements of which of the following organizations?
   a. The AICPA.
   b. The PCAOB.
   c. The SEC.
   d. All of the above.

Multiple-
Choice

28. A member receives a wedding present from an audit client. The value of the gift exceeds the firm's policy on gifts. Which of the following is true?
   a. Independence is not impaired because it is a wedding present.
   b. Independence is not impaired if the gift is disclosed to the firm.
   c. Independence is not impaired if the gift is disclosed to the firm and to the SEC.
   d. Independence is impaired.

Multiple-
Choice

29. Which of the following is true for an agreed-upon procedures engagement?
   a. The definition of covered member is the same for an audit engagement as for an agreed-upon procedures engagement.
   b. The definition of covered member is less inclusive for an agreed-upon procedures engagement.
   c. The definition of covered member is more inclusive for an agreed-upon procedures engagement.
   d. Independence is not required for agreed-upon procedures engagements.

Multiple-
Choice

30. A CPA has begun an engagement to issue a review report for a client. Independence would be impaired if a member has which of the following?
   a. A material indirect interest in a client.
   b. A direct financial interest in a client.
   c. Either a. or b.
   d. Neither a. or .b.

Multiple-
Choice

31. A CPA firm is in an alliance with a public company in an alternative practice structure (APS). In addition to owners of the CPA firm, which category of individuals are subject to all of the same independence requirements as the owners/members?
   a. Direct superiors.
   b. Indirect superiors.
   c. Both direct and indirect superiors.
   d. Neither direct nor indirect superiors.

Multiple-
Choice

32. A firm should do which of the following with respect to quality control systems?
    a. Periodically obtain written representations from all professional personnel that affirm that the individual complied with independence policies.
    b. Designate a competent person or group as responsible for resolving questions on independence.
    c. Establish requirements for documentation of the resolution of independence questions.
    d. All of the above.

Multiple-
Choice

33. An auditor's independence with respect to an employee benefit plan is impaired whenever the auditor
    a. Has a material indirect financial interest in the plan.
    b. Serves as an investment advisor to the plan.
    c. Serves as the director of a plan sponsor.
    d. All of the above.

Multiple-
Choice

34. An audit partner in the Boston office of CPA Firm has a spouse who is the chief financial officer of ABC Company. ABC Company has just become a client of CPA Firm's Boston office. The partner will not participate in the engagement. Which of the following is correct concerning the relationship between CPA firm and ABC Company?
    a. Independence is impaired under AICPA and SEC requirements.
    b. Independence is impaired under AICPA, but not SEC requirements.
    c. Independence is impaired under SEC requirements, but not AICPA requirements.
    d. Independence is not impaired under AICPA or SEC requirements.

Multiple-
Choice

35. Which of the following would impair independence without regard to materiality?
    a. A direct financial interest.
    b. An indirect financial interest.
    c. Both a. and b.
    d. Neither a. nor b.

Multiple-
Choice

36. An audit manager invests in a nonclient mutual fund that holds stock in one of the audit manager's clients. Which of the following is true?
    a. Independence is impaired if the value of the stock is material to the member.
    b. Independence is impaired if the value of the stock is material to the member's firm.
    c. Independence is impaired if the value of the stock is material to the client.
    d. All of the above.

Multiple-
Choice

37. If the auditor is not independent, then which of the following is true about the audit?
    a. The procedures performed by the auditor must be more extensive than those performed if the auditor were independent.
    b. The SEC must be notified before the audit opinion can be issued.
    c. The final statements would be considered unaudited.
    d. None of the above.

Multiple-
Choice

38. Material cooperative arrangements are
    a. Prohibited by both the AICPA and SEC.
    b. Prohibited by the AICPA, but permitted by the SEC.
    c. Prohibited by the SEC, but permitted by the AICPA.
    d. Permitted by both the AICPA and SEC.

Multiple-
Choice

39. Under AICPA requirements, independence would be impaired in which of the
    following situations?
    a. A third-party litigant, such as an insurance company, brings litigation
        against a member in the name of the client under subrogation rights.
    b. The client and the member agree to binding arbitration to avoid litigation.
    c. A client sues member but settles out of court.
    d. All of the above.

Multiple-
Choice

40. Which of the following CPAs would need to maintain integrity and objectiv-
    ity?
    a. An audit manager who works only on audits of small companies.
    b. A corporate controller.
    c. A sole practitioner who does only tax returns.
    d. All of the above.

Multiple-
Choice

41. Under the AICPA rules, which of the following relatives of an audit manager
    would impair independence if he/she owned 5% of equity securities in a
    client?
    a. Father.
    b. Sister.
    c. Stepson.
    d. All of the above.

Multiple-
Choice

42. An audit partner inherits stock in a client from his great-uncle. Under SEC
    rules, this unsolicited financial interest must be disposed of not later than
    ____ days after the partner has knowledge of and the right to dispose of the
    interest.
    a. 30
    b. 60
    c. 90
    d. 180

Ethics for CPAs CPE Course

Record your CPE answers on the answer form provided below and return this page for grading.

Mail to:

John Wiley & Sons, Inc., 7222 Commerce Center Drive, Suite 240, Colorado Springs, CO 80919

***Ethics for CPAs* CPE Director**

PAYMENT OPTIONS

☐ **Payment enclosed ($59.00).**
(Make checks payable to John Wiley & Sons, Inc.)
Please add appropriate sales tax.
Be sure to sign your order below.

Charge my:

☐ American Express ☐ MasterCard ☐ Visa

Account number _____

Expiration date _____
Please sign below for all credit card orders.

Signature _____

NAME _____

FIRM NAME _____

ADDRESS _____

PHONE ( ) _____

CPA STATE LICENSE # _____

ISBN 0-471-45737-X

SEE THE OTHER SIDE OF THIS PAGE FOR THE CPE FEEDBACK FORM.

CPE ANSWERS

1. ___	2. ___	3. ___	4. ___	5. ___	6. ___	7. ___	8. ___	9. ___	10. ___
11. ___	12. ___	13. ___	14. ___	15. ___	16. ___	17. ___	18. ___	19. ___	20. ___
21. ___	22. ___	23. ___	24. ___	25. ___	26. ___	27. ___	28. ___	29. ___	30. ___
31. ___	32. ___	33. ___	34. ___	35. ___	36. ___	37. ___	38. ___	39. ___	40. ___
41. ___	42. ___								

Ethics for CPAs CPE Feedback

1. Were you informed in advance of the

   a. Course objectives? **Y   N**
   b. Requisite experience level? **Y   N**
   c. Course content? **Y   N**
   d. Type and degree of preparation necessary? **Y   N**
   e. Instruction method? **Y   N**
   f. CPE credit hours? **Y   N**

2. Do you agree with the publisher's determination of

   a. Course objectives? **Y   N**
   b. Requisite experience level? **Y   N**

      c. Course content? **Y   N**
      d. Type and degree of preparation necessary? **Y   N**
      e. Instruction method? **Y   N**
      f. CPE credit hours? **Y   N**

3. Was the content relevant? **Y   N**

4. Was the content displayed clearly? **Y   N**

5. Did the course enhance your professional competence? **Y   N**

6. Was the course content timely and effective? **Y   N**

How can we make the course better? If you have any suggestions please summarize them in the space below. We will consider them in developing future courses.

_____

_____

_____

_____